The Independent Trade Unions, 1974 — 1984
Ten Years of the South African Labour Bulletin

The Independent Trade Unions, 1974 — 1984

Ten Years of the South African Labour Bulletin

Edited by Johann Maree

RAVAN PRESS

Johannesburg

Published by Ravan Press (Pty) Ltd
P.O. Box 31134, Braamfontein 2017, South Africa

First impression 1987

© Copyright Johann Maree 1987

Cover photograph: Wendy Schwegmann

ISBN 0 86975 307 X

Printed and bound by Citadel Press, Lansdowne, Cape

B365/S

Contents

Abbreviations

A.F.C.W.U.	— African Food and Canning Workers' Union
A.H.I.	— Afrikaanse Handelsinstituut
A.N.C.	— African National Congress
ASSOCOM	— Associated Chambers of Commerce
BAWU	— Black Allied Workers' Union
C.C.O.B.T.U.	— Consultative Committee of Black Trade Unions
C.T.M.W.A.	— Cape Town Municipal Workers' Association
CUSA	— Council of Unions of South Africa
C.W.I.U	— Chemical Workers' Industrial Union
ERAB	— East Rand Administration Board
F.C.I.	— Federated Chambers of Industry
F.C.W.U.	— Food and Canning Workers' Union
FOSATU	— Federation of South African Trade Unions
GAWU	— General and Allied Workers' Union
GAWU	— Glass and Allied Workers' Union
I.A.S.	— Industrial Aid Society
I.M.S	— Iron Moulders' Society
MAWU	— Metal and Allied Workers' Union
NAAWU	— National Automobile and Allied Workers' Union
NUM	—National Union of Mineworkers
NUSAS	— National Union of South African Students
N.U.T.W.	— National Union of Textile Workers
R.T.V.E.W.U.	— Radio, Television, Electronic and Allied Workers' Union
SAAWU	— South African Allied Workers' Union
SACTU	— South African Congress of Trade Unions
SACWU	— South African Chemical Workers' Union
S.A.L.B.	— South African Labour Bulletin
SEIFSA	— Steel and Engineering Industries Federation
T.M.S.A.	— Telephone Manufacturers of South Africa
TUACC	— Trade Union Advisory Coordinating Council
TUCSA	— Trade Union Council of South Africa
UMMAWSA	— United Metal, Mining and Allied Workers' Union of South Africa
U.T.P.	— Urban Training Project
W.I.P.	— Work In Progress
W.P.W.A.B.	— Western Province Workers' Advice Bureau

Introduction

This book reflects the first vital ten years of the democratic trade union movement from 1974 to 1984 as recorded by the *South African Labour Bulletin (S.A.L.B.)*. The *Bulletin's* origin and first years of existence, as Webster explains in the Prologue, were closely associated with the democratic trade union movement. The book therefore also commemorates ten years of production of the *Bulletin*.

The term 'independent trade unions' which appears in the title of the book and is used throughout the text requires clarification right at the outset in view of the changing political situation in South Africa. When the term 'independent trade unions' was coined by the *Labour Bulletin* in 1977[1] it was used to distinguish the black, predominantly African, unions that emerged in the early 1970s and were free from control of white unions, from those African unions that appeared contented with such controls.* Over time the meaning of 'independent' broadened out to incorporate trade union autonomy from both the state and employers. It is in this broad sense that the term 'independent trade unions' is used through this book.

However, as the debate whether trade unions should form alliances with other movements came to the fore, the term 'independent' started acquiring a new connotation, namely being independent of the

* Throughout this book the four main population groups into which the state has divided the country's people are referred to as the African, coloured, Indian (or Asian) and white groups. The term 'black' is used to refer collectively to Africans, coloureds and Indians, except when using official terminology when it refers only to Africans. The use of the term coloured instead of so-called coloured or 'coloured' is used to streamline publication. It in no way implies recognition that they constitute a separate race or national group.

national liberation movements. In view thereof the *South African Labour Bulletin* decided in August 1986 to refer to these unions as the 'democratic unions' instead.[2] Since the term 'independent' did not have this connotation for the decade which this book covers it was decided to refer consistently in the book to the democratic unions as the independent unions.

The readings in this book, selected from the first ten volumes of the *South African Labour Bulletin*, were chosen to depict the emergence, growth and struggles of the independent trade union movement. But the unions operated in the wider South African society with external forces acting on them. These forces were sometimes supportive, but often very hostile to the unions. Readings that demonstrated how these external forces impinged on the unions and how the unions responded to them are therefore also included. The readings are accordingly arranged into five parts each containing a different theme. They are:

1 the emergence of the independent trade union movement which focuses on the struggles of the unions to establish themselves in the early 1970s, the issues they were facing in the 1980s, and what they had achieved up to 1984;

2 industrial conflict and strikes which the independent unions had engaged in during the period under consideration. The epoch-making 1973 Durban strikes are not included in the book since the *Labour Bulletin* was only started in 1974 and its founding body, the Institute for Industrial Education, had itself published a book on the Durban strikes.[3] The historical significance of the strikes to the trade union movement and the mutual effect that the strikes and the unions had upon each other is made clear in the overview to this part;

3 the major industrial relations laws and their significance for the unionisation of Africans as well as their impact on the independent trade unions are examined in Part III. The role of the repressive apparatuses of the state on the independent unions also come under the spotlight;

4 the intensive, and at times heated, debate between the independent unions on the appropriate strategy towards the state and legislation, as reflected in the registration debate constitutes the fourth theme of the readings. This debate was carried exclusively in the pages of the *South African Labour Bulletin;*

5 the political role of the independent trade unions for the period

under review constitutes the final theme of the book. The readings consist mainly of statements by leaders of the unions on what they perceived to be the appropriate political involvement of the unions. The last reading however examines the crucial role of the independent unions in the stayaway on the east Rand in November 1984. It indicated a new preparedness on the part of those unions which had mainly concentrated on shop-floor issues, to take up political issues .

The book also contains an index of the first ten volumes of the *South African Labour Bulletin*, the first and only index of the *Bulletin* to date.

In order to present an outline of the major developments during the ten year period and to place the readings in their historical context, overviews to each of the five parts have been written by members of the Editorial Board of the *Bulletin*. Consequently this book presents a fairly comprehensive coverage of the development of the independent trade unions in their first ten years of existence as well as of the milieu in which they were operating.

The readings in this book have been reprinted from the *South African Labour Bulletin* without any editing other than shortening some of the pieces. They therefore reflect the realities as they were perceived by the authors at the time of writing. The book thus provides a rather unique insight into both the history of the democratic unions as well as the history of ideas about the unions.

Owing to a production delay of more or less two years from the time the manuscript was submitted to the publishers, the overviews written by the editors do not reflect or mention some of the more recent developments in the democratic trade union movement such as the formation of the Congress of South African Trade Unions (COSATU) and the National Council of Trade Unions (NACTU). They only cover the first ten years of the unions up to 1984, ten years which are however crucial to understanding the democratic trade union movement.

Johann Maree
July 1987

Notes

1 See *S.A.L.B.* III, 4 (January/February, 1977), pp. 7-13.
2 See *S.A.L.B.,* XI, 7 (August, 1986), pp. 1 and 125.
3 Institute for Industrial Education, *The Durban Strikes 1973* (Ravan Press, Johannesburg, 1974).

Ten Years of the South African Labour Bulletin

Eddie Webster

The origins of the *S.A.L.B.* lie in the re-emergence of working class action and organisation in Durban in the early 1970s. On 30 May 1973, three months after the wave of spontaneous mass action by 100 000 black workers, a group of sympathetic trade unionists, students and academics from the University of Natal (Durban), met in the James Bolton Hall in Durban to inaugurate the Institute for Industrial Education (I.I.E.). Harriet Bolton, Secretary of TUC-SA's Garment, Textile and Furniture unions opened the meeting and explained how the project had come about. She said that workers lacked formal knowledge of trade unionism as they had neither the time nor the money to study. She said a school should be formed which would educate workers about their rights. Foszia Fisher, who was later to become the secretary of the I.I.E., then proposed:

a) that a correspondence course be established to help workers understand the social and economic situations in which they operated,

b) that a resource centre be established to provide the unions with background material and information.

It was from this second component of the I.I.E. project that the idea of a journal on labour was to emerge. On 30 July 1973, the I.I.E. sub-committee proposed that a newsletter be published 'tentatively called *Labour Bulletin* — containing general information on trade unionism at home and abroad, book reviews, topical discussions and analyses of economic trends (like inflation)'.[1]

On 11 August a working committee was set up consisting of Omar Badsha, Halton Cheadle, Foszia Fisher, Dave Hemson, Eddie Webster and Harriet Bolton, to run the day-to-day affairs of the I.I.E. It was this committee that was to undertake the initial planning of the *Bulletin*, appoint the first editor and solicit material for the first few editions. The *South African Labour Bulletin (S.A.L.B.)* was, then, never conceived of as a mere academic exercise. It was directly linked to the emerging labour movement and was concerned both to record its struggles and serve its needs. From its inception it contained a tension; was it an instrument of the emerging unions or was its role that of independent critic? It was, of course, to develop a degree of independence over the years as it began to serve a wider constituency of persons concerned with understanding this movement.[2] But it always retained those early links and continued to draw its material and audience from people sympathetic to that movement. It can be seen, in fact, as a mirror of ten years of the workers' movement in South Africa.

During these ten years 78 editions of the *S.A.L.B.* have been published. The content of these editions fall roughly into five phases — phases that mirror developments in the history of the emerging unions.

Phase One

During this phase, which covers the first five editions, the *S.A.L.B.* had close links with the day-to-day activities of the new unions in Durban and attempted to reflect their activities in its pages. The driving force behind much of the material was the banned political science lecturer from the University of Natal, Richard Turner, whose particular brand of theory and practice was to influence and shape the *S.A.L.B.* during this phase.

Appropriately the first edition of the *S.A.L.B.*, published in April 1974, was on the case for African trade unions. At this stage trade union recognition, which had been denied under the Industrial Conciliation Act, was the central issue for these new unions. The next four editions published regular reports on the organising activities of the new unions and accounts of struggles for recognition. The *S.A.L.B.*

was seen during this phase, as an important outlet for the viewpoint of these unions. Two of the first five issues were banned by the Publications Control Board. The reasons given were that the *S.A.L.B.* was 'promoting workers' unrest' and opposition to the government's alternative to trade unions for black workers, the liaison committee system.

It is perhaps an indication of the close links of the *S.A.L.B.* with these new unions that after the first few editions, the editors were to debate whether some editions should not be introduced in Zulu.

Phase Two

Within the first six months of the *S.A.L.B.*'s existence an intense debate over the relationship between education and organisation was to emerge. In essence, the new unions were struggling to survive in a harsh political and economic climate and saw the I.I.E. as a resource that needed to direct its energies more concretely to building shop-floor leadership. The I.I.E. was eventually brought directly into the educational work of the unions.[3] The *S.A.L.B.*, however, was to experience a different history as it carved for itself a distinct niche almost exclusively among university academics linked through education and research to the emerging unions. This can be seen in the changing nature of the content of the *S.A.L.B.* volume one, number six, published in late 1974, carried articles on the early history of the I.C.U. and reflected the intellectual interests of the new school of radical South African historiography that emerged in the early 1970s. However throughout 1975 the *S.A.L.B.* retained the close links with the unions that marked its origins. For example volume two, number five was banned for carrying an article on the struggle for recognition at Leyland.

This phase ended rather abruptly in December 1975 when two of the editors were arrested under the Terrorism and Suppression of Communism Acts. The state was, in the coming year, to embark on a sustained offensive against the leadership of the new unions, which culminated in the banning of 26 unionists in November 1976. The *S.A.L.B.* was to survive this period of repression by retreating into the university and becoming more of an academic journal.

Phase Three

This third phase could be categorised as one of retreat when the *S.A.L.B.* established its independence from the I.I.E. and became more firmly based in the universities. It was also a period of intellectual growth as labour became a focus of serious academic attention in the universities for the first time and the *S.A.L.B.* widened its editorial board to include academics from the Universities of the Witwatersrand and Cape Town. Significantly these new editors brought into the *S.A.L.B.* different perspectives and experiences making the *Bulletin* more of a national journal. During this period from 1976 to 1979, the *S.A.L.B.* pioneered the academic study of labour through editions on unemployment (IV, 4), the labour process (IV, 7), industrial health (IV, 9 and 10) and international labour (V, 8). In 1978 the *S.A.L.B.* brought out a book of fourteen past articles on South African labour history, as part of an attempt to meet this growing demand for material on labour.[4]

Phase Four

A new phase in the history of the *S.A.L.B.* was to begin in late 1979 when working class militancy re-emerged in the post-Wiehahn period. A new editor had been appointed in mid-1979, Merle Favis, and she grasped the opportunity of redefining the *S.A.L.B.* as a journal that would, once again, record the day-to-day struggles of workers more closely. In September 1980 the *S.A.L.B.* brought out an edition on the strikes at Ford (VI, 2 and 3) and in December 1980, the *S.A.L.B.* began a strike series. The first edition (VI, 5) focused on the 1980 cotton workers' strike in Pinetown and the meat workers' strike in Cape Town. The second edition (VI, 6) focused on strikes in Putco, the media, and Allied Publishing. The third edition focused exclusively on the Johannesburg municipal workers strike of 1980 (VI, 7).

The *S.A.L.B.*'s growing institutional autonomy led it, during this phase, to develop more clearly its role as an independent critic. This was most evident in the articles by Maree where he critically evaluated the organising activities of NAAWU in the Ford dispute (VI, 2 and 3) and SAAWU in East London (VII, 4 and 5). Both articles were to re-open the debate on the relationship of the intellectual to the workers' movement. Above all, this phase of the *S.A.L.B.* was shaped by the shift in state strategy towards black workers and the intense debate around the workers' response to this. The *S.A.L.B.* had given fifty typed pages of evidence to the Wiehahn Commission in January 1978 and had carried a detailed critique of the commission's findings in April 1979 (V, 2).

In November 1979 we received a memorandum from the Western Province General Workers' Union strongly critical of the decision of some groups, such as FOSATU, to register. After considerable debate we published the memo in volume five, number four (November 1979). This was to trigger off an acrimonious debate inside the *S.A.L.B.* Two positions were reflected in the pages of the *S.A.L.B.*; those who saw the decision to register as tactically wise (Fine, De Clercq and Innes in VII, 1 and 2) and those who saw it as surrendering to state control (Haysom and Hirsch, Nicol in VII, 3). This debate was to be a turning point in the *S.A.L.B.* Not only did the *S.A.L.B.* provide the only written record of this important debate, but it was also to establish the *S.A.L.B.* as a genuinely independent forum for the emerging trade unions opening up a new phase in our history.

Phase Five

This new phase coincided with the unity talks that began in August 1981 in Langa when support grew for a more united trade union movement. The wave of detentions of trade unionists in 1981, including our editor, Merle Favis, was to underline the need for unity within the labour movement. This commitment of the unions to a united movement enabled the *S.A.L.B.* to play more effectively its central role of recording the struggles inside the movement and providing background information on issues of broad interest to the labour movement. This has taken a number of different forms:

a) In late 1981 we began a briefing section in the *S.A.L.B.* that has proved highly successful. In these briefings we have tried to capture key issues in labour in summary form.

b) At the beginning of 1982 we appointed a research officer, Jeremy Baskin, who, in the fifteen months he was with us, transformed our coverage of contemporary labour by writing a number of in-depth articles.

c) We have been able to run more articles of practical value to the labour movement such as studies that look at maternity agreements in other countries or compare different health and safety agreements.

d) In 1983 the offices of the *S.A.L.B.* were moved to Johannesburg under the direction of the subsequent editor, Doug Hindson. They were kept separate from any trade union grouping, with regular funding and proper office equipment.

The *S.A.L.B.* is now well placed to continue critically to reflect and serve the needs of the emerging trade union movement under the new editor, Jon Lewis. We feel we have fulfilled our intention, first stated ten years ago, to help workers understand the social and economic situation in which they operate. We have not always done this in ways with which the trade unionists have agreed and certainly not in ways in which we foresaw when we first gathered to discuss the idea of a bulletin on 30 May 1973. The role of the intellectual within the workers' movement is one of on-going debate.

A crucial question raised by this account of '*Ten Years of the South African Labour Bulletin*' is about the effect which our increasingly institutional autonomy has had on our capacity to play a role within the worker's movement. Has the lack of direct union control made us too 'academic' or has our independence from any specific union group, and the wider range of links that accompanied this, strengthened our capacity to play a supportive but critical role?

Our only regret, as we celebrate ten years of the *S.A.L.B.*, is that we do not have with us Richard Turner, who played a vital part in the foundation of the *Bulletin*. His untimely death by an assassin's bullet in the early morning of 8 January 1978, deprived us of a remarkable colleague. Our best tribute to Rick, and warning to the assassin, is that his ideas and commitment to a nonracial democratic workers' movement live on in the pages of the *S.A.L.B.*

June 1984

Notes

1 Minutes of the I.I.E. sub-committee, 30 July, 1973.

2 See J. Maree, 'The Institute for Industrial Education and Worker Education', *S.A.L.B.*, IX, 8, (July, 1984), pp. 86-87.

3 Ibid., pp. 80-86.

4 *Essays in South African Labour History*, edited by E. Webster (Ravan Press, 1978).

Part I

Overview: Emergence of the Independent Trade Union Movement

Johann Maree*

The emergence of the independent trade union movement from 1973 to 1984 can broadly be classified into three eras. The first era from 1973 to 1976 was a struggle for survival as the unions battled to obtain recognition in a hostile environment, with both the state and capital opposed to their very existence. At the end of this period the survival of the movement was by no means assured due to severe political and economic setbacks received during 1976. But the movement did survive and the second era from 1977 to 1979 was one of reconstruction and consolidation. During this time the unions managed to establish themselves firmly at a small number of companies. The third era from 1980 to 1984 was one of rapid expansion after the state had switched to a policy of recognising African trade unions in 1979 and a resurgence of black worker militancy from 1980 onwards. After the first decade of their existence the independent trade union movement had thereby succeeded in establishing itself as a powerful and growing force in South Africa.

Struggle for survival 1973-1976

Origins and formation
With the destruction of the South African Congress of Trade

* Ari Sitas assisted with the editing of readings in this section.

Unions (SACTU) by the state in the early 1960s, African trade unions virtually ceased to exist and strikes receded almost totally in South Africa. After some indications of African working class discontent in 1971 and 1972 the industrial calm was shattered in Durban in January 1973. A strike wave hit the industrial complexes as at least 61 000 African workers and a much smaller number of Indian workers went on strike in demand of higher wages.[1]

The most significant immediate consequence of the strike wave was that masses of militant African workers poured into newly founded working class organisations in Durban and Pietermaritzburg. This heralded the start of the resurgence of African trade unionism in the country as a whole even though tentative steps had already been taken to revive African trade unions in the major industrial centres.

Although the independent trade unions were started under circumstances unique to each centre, most of them had three characteristics in common. Firstly, for fear of state repression the first working class organisations to emerge were not trade unions, but bodies that seemed less challenging to the state and capital. The institutions that emerged as forerunners of the independent unions were the General Factory Workers' Benefit Fund (G.F.W.B.F.) in Durban and Pietermaritzburg, the Urban Training Project (U.T.P.) and the Industrial Aid Society (I.A.S.) on the Witwatersrand, and the Western Province Workers' Advice Bureau (W.P.W.A.B.) in Cape Town.

Secondly, the initiative for the formation of the unions came primarily from intellectuals outside the ranks of the black working class although this was done in conjunction with former trade unionists. The G.F.W.B.F., W.P.W.A.B. and I.A.S. were founded by students belonging to Wages Commissions and academics from the Universities of Natal, Cape Town and Witwatersrand along with a few sympathetic officials in the Trade Union Council of South Africa (TUCSA) and former SACTU organisers. Wages Commissions were at that time being established under the auspices of the National Union of South African Students (NUSAS) on all the major English-speaking university campuses with the intention of aiding African working class organisation. The origin of the U.T.P. was somewhat different as ex-TUCSA trade unionists who strongly supported African trade unionism took the lead in establishing the U.T.P.

Thirdly, the founders of the independent union movement had in common a commitment to create democratic trade unions. Although there were different approaches between the leaders, they were by and large committed to building up democratic unions by means of active worker participation at the work-place and worker control of union affairs and officials. The democratic goal proved to be a long and difficult task, but was beginning to be realised by the end of the 1970s.[2]

Most of the unions practised a form of nonracialism in that the leadership included whites, Africans, Indians and coloureds even though the membership of the unions was initially exclusively African. The unions serviced by the U.T.P., however, adhered exclusively to African leadership, but even so a few whites played a prominent role in the U.T.P. In addition a clearly black consciousness oriented union, the Black and Allied Workers' Union (BAWU), was founded in 1973,[3] but did not play a prominent role during the 1970s.

Initial organisational experiences and strategies

The initial organisational experiences and strategies of the independent union groupings varied quite markedly from each other. This was due to the different conditions facing the unions in each of the regions and because of distinctions between the founding bodies.

Natal was most markedly unlike the other regions. The strike wave of early 1973 followed by a smaller one in January 1974 raised African working class consciousness as they poured into newly formed unions. Consequently union membership in Durban and Pietermaritzburg grew rapidly. By June 1974, only eighteen months after the Durban strikes had commenced, the General Factory Worker Benefit Fund membership stood at 22 000 while signed up membership of the four unions founded by then had risen to over 10 000. These bodies had grouped themselves together into the Trade Union Advisory and Coordinating Council (TUACC).

The TUACC unions' initial organisational strategy was one of signing on mass membership, but it changed after worker militancy receded from about the second half of 1974. The new strategy placed an emphasis on trade union democracy by means of in-depth work-place organisation with shop stewards being given a key role. As Webster shows (Reading Two) they were to be made responsible for recruiting, organising and representing workers in their departments.

However, it was not until after 1977 that all the TUACC unions fully adopted the new strategy. Webster's survey of TUACC unions' members in 1975 also provides a valuable and rare insight into the workers' attitudes towards their unions and political leaders.

In Cape Town and the Witwatersrand there were no equivalent strike waves and membership of the organisations progressed much more slowly. African workers' fears, in the light of their previous experiences, that joining trade unions would automatically entail state repression, had to be overcome first.

The two organisations that operated on the Witwatersrand adopted very different approaches. The U.T.P. was started about three years before the I.A.S. and in a relatively short time it had revived two African unions, was servicing another, and had helped African workers to establish seven new unions. Thus it was servicing no less than ten African unions by the end of 1975. Once established, these unions increased in size fairly rapidly: by November 1976 signed-up membership of seven of the U.T.P.-serviced unions totalled no less than 19 338. These unions had grouped themselves together into an ad hoc body, the Consultative Committee of Black Trade Unions. By contrast, the I.A.S. had only succeeded in getting one union, the Metal and Allied Workers' Union (MAWU), off the ground by that time. The reasons for the different initial experiences of the two organisations have been ascribed to the former trade union experience of the U.T.P. officials plus the fact that they commenced organising in the east Rand where workers had a higher working class consciousness.

In Cape Town the W.P.W.A.B. adopted a strategy from the start to form statutory works committees and to assert pressure on management to recognise and negotiate with the works committees. As Horner shows (Reading One), the works committees were not used as an alternative to trade union recognition, but as a means of building up a general workers' union by uniting all the works committees in a common worker organisation. This form of organisation was also chosen because works committees were democratically elected and could enhance worker participation on the shop-floor.

Union setbacks in 1976

Early in 1976 the union groupings were all fairly well on the way to firmly establishing themselves. However during 1976, particularly in the second half of the year, the independent unions received severe setbacks.

Firstly, the Soweto uprising of June 1976 and the subsequent upheavels severely disrupted the independent unions' organisations on the Witwatersrand and Cape Peninsula.

Secondly, the economy slumped to its lowest growth level since the Second World War in the wake of the Soweto uprising and the preceding international recession. The independent unions were subsequently hard hit as workers were laid off during 1976 and 1977.

Thirdly, conflicts between management and two of the independent unions on the Witwatersrand in 1976 ended in defeats for the unions and effectively destroyed their organisational bases. (See Reading Five in Part Two for one of these conflicts.)

Fourthly, in November 1976 the state imposed the most repressive measures yet taken against the independent unions when it prohibited the participation of twenty two activists in the organisations by imposing banning orders on them. Although the bannings were probably in part due to the upheavals caused by the Soweto uprising, the state appeared intent on undermining, if not destroying, the independent African trade union movement.

Due to the events and circumstances in 1976 the independent unions were at their lowest ebb since being founded. On the Rand and in the western Cape especially, the unions' operations were completely ruptured by the end of 1976.

Reconstruction and consolidation 1977-1979

However, the independent unions had sufficient resilience and depth of leadership to survive the adverse conditions and attacks by a hostile state. The unions had laid the foundations for their recovery during the preceding four years through their organisational methods involving shop stewards as well as rank and file participation.

In Cape Town the Workers' Advice Bureau was back on its feet again by April 1977. It soon thereafter successfully transformed itself by placing control of the organisation in the hands of a Controlling Committee comprising elected factory representatives. It appropriately changed its name to the Western Province General Workers' Union and later to the General Workers' Union (G.W.U.) when it started organising in other regions. In 1977 the Food and Canning Workers' Union, which was founded in 1941 with its head office in Cape Town, obtained a new lease of life after going through a period of decline over the preceding decade.[4]

In the Transvaal the Consultative Committee of Black Trade Unions did not only suffer severe setbacks from the bannings, but was subsequently disrupted by considerable conflict within and between the unions. By 1979 the tensions were resolved when two of the unions split and a further two severed their relationship with the Consultative Committee. MAWU in the Transvaal had to rebuild itself almost from scratch by organising completely new factories. This was successfully done over the next three years by concentrating on intensive shop-floor organisation at a limited number of factories and entering into very few strikes.

The Natal TUACC unions consolidated themselves by similarly concentrating on in-depth organisation at a limited number of factories from 1977 to 1979. The unions carefully chose the companies which were subsidiaries of multinational corporations. While the unions' main efforts were directed at shop-floor mobilisation, they all conducted fairly intensive international campaigns in their efforts to gain recognition at these companies.

Thus at the end of 1979 the independent trade unions had successfully established a small but secure base. They had managed to sign five recognition agreements with companies, but were organising at a considerably larger number of enterprises.

A first step towards trade union unity was taken in April 1979, when the Federation of South African Trade Unions (FOSATU) was established. TUACC, the motor unions which subsequently amalgamated into one union, namely the National Automobile and Allied Workers' Union (NAAWU) and the four break-away unions from the Consultative Committee of Black Trade Unions combined to form a national federation. The following year the remaining unions in the Consultative Committee, with the exception of the Commercial Catering and Allied Workers' Union (CCAWUSA), formed another federation, the Council of Unions of South Africa (CUSA). CUSA has continued to organise almost only African workers whereas FOSATU and the other independent unions remained open to all workers. With a few notable exceptions such as NAAWU and the Food and Canning Workers' Union, the unions have remained predominantly African.

Rapid expansion 1980-1984

After 1979 African unions expanded rapidly. This was in part due to the state's switch in policy to recognise African unions after the Wiehahn Commission's first report in 1979. (See the Overview of Part Three.) Unions subsequently found it easier to gain recognition from employers. It was also due to a heightened political consciousness and militancy on the part of the African working class in the 1980s.

Thus many new unions emerged after 1979. They tended to grow rapidly and some have become very prominent. The National Union of Mineworkers (NUM) is one of the most significant new unions. It was only started in 1982 by CUSA, but by the end of 1984 it had a membership of 110 000 (45 000 of them paid-up) and had signed 29 recognition agreements.[5]

Another union that emerged into prominence in the early 1980s was the South African Allied Workers' Union (SAAWU). Although it had come into existence earlier when BAWU split in 1979, SAAWU expanded rapidly only when it took root in East London where it could build on a long tradition of black political resistance. Reading Three shows that SAAWU was overtly political and strongly challenged the independence of the Ciskei as a separate ethnic state. As a result it experienced extremely harsh repression and consequently suffered severe setbacks.

The rapid expansion after 1979 of the independent trade unions that emerged from 1971 onwards is illustrated in table one.[6]

During the four year period from the end of 1979 to the end of 1983 signed-up membership of the emerging independent unions went up more than fourfold from about 70 000 to almost 300 000 while claimed membership, a considerably less reliable indicator of union size and strength, increased more than fivefold to 298 000. But the unions made their most impressive headway in gaining formal recognition from companies. This is indicated by the enormous increase in the number of signed recognition agreements: between 1979 and 1983 they increased from a mere five to no less than 406 with the FOSATU unions accounting for 285 or seventy percent of the agreements.

Table 1

Growth of Emerging Independent Trade Unions 1979-1983[a]

	FOSATU	CUSA	CCAWUSA	G.W.U.	SAAWU	OTHER[b]	TOTAL
Membership 1979							
Signed-up	30 100	32 050	3 500	4 500			70 150
Claimed					29 000	20 000	49 000
1983							
Signed-up	106 460	140 592	40 500	12 000			299 552
Claimed					100 000	198 000	298 000
Signed agreements							
1979	3	0	1	1	0	0	5
1983	285	62	7	13	11	20	406

Notes:

a) This table does not include independent unions, such as the Food and Canning Workers' Unions (A./F.C.W.U.) and the Cape Town Municipal Workers' Association (C.T.M.W.A.), that already existed before the 1970s. In 1983 their signed-up membership was 20 000 and 10 445 respectively.

b) The ten largest unions that claimed 97% of the membership for 1983 in this column are:
   Black Allied Workers' Union — 86 000,
   Public Servants' League — 24 000,
   General and Allied Workers' Union — 20 600,
   Black Allied Mining and Construction Workers' Union — 15 000
   National Sugar and Refining and Allied Industries Employees'
   Union — 13 000 members and twelve recognition agreements,
   Black Health and Allied Workers' Union of S.A. — 10 000,
   National General Workers' Union — 6 000,
   African Allied Workers' Union of S.A. — 4 900,
   Orange-Vaal General Workers' Union — 2 600.

To retain a perspective on these rapid advances, it is necessary to bear in mind that the independent unions that emerged after the 1970s had only organised roughly seven percent of the total black, that is, coloured, Asian and African labour force, by 1983. When sectors harder to unionise, namely agriculture, forestry and fishing, domestic workers and state employees are excluded, the proportion of the African labour force unionised by the end of 1982 was still only sixteen percent.[7]

The independent unions have continued to concentrate their efforts on strong shop-floor organisation. They have consolidated their positions by negotiating and signing recognition agreements with many companies. The agreements usually contain the right to negotiate wages and working conditions at plant level, as well as procedural agreements such as grievance, dismissal and retrenchment procedures. The unions are challenging arbitrary managerial prerogative in the work-place. The prerogative that has most clearly been challenged is management's power to dismiss workers unilaterally. In particular the power of foremen to fire workers arbitrarily has been curtailed.[8]

Another aspect that the unions commenced to take up meaningfully as part of the collective bargaining process in the 1980s has been occupational health and safety in the work-place, particularly in the mining industry. With the technical aid of service groups such as the Industrial Health Research Group in Cape Town and the Health Information Centre and Technical Advice Group in Johannesburg the independent unions have taken up concrete struggles on health and safety in the work-place. These have included the right to refuse dangerous work on the mines, challenging statutory health and safety structures which attempt to pre-empt worker organisation, and ensuring compensation for workers whose health had been impaired due to occupational diseases or injuries.[9]

The policy and practice of many of the independent unions to place a strong emphasis on an active role for shop stewards in the work-place and the union advanced to a new level on the east Rand when a shop stewards' movement emerged in 1981. As Baskin shows (Reading Four) the first one to emerge was the Germiston shop stewards' council which was founded with the aim of organising factories in the region because of the immense shortage of organisers due to the rapid expansion of FOSATU unions, especially MAWU, in the region.[10]

A neglected issue in the independent trade unions until well into the 1980s has been the gender division of labour in the work-place and the household. Not only does this place heavy burdens on black working class women, but it also hampers the proper participation of women in trade union organisation. Some unions in FOSATU had started to take up this issue by 1983.[11] CCAWUSA took up the issue of rights for working mothers and managed to gain the first health and safety agreement for pregnant and nursing mothers in 1985.[12]

The 1980s also saw the first meaningful engagement of the independent trade union movement in politics. Even the independent unions that had adopted the strategy of first building their power at the point of production and concentrated all their effort on work-place organisation, started taking up political issues beyond the shop-floor. The two-day stayaway on the Rand in which the independent unions participated heralded a new era in their political role. (See Part Five on trade unions and politics.)

The need for greater unity amongst the independent unions became more apparent in the 1980s. A strong move towards unity amongst most of the major independent unions gained momentum from 1983 onwards.[13] At the end of 1984 negotiations to form a new federation were well advanced. Once formed the federation could potentially bring together industrial unions of black workers organising nationally in the mining, engineering, transport, docks, food and textile industries for the first time in the country's history. Such a new federation suggests that the independent unions will probably enter a new era as the federation is likely to become a truly powerful working class organisation in South Africa.[14]

August 1985

Notes

1 Institute for Industrial Education, *The Durban Strikes 1973*, (Ravan Press, Johannesburg, 1974), pp. 57-58.

2 See J. Maree, 'Democracy and Oligarchy in Trade Unions: the Independent Trade Unions in the Transvaal and the Western Province General Workers' Union in the 1970s', *Social Dynamics*, VIII, 1 (June, 1982), pp. 45-52.

3 See S. Nolutshungu, *Changing South Africa*, (David Philip, Cape Town, 1983), pp. 197-9.

4 For the decade preceding 1976, see R. Goode, For a Better Life. The Food and Canning Workers' Union 1941 to 1975, B.A. Honours Dissertation (Economic History), (University of Cape Town, 1983), ch. 4.

5 *Financial Mail*, 25 January, 1985, p. 49.

6 Table 1 is compiled from: S. Miller, Trade Unions in South Africa 1970 — 1980:

Directory and Statistics, *SALDRU Working Paper No. 45*, (University of Cape Town, 1983); and P. Lundall, I. Schroeder and G. Young, *Directory of South African Trade Unions: a Complete Guide to All South Africa's Trade Unions*, (SALDRU, University of Cape Town, 1984).

7 National Manpower Commission, 1984, *Report on an Investigation into the Levels of Collective Bargaining and Works Councils, the Registration of Trade Unions and Employers' Organisations and Related Matters, and the Industrial Court*, Report 3/1984, pp. 48-9. Note that official statistics exclude Africans from the independent ethnic states. These are Transkei, Ciskei, Bophuthatswana and Venda.

8 E. Webster, 'A New Frontier of Control? Case Studies in the Changing Form of Job Control in South African Industrial Relations', *Carnegie Conference Paper* No. 111, (University of Cape Town, 1984), pp. 12, 14, 16.

9 See T. Adler, 'The Prevention of Occupational Diseases and Industrial Accidents in South African Industry', *S.A.L.B.*, IV, 9 and 10, March 1979, pp. 55-65, for an early example of union concern with workers' compensation; J. Myers and M. Steinberg, 'Health and Safety Organisation: a Perspective on the Machinery and Occupational Safety Act', *S.A.L.B.*, VIII, 8 and IX, 1 (Sept.-Oct., 1983), pp. 79-95, on the implications of the act for trade unions; and *S.A.L.B.*, IX, 7 (June, 1984), which focuses on occupational health and safety. For an overview of the stage reached by the independent unions in 1983 and 1984, see J. Myers and M. Steinberg, 'Health and Safety: An Emerging Issue on the Shop-floor', in *South African Review Two*, edited by SARS, (Ravan, 1984); and J. Maller and M. Steinberg, 'Health and Safety: an Issue in Industrial Relations', in *S.A.L.B.*, IX, 7 (June, 1984), pp. 60-75.

10 See M. Swilling, 'The Politics of Working Class Struggles in Germiston, 1979-1983, *History Workshop 1984*, (University of the Witwatersrand, 1984), pp. 26-41.

11 See Johannesburg Correspondent, 'Workshop on Women', *S.A.L.B.*, IX, 3 (December, 1983), pp. 7-17.

12 See 'DOCUMENT: CCAWUSA Maternity Agreement', *S.A.L.B.*, X, 2 (October-November 1984), pp. 109-15; and J. Daphne, 'Maternity Rights: CCAWUSA Shows the Way', *S.A.L.B.*, X, 5 (March-April 1985), pp. 15-16.

13 D. Hindson, 'Union Unity', *S.A.L.B.*, VIII, 6 (June 1983), pp. 9-14.

14 See C. Charney, 'Trade Union Unity Moves: Evaluating the Strengths', *Work in Progress* 27, (1983), pp. 4-7, for a 1983 perspective on the new federation.

Reading 1. (1976)

The Western Province Workers' Advice Bureau*

Dudley Horner

A more general strategy for the organisation of workers than the industrial union approach, is what distinguishes the Western Province Workers' Advice Bureau from other organisations in the country which are organising African workers. Prior examination of the rationale for this different approach is, thus, a necessary requirement for assessing the Advice Bureau's achievements.

In the first place, although the Bureau is open to all workers, only African workers have thus far joined it. The position of the African worker in the western Cape has particularly peculiar characteristics because the area falls within what the authorities have decreed a 'coloured labour preference area'. This means that no employer can employ an African worker without first applying to the Department of Labour for an unemployed 'coloured' worker to fill the vacant post. If no 'coloured' worker is available, the department issues a certificate to this effect and sanctions the employment of African labour. While this policy is obviously an important obstacle in the path of African/'coloured' worker unity, its practical application over many years has ensured that the vast mass of African workers in Cape Town have remained either unskilled labourers or semi-skilled operatives engaged in tasks for which relatively little training is required. The exceptions are the

* First published in *S.A.L.B.*, III, 2 (September, 1976), pp. 74-79.

few professional people, teachers for example, and salesmen, clerks and minor bureaucrats, who together constitute a tiny fraction of the city's African labour force.

A second factor, which aggravates the insecurity of African workers in Cape Town is the severe restriction of their residential rights. Some ten years ago, the government 'froze' the African labour complement of Cape Town and, since that time, it has been impossible for any Africans, other than children born to people legally resident then, to become permanent legal residents of the city. This has meant that the proportion of migrant workers from the Transkei and Ciskei has risen tremendously. The fact that the contracts of these migrants are valid for one year only, after which period they are obliged to return to their places of origin and await new or renewed contracts, tends to keep these workers in relatively unskilled jobs. This leads to a great deal of inter-industry mobility which in turn reinforces their unskilled status. The uncertainty attached to migrant status coupled with vast reservoirs of unemployed people in the Transkei and Ciskei, exacerbates an already insecure job situation.

The aims and the work of the Advice Bureau must be seen against this background. The inter-industry mobility of the relatively unskilled worker, either from choice or — in the case of the migrant worker — from necessity, is of crucial importance. In most industries the African worker has, thus far, been taught a few basic skills only and this fact places him at a serious disadvantage on the bargaining front. At a number of factories, and Cape Town is not exceptional on this score, employers, with little inconvenience to themselves, have been able to dismiss their entire complement of unskilled labour and hire migrant workers as replacements. The displaced seek other jobs wherever available, but often in different industries from those in which they had previously been employed.

Historically the trade union, whether craft or industrial, developed mainly because skills acquired by workers in particular industries provided them with an effective weapon in negotiations with their employers. This does not appear to be true of relatively unskilled workers. The absence of this basic motive for incorporating workers into industrially based organisations, has led the Advice Bureau to conclude that such an approach affords inadequate protection for relatively unskilled workers. In short, the real need is for a more general organisation reflecting the numerical strength of these workers and compensating for their lack of bargaining power based on acquired skills. An organisation of this kind could provide workers with the base they need as they move from job to job or industry to industry, thus ensuring some continuity of interest in spite of mobility.

Of course, certain workers in specific industries would have particular needs and concerns from time to time, because their wages and working conditions are determined industrially by industrial councils or wage determinations. The most general organisation would not prevent workers from coming together, *within this broad base*, to formulate common demands or discuss particular grievances, according to the dictates of a specific situation. This is in fact the policy adopted by the Advice Bureau.

At the work-place the Bureau organises workers in factory committees, duly elected by the workers themselves, and encourages their registration as 'works committees' in terms of the Bantu Labour Relations Regulation Act. This tactic has received criticism from many quarters. The Bureau's view is that registration helps workers gain management recognition. Obligatory legal recognition of this sort provides them with a channel for direct negotiation with their employers. Without this legal sanction it would have been very difficult to get management to recognise the Advice Bureau during the early stage of its development. Then, too, registration may provide some protection against victimisation for committee members. It is true that there have been cases where the act's provisions aimed at preventing victimisation have had little practical value, but it could be argued that victimisation of committee members may have been more serious if they had not been legally registered.

The Advice Bureau, nevertheless, certainly does not contend that registration of a factory committee as a 'works committee' is the principal or essential requisite for sound worker organisation at the work-place. The basic requirements are a united, educated and trained labour force with an elected committee, continuously responsible to the workers and maintaining well-established organisational connections with other committees. In this context the argument for or against registration is immaterial.

We turn, in the light of our earlier sketch, to an examination of the Advice Bureau's methods of organising workers, and its achievements, since its foundation some three-and-a-half years ago.

The Bureau consists, constitutionally, of individual members who elect annually an executive committee, and a board of trustees which functions in an advisory capacity. In the first two years of its existence it employed a single secretary/organiser, but later expanded its personnel to two organisers and an office administrator who handles individual worker complaints.

On paper, membership of the Bureau stands between five and six thousand members organised in factory committees in approximately fifty different establishments. In practice, however, the active membership is about one-quarter of total membership. The reason for this is that many of the factory committees which had initially been organised (which were located mainly in the commercial rather than the industrial sectors) 'dropped out' of ongoing active involvement. They tend to make use of the Bureau only when specific problems arise at their places of work.

There are a number of causes for factory committees withdrawing active support. One cause, experienced by other worker organisations also, is that active membership which tends to increase when particular demands are being pressed, falls off after settlement has been reached. Another is that the Bureau's educational and training programme for committees was haphazard in the beginning and took time to develop properly. However, the main reason for dwindling support from factory committees which the Bureau had originally organised, is that these committees were not concretely involved in the organisational structure. An executive committee elected annually probably could not really achieve the necessary degree of active participation. What happened, inevitably, was that some factory committees were not represented on the executive while newly organised committees could not be brought onto the executive immediately. A further factor was that the executive committee, unsurprisingly, tended to regard itself as responsible to the annual general meeting of workers and was thus in some danger of divorcing itself from the needs and interests, as well as the control, of workers on the factory floor.

In an effort to redress these faults the Bureau evolved a controlling committee of elected representatives of African workers at establishments which had been organised. This committee meets every week and presently consists of representatives of thirteen factories employing about 3 000 workers, mainly from the iron, steel and engineering industries, and the construction industry. The aim is to have representatives of workers at all organised establishments.

The Advice Bureau has, until recent times, encouraged committees at organised factories to negotiate with management, direct. It has not pressed for recognition of the Bureau itself. In practice, circumstances at a particular factory, and demands and objectives arising from the situation there, have been discussed with other factory committees and with Advice Bureau organisers. These have then been pursued by the committee in question in its negotiations with management. The Bureau has only been directly involved in disputes when workers required that legal action be taken. It has, however, taken up individual worker grievances and it was twice involved with management's consent, and at the workers' request, in direct negotiations between factory committees and management. In time, as the organisation develops a firm foundation among workers on the factory floor, it is likely that management will be presented with demands for recognition.

In examining the achievements of the W.P. Workers' Advice Bureau since its inception, one faces the inevitable problem that young organisations tend to be more subjective than objective in their early years. Nevertheless, it remains true that many workers have been assisted with individual problems and grievances. Furthermore, there have undoubtedly been many factories where committees have been helped to negotiate higher wages and better working conditions. However, the most important achievement has probably been the establishment of the beginnings of sound, representative organisation among African workers in Cape Town where before none had existed.

Reading 2. (1979)

A Profile of Unregistered Union Members in Durban*

Eddie Webster

This survey, based on interviews conducted in late 1975, is an attempt to give a clear statistical and attitudinal portrait of the African members of three unions affiliated to the Trade Union Advisory and Coordinating Council (TUACC) in Natal.[1]

Profile of unions surveyed

Table 1 is a detailed profile of the trade unions surveyed: the Chemical Workers' Industrial Union (C.W.I.U.), the Metal and Allied Workers' Union (MAWU), the National Union of Textile Workers (N.U.T.W.).[2]

They were all formed in the wake of the mass strikes in Durban in 1973 (although the C.W.I.U. was only officially formed in 1974, it started accepting members from late 1973). They are all affiliated to the Trade Union Advisory and Coordinating Council (TUACC) and have been influenced by that body's emphasis on the need for strong shop-floor representation. This can be seen in Table 1 where the ratio of paid-up members to shop stewards is: (see p. 19).

* First published in a more extended form in *S.A.L.B.*, IV, 8 (January-February,1979), pp. 43-74.

TABLE 1: PROFILE OF UNIONS SURVEYED IN 1976

		C.W.I.U.	MAWU	N.U.T.W.
1.	Year founded	1974	1973	1973
2.	Secretary	Mr O. Badsha (1975) Ms N. Dlamini (1976)	Mr A. Mthetwa (1976) (banned) Ms J.R. Nala (1977)	Ms J.R. Nala (1976) Mr O. Zuma (1977)
3.	Chairperson of Branch Executive Committee (BEC)	Mr Mbuto (1976) Mr Mpamulu (1977)	Ms B. Tshaba-lala	Mr Manyathi (1976) Mr Mkize (1977)
4.	Locals/ Branches	Jacobs, Pine-town & Dal-bridge	Johannesburg PMB., Dal-bridge	Jacobs, Pine-town & Dal-bridge
5.	Industry covered	chemicals, soaps & candles, oils refinery, pharm-aceuticals, including plas-tics, perfume, paints	metal (engineer-ing, motor manu-facturing)	textiles: blankets, cotton, wool synthetic fibres
6.	Paid Officials	4 (including 1 part-time) (since 1977, 2 paid officials)	6 (including 1 part-time) (since 1977, 1 or 2 paid officials)	4
7.	Shop stewards	48	86	80
8.	Membership:			
	Signed-up	2 900	5 000	6 000
	Paid-up	900	1 000	2 000
	% paid-up	31%	20%	33%
9.	Estimated potential membership in the industry: % signed-up membership	8%	2,5%	40%
10.	Attendance at Annual Meeting	Not available	500	500
11.	Ratio of signed-up members:			
	to paid officials	880:1	940:1	1 500:1
	to shop stewards	60:1	58:1	75:1
12.	Ratio of paid-up members:			
	to paid officials	270:1	190:1	500:1
	to shop stewards	19:1	12:1	25:1
13.	Entrance fee	50 cents	50 cents	50 cents
14.	Annual Sub-scription	R10.40	R10.40	R10.40

         C.W.I.U.   19:1
         MAWU   12:1
         N.U.T.W.   25:1

They all have links with the international trade union movement and the MAWU has been represented on the International Metalworkers' Federation's Coordinating Council from its inception in South Africa.

Profile of union membership

All three of the unions could be classified as industrial unions as they cater for all workers in a single industry irrespective of their race, craft, occupation or grade of skill. Furthermore, the vast bulk of union membership (between eighty and ninety percent) are either unskilled or lower semi-skilled.

Most members (64%) are between thirty and 49 years of age although the N.U.T.W. does have a significantly higher proportion of members between the age of twenty and 39 (72%) than does the C.W.I.U. (42%) and MAWU (35%).

Most members (77%) have a primary school education. However the N.U.T.W. has significantly less members with no education and a higher proportion with Form I, II and III, than the other two unions. This is most probably the result of the higher proportion of younger workers in the N.U.T.W.

Seventy two percent of the union membership had been working in the same job for over two years although only a small percentage stayed on for over ten years (ten percent). The survey suggests, therefore, that union members are relatively stable in their jobs.

Most union members earned between R20-R30 per week. As much as 23% of all union members earned less than R20 and in the N.U.T.W., twenty percent earned less than R15 per week. These figures are similar to those of the Natal Employers Association (N.E.A.) annual wage survey for the year ending 1 May 1975 where they found that the average wage for adult male labourers was R24 per week.

Most of the union members (54%) were born in the rural areas (reserve or 'white' farming areas), twelve percent in peri-urban areas, and 34% were born in Durban. As many as 65% had been working in Durban for more than fifteen years, and only 24% for less than ten years. It is quite likely then that nearly two-thirds of the sample qualify for permanent urban residence either under Section 10, (1) (a) or 10, (1) (b) of the Black (Urban Areas) Consolidation Act.

Recruitment

We were interested in the degree of continuity of membership between the present unions and their fore-runners in the past. We asked respondents whether they had ever been members of trade unions before. One said he had been a member of the I.C.U., a general union prominent in Natal in the 1920s which continued on a loose basis until the 1930s. Eleven percent of the sample had belonged to SACTU — the trade union wing of the Congress movement active in the late 1950s and early 1960s. It ceased to be active publicly in South Africa in 1964 after a wave of bannings and state harassment. It was interesting to note that many respondents were aware of this and said that they had been reluctant to join the present unions because of SACTU's experience of banning, exile and banishment. They contrasted SACTU's concentration on politics on a national level, with the present unions' concern with the day-to-day issues in the factory, and their stress on the need to resolve complaints through shop stewards, and not at the trade union offices.

Our impression was that there existed in the factories a network of informal leadership who had past experience of the repression of formal organisation and who discussed the wisdom of re-establishing trade unions. In some cases they had been members of SACTU or, more recently, they had participated in the wave of strikes in 1973. As the authors of *The Durban Strikes 1973* argue, 'The spread of spontaneous action of this kind (such as the mass action of 1973) will almost certainly depend upon and be influenced by pre-existing informal communication networks, such as friendship groups, "homeboy" groups, groups of people who habitually commute together and so on'.[3] In addition most of those interviewed belonged to informal groups who pool their income such as stokfel or maholisana.[4]

Respondents were asked how they had heard about the present union. Forty three percent mentioned workmates at their place of employment, 25% mentioned hearing about the union in the township and 32% were approached directly by a union organiser at their factory gate.

They were then asked an open-ended question on why they decided to join the union once they got to hear of it. They often gave more than one reason and we decided to categorise the answers under three headings: benefits offered by the union; improvement of wages; and defence of the workers' dignity and rights. This last reason was often expressed in terms of the need for workers to get together to defend their rights. Fifty nine percent gave the last category as their reason for joining the union.

This is a typical reply:

> I had known of the advantages of the union. The employers know of the advantages of the union too and fear them. They know how they (management) rob people of the monies due to them. That is why they do not want anybody who is a member of a trade union. I felt the union would aid me in times of dispute with the management. But more than this there is a need for the workers themselves to be a strong block that will force management to recognise our rights. The union must be so strong that if anything happened to one of its members they must fight to the last degree.

Thirty four percent singled out union benefits (funeral, medical and legal aid) as a reason for joining the union. Seven percent mentioned wages specifically.

Initially unions recruited members on a mass basis. MAWU stated this change in their report to TUACC in August 1975 in these terms:

> Previously organisation had been based on a mass drive for membership without a thorough assessment of the direction of the union or the consequences of such a drive. The heightened militancy of Durban workers following the strikes made the mass organisational drive appear successful, but the subsequent lessening of militancy on the workers' part and the need to train suitably qualified personnel to deal with the problems of the union have necessitated a reassessment of strategy. Broadly speaking, this reassessment had resulted in two major changes in strategy:
> a) Decentralisation.

b) Concentration of resources upon a few carefully selected factories.

Decentralisation
This has taken two directions:
1) The union officials now concentrate primarily upon training of workers in shop stewards' committees, making it in turn the responsibility of these shop steward committees to recruit and organise members, and to collect subscriptions. Regular meetings of shop stewards from particular factories are held and training is integrated with the ongoing organisation process at these factories.
2) The office in Jacobs was established in order to encourage more participation in union affairs by members whose place of work is in that area.

Concentration of resources
(A number of factories are then mentioned).

Problems facing Africans in the work-place

The most common problem mentioned was victimisation and arbitrary action against African workers (38%). Respondents said it was difficult to prove victimisation for trade union activity, as it was often done in the form of 'redundancy'. If the factory has to go on to short time, they said, it is the union activists who are laid off first. Another important form of victimisation mentioned by respondents is that applied to contract workers. A contract worker who is dismissed has to return immediately to the rural areas. With the present rate of unemployment this will mean that he is not likely to have his contract renewed and will have to remain in the rural areas. One respondent said management used the contract system to 'weed-out' trade unionists by simply not re-employing them when their contracts expire.

In addition respondents mentioned, under the broad heading of 'victimisation and arbitrary action', a range of actions on management's part that they felt showed either management's lack of conception of them as human beings or management's arbitrariness. Here reference was frequently made to the fact that management gave preference in promotion to Indians. Many spoke of this tendency as if it were a deliberate attempt to divide the working class.[5] Clearly Indian-African hostility is a potential problem for unions concerned with attempting to establish nonracial solidarity, but this problem should not be exaggerated. The unregistered textile union had complete cooperation from the local branch of the registered, largely Indian and coloured union (T.W.I.U.) until the head office in Cape Town ruptured relations in 1976 after the bannings of some TUACC officials. The main reason for the cooperation of the local branch of T.W.I.U. was that only about fifteen percent of the workers in the textile industry are eligible to belong to the registered union i.e. are Indian. On its own this union would be very weak, so it needs to cooperate with the much larger unregistered union. It seems, therefore, not unreasonable to postulate that if there were freedom of association, and Africans and Indians could join common unions, they would do so if *only* because of the economic benefits of collective bargaining. There is evidence of precisely this kind of solidarity emerging in the Smith and Nephew factory, where, when the T.W.I.U. head office withdrew cooperation from the unregistered N.U.T.W., the majority of Indian workers in that factory chose to join the unregistered union. In this situation their class interest lay clearly in inter-racial working class solidarity.

The next most common problem mentioned (35%) was low wages. This problem was often accompanied by complaints about the growing number of unemployed Africans and the numbers being laid-off.

The lack of recognition of trade union representatives by management was the third most common problem mentioned (twelve percent) by respondents. The ineffectiveness of liaison committees and the 'planting' of informers to try and divide workers was also frequently mentioned.

All three of the unions were, at the time of the survey, conducting negotiations with management over recognition in some of the factories where they were organised. Some of these negotiations had already broken down by the time the survey was completed. In all cases management evaded recognition by promoting works or liaison committees as *alternatives* to the trade unions.[6]

Dangerous work conditions (eight percent) was raised in strong emotional terms by some members particularly those working with chemicals.

Members' perceptions of the unions

When asked whether the union was helping to overcome their problems nearly half (49%) answered clearly in the affirmative. Only three percent said no while 45% felt that the union's performance could not be judged because it was not recognised and its members were vulnerable to victimisation if they tried to solve workers' problems. Here is an example of this type of response to the question.

> This is very difficult because most of the things need an open challenge, yet we can't do it because we can then be exposing ourselves to victimisation by police and management.

TABLE 2: 'WHAT DOES THE UNION NEED TO MAKE IT EFFECTIVE?'

	Recognition through unity	More involvement in factories	Increased members	Links with Kwa-Zulu	More militant	Other	Total
	%	%	%	%	%	%	%
C.W.I.U.	33	39	17	0	0	11	100
MAWU	27	35	15	0	4	19	100
N.U.T.W.	50	28	9	2	2	9	100
Total	39	33	13	1	2	12	100

When asked how the union could become more effective, 39% mentioned the need for greater unity and discipline to win recognition. Thirty three percent mentioned the need for the union to have more contact with its members in the factories by taking up specific issues (see Table 2).

Maintaining contact between organisers and members is made particularly difficult by the long distances organisers have to travel, which is in part the result of the Group Areas Act. Transport costs are the second largest item next to wages for most unions. Organisers have to work four regular evenings a week attending shop steward meetings. The unions thus spent a great deal of time and money developing factory structures in an attempt to consolidate support in the factory and establish the shop steward as the key link between the union office and the shop-floor.

An interesting feature of members' responses to this section of the questionnaire is that only two percent of the membership felt the union needed to become more militant. Many of them stressed the extent to which the unions had taught them to exercise their collective power in a disciplined and cautious way.

Factors inhibiting membership growth

The percentage of the potential work-force in each industry which is organised by the unions is low except for the N.U.T.W. (forty percent). We asked respondents, therefore, why more workers did not join the union.

Fear of intimidation from employers and from the state was the reason 44% of the respondents gave when asked why more workers did not join the union.

> They fear employers who always give an impression that the unions are dangerous and adventurous bodies and threaten to dismiss anyone who joins the union.
> They have fear of the police. The police consider the union as the same thing with the Congress (A.N.C.) because it fights against oppression.
> When the organisers make explanations they put it clearly that the union is not registered. As a result many people keep away and interpret 'not registered' as meaning 'illegal'.
> Africans consider it illegal to join the union or something that ultimately leads one to trouble or confrontation with the police.
> Many believe there can be informers within the union membership which at a later stage can lead to some ill information oozing out to the

police or management, leading to arrests.

One member interviewed described how he hides his union card at work because he is afraid of informers. There seemed, he said, to be general agreement that you can only talk about unions to those whom you can trust.[7]

These fears have a clear base in objective experience. Not long after the survey was completed the secretary of MAWU was banned for five years under the Internal Security Act and the secretary of N.U.T.W. was detained under the Terrorism Act for nine months then released without any charges being laid. In January 1974 four Durban trade unionists were banned. In November 1976, 26 men and women involved with African worker organisation were banned. In the textile industry alone 27 trade unionists have been banned since 1950.

The second largest category of responses (33%) to the question why more workers did not join the union was amongst those who felt there was basic pessimism about any chances of survival of unions. These two responses sum up this category:

> We Africans do not have good knowledge of the unions. Unions all the time have been considered by us as something we are not allowed to participate in or found. Many people do not consider the African unions to be having any future as it is.
>
> As they understand it, it is something for the whites. Some people do not believe that there are any means by a black man that can make a white man either change his attitude or yield to some force by a black man. Hence you find some people saying 'What can Buthelezi do for me? He is black and can't get anywhere'.

A considerably smaller proportion (eleven percent) attributed lack of support of the union to corruption among union officials.

> Many people have had their monies collected by people who later disappear. This has led to distrust of them who form unions.

Membership maintenance

Two thirds of the sample were members whose subscription fees had lapsed, i.e. they were 28 weeks in arrears. These figures are similar to the proportion of paid-up members in Table 1: 31% in the C.W.I.U., twenty percent in MAWU and 33% in N.U.T.W. They were asked why they stopped paying their subscriptions.

The most frequent reasons (forty percent) given for ceasing to pay subs were personal factors unrelated to the union. These included such factors as financial difficulties, changing jobs, being too busy with family affairs, etc. (The answer to this particular question must be treated with caution — although the interviewer made it clear that he was not from the unions, it is possible that some would have given reasons that would not offend the union.) Twelve percent stopped paying because they believed that the union had been inefficient. Six percent were disillusioned in general with the unions' progress. This response typifies this category:

> This union is useless and fails to respect its promises. I hate such things.
> We are in a bad position. We need help from people, not to be cheated.

The collection of subscriptions is clearly a problem for the unions. The Industrial Conciliation Act allows employers to make check-off (or stop-order) deductions on behalf of the registered trade unions against the wages of employers (Sec. 51/3). This facility is denied Africans, which in terms of the Bantu Labour Act, is made illegal (No. 67 of 1964; Sec. 16/11). (The implications of the recent abolition of Section 16 is not yet clear.) Unregistered unions are forced to collect dues by one of the four following methods:
a) organisers can visit the work-place if they have access to it, or else, stand at the factory gates,
b) they can try and develop a sufficiently cohesive shop steward committee to collect the dues at the work-place,
c) they can get subscriptions indirectly in conjunction with a life insurance scheme,
d) workers pay membership fees at the union offices.

Amongst the TUACC unions only b) and d) are used.

The unions and politics

The debate about the relationship between trade unions and political parties is a long-standing one in the labour movement. Amongst African workers in South Africa it has taken a particularly controversial form because of the tendency of working class organisations to link up with the movement for national liberation. For example, in 1955 SACTU was formed with the specific intention of engaging in 'political unionism' and linked up with the Congress movement in its national political campaigns.

The TUACC affiliated unions have eschewed any involvement with the nationalist movement and have been concerned to establish an independent trade union organisation. However, nationalist politics remain crucial areas of interest for African workers and we were concerned to establish what perception of present and past leadership union members had.

TABLE 3: 'CAN YOU THINK OF A LEADER PRESENT OR PAST WHO CAN OR COULD IMPROVE THE POSITION OF AFRICAN WORKERS?'

Unions	Lutuli	G. Buthelezi	Mandela	M. Mabhida	Others	Total
	%	%	%	%	%	%
C.W.I.U.	58	8	0	17	17	100
MAWU	42	25	17	8	8	100
N.U.T.W.	40	24	8	4	24	100
Total	44	19	10	8	19	100

Table 3 indicates that Chief Albert Lutuli, President General of the A.N.C. until his death in 1967, remains the most popular nationalist political figure. Not surprisingly, since Durban is a predominantly Zulu-speaking area, Chief Gatsha Buthelezi, Chief Minister of KwaZulu, was rated second, followed by Nelson Mandela, the jailed leader of the A.N.C. (what support A.N.C. leaders would have if they were free to campaign for that organisation is a crucial question which clearly we could not answer). Moses Mabhida, a SACTU leader in the 1950s and early 1960s was seen by some as a leader of African workers.

The attitude of union members to Chief Buthelezi is of particular interest because of Buthelezi's overtures to the trade unions in 1975 to join the newly established Inkatha movement. The trade unions were concerned to maintain the independent position mentioned earlier and decided not to join but encouraged individual members to join if they so wished. The survey clearly shows the widespread support Buthelezi has amongst workers: 87% said they think of him as their leader.

However, if age is taken as a variable a clear tendency for the younger members to be critical of Buthelezi is noticeable. Those who are critical say that he is not a 'workers' leader' or they say that he has made promises but nothing has come about.

Conclusion

The evidence presented in this survey seems to suggest that the *necessary* conditions for effective trade unions now largely exist among the members of these three unregistered trade unions. These conditions involve, essentially, the existence of a body of life-long wage earners, dependent on wages and aware of the benefits of collective bargaining. We have shown that members in this sample are relatively stable in their jobs and join unions to try collectively to improve their wages and work conditions. These are the necessary conditions; the sufficient conditions for effective trade unions involve the readiness of both management and the state to allow the emergence of collective organisation in the work-place and a willingness to recognise and negotiate with its leadership on a permanent basis. We suggested earlier that some changes in this direction are discernible; in Durban, as yet, only one company, Smith and Nephew, has been prepared to enter into a negotiated agreement with a trade union, N.U.T.W.

However, a central dilemma for these members remains. When asked whether the union was helping members to overcome their problems, nearly half (45%) of the respondents said the union could not be judged because it was not recognised. There is no evidence that they rejected the union per se; they seemed to accept the necessity for a strategy based on the day-to-day issues in the factory rather than national political issues. For the present, in as much as they have a 'political consciousness', it is a politics of the factory — what Beynon had called a working class factory consciousness.[8] Their commitment to the union arises, not so much from the benefits it offers, but because they believe it will help them in their struggle in the work-place where conflict takes place with management over control of the job.

Yet, as Table 3 indicates, members still retain a loyalty to certain national political figures, and many, as a response to certain pressures, increasingly turn to more 'political' forms of involvement. However, what forms such political involvement could take, and what the relationship between work-place organisation and the working class party should be, is an issue which must be left to another occasion.

Notes

1 Although the bulk of the survey data was drawn from a conventional questionnaire, some information on the unions was derived from my 'participant observation' in the unions over the period 1973 to 1975 when I served on the Working Committee of the Institute for Industrial Education (I.I.E.), the educational wing of the Trade Union Advisory and Coordinating Council (TUACC).

   Acknowledgement is made to the S.A.I.R.R. for financial assistance and to Judson Kuzwayo for conducting the interviews.

2 Most of these statistics are derived from Appendix A. 1 and A. 2 in John Lewsen, Black Trade Unions in South Africa, unpublished M.B.A. dissertation, University of Witwatersrand, 1976.

3 *The Durban strikes 1973*, (I.I.E., 1974), p. 92.

4 For similar information on 'informal groups' among African workers in Durban see E. Webster, 'A Research Note on Consciousness and the Problem of Organisation' in L. Schlemmer and E. Webster, *Change, Reform and Economic Growth in S.A.*, (Ravan Press, 1977), p. 229.

5 For a discussion of similar alleged preferential treatment towards Indians by management see E. Webster, 'The 1949 Durban Riots' in P.L. Bonner, *Working Papers in Southern African Studies*, (Institute of African Studies, 1977).

6 For two short case studies of management's attempts to evade recognition by promoting works and liaison committees see E. Webster, 'Management's Counter-Offensive' *S.A.L.B.*, II, 3 (1975), pp. 33-34.

7 For further information on 'company spies' see the cross-examination by the defence of the Wentex employee in the State vs Mbali, *S.A.L.B.*, II, 9-10 (1976), pp. 54-57.

8 'A factory class consciousness' Beynon says, 'understands class relationships in terms of their direct manifestation in conflict between the bosses and the workers within the factory. It is rooted in the work-place where struggles are fought over the control of the job and the 'rights' of managers and workers. In as much as it concerns itself with exploitation and power it contains definite political elements. But it is a politics of the factory'. H. Beynon, *Working for Ford*, (Allen Lane, London, 1973), p. 98.

Reading 3. (1982)

SAAWU in the East London area: 1979-1981*

Johann Maree

Introduction

SAAWU, the South African Allied Workers' Union, is at present a
highly significant workers' organisation as a nonracial independent
trade union led entirely by Africans and overtly political in its pro-
nouncements. It is also faced by a unique situation in the East London area. Most of its members live in Mdantsane which is in the
Ciskei, but work in industries located in South Africa. As a result
SAAWU is locked in a struggle against a triple alliance in the
Border region. The triple alliance comprises the South African and
Ciskeian states and many regional employers. All three work closely together to undermine and, if possible, to destroy this independent worker organisation, but its members and leaders are display-
ing a remarkable endurance and tenacity. By the end of 1981, after
three years of existence, it still appeared to be a vibrant movement
with popular support from African workers in the region.

The aims of this article are to outline the development and
growth of SAAWU and to assess its strength and viability in East
London and its environs.

*First published in a more extended form in *S.A.L.B.*, VII, 4 and 5
(February, 1982), pp. 34-49.

History of SAAWU

a) From origins to 1980

The birth of SAAWU can be traced to a National Conference of the Black Allied Workers' Union (South Africa), (BAWU) in March 1979 in Durban. During the course of 1978 a split had developed in BAWU over the representation of the union overseas by Drake Koka, a founder of BAWU, who was in exile. The split divided between those who supported him and the black consciousness philosophy and those who opposed him and favoured nonracialism. His supporters were mainly from the Johannesburg and Newcastle branches and his opponents from the Durban and East London branches. The National Conference decided to expel the Johannesburg and Newcastle officials and to change the name of the organisation to the South African Allied Workers' Union (SAAWU).[1] Thozamile Gqwetha, who was present at the meeting as national organiser from East London, subsequently explained why SAAWU adopted a nonracial principle: 'We believe the country has a nonracial future and we must therefore be totally nonracial.'[2]

Although Gqweta deserves the credit for the founding and growth of SAAWU in the East London region, the history of Africans in the area provided a fertile and well-tilled soil for SAAWU to grow in.

SAAWU's support consequently shot up in 1980. Five months after opening the union offices the claimed membership had grown from 5 000 to 15 000. The South African state was so concerned about the growing popularity and strength of SAAWU, an unregistered trade union, that the Minister of Manpower, Fanie Botha, flew to East London in October and urged employers in a closed meeting to 'hold out against the union' and not to recognise it.[3]

In November SAAWU achieved its first major break through when Chloride (S.A.) agreed to recognise it after a ballot in which 95% of the workers at the plant voted in favour of representation by SAAWU. It constituted the first formal recognition of SAAWU by a company in East London thereby shattering the attempted united stand against the unregistered union.

b) 1981

During 1981 SAAWU entrenched itself more thoroughly at the

work-place by securing a number of informal and formal recognitions. In March SAAWU achieved another major break through when Johnson and Johnson agreed to formal recognition after a referendum in which 93,5% of workers voted to be represented by the union. At that time the union also announced that K.S.M., a South African owned milling company was soon to recognise SAAWU.

Increased recognition for SAAWU did not mean that its members did not get involved in industrial conflict. There were strikes of major significance during the year. On 9 February, 92 workers at Wilson-Rowntree were fired for going on strike because of the dismissal of three workers in the toffee department over a job dispute. By a fort-night later a further 412 workers had gone on strike in support of the initial 92. They were also dismissed bringing the total workers out on strike to 504 which constituted half of the African work-force at Wilson-Rowntree.[4] As a result of this SAAWU called for a consumer boycott in March.

Other major strikes followed during the year. In October two strikes took place. At Johnson and Johnson 550 African workers went on strike after the company had dismissed an employee, Tempi, for allegedly stealing two toilet rolls. The strike followed within a few months of signing an agreement between the company and SAAWU, but the union appeared to have been caught out in the agreement. While SAAWU's striking workers held mass meetings at which they resolved not to return to work until Tempi had been reinstated, management resolutely stuck to the terms of the agreement claiming that the workers had gone on strike before exhausting all agreed procedures and that negotiations could not proceed until workers were back at work. A week after the strike commenced Johnson and Johnson placed a full page advertisement in the *Daily Dispatch* which set the following day as a deadline for workers to return or be fired. As a result the workers backed down from their demands on the advice of Gqweta at a mass meeting and returned to work whereafter negotia-tions on the reinstatement of Tempi commenced.

At Dunlop Flooring 500 African workers were fired for going on strike over a pensions dispute. Dunlop Flooring management commenced soon afterwards to recruit new labour, but appeared to experience difficulty finding suitably qualified labour.[5] As a result they first turned to the Ciskei Manpower Centre in Mdantsane to assist in recruiting. When this proved inadequate the Ciskei Central Intelligence Service (C.C.I.S.) acted as a recruiting agent and screened

150 work seekers who applied. Brigadier Charles Sebe, head of the C.C.I.S., explained the involvement of Ciskeian security police in the recruitment by saying that workers who had lost their jobs at Wilson-Rowntree for striking and were subsequently hired at Car Distributors Assembly (C.D.A.) were involved in a strike at C.D.A. Consequently 'some industrialists have come to realise the need for screening'. His department was committed to 'eliminating this element' and he relied on 'industrialists to cooperate with us in stamping out this evil'.[6]

The repression intensified in September when the Ciskei security police detained 205 trade unionists, mostly SAAWU members, upon their return in three buses to Mdantsane from a union mass meeting in East London.

Events took an ominous turn on 31 October when a fire mysteriously destroyed the home of Gqweta's parents killing his uncle and, a few days later, his mother who died from serious burn wounds. As mourners returned in buses to Mdantsane from the funeral, attended by about 5 000 people, armed police ordered them to disperse. When they did not do so the police opened fire on the defenceless crowd wounding several and killing Deliswa Roxiso, a close friend of Gqweta.

SAAWU's principles, policy and practices

Principles

SAAWU's spokesmen state that it is a nonracial trade union committed to mass participatory democracy. During the Johnson and Johnson strike Sisa Njikelana said 'We believe in mass participatory democracy which means the workers and not the union officials dictate what action is to be taken.'[7] Although SAAWU is seen as a trade union it is also considered to be tied to the community. Every person interviewed linked it with the community: 'SAAWU is a trade union dealing with workers who are part and parcel of the community. Transport, rents to be paid, are also worker issues. I see SAAWU as a trade union. There's no doubt about it. The problems of the work-place go outside the work-place. If you are underpaid it goes at home or the community.'[8]

SAAWU's strength is considered to lie in the shop-floor and it is viewed as a force through which to obtain political rights. Said one member: 'Trade unionism is new to us, but a backbone to obtain our rights'.

Policy

SAAWU considers itself to be an unregistered federation of trade unions. It is strongly opposed to registration because it fundamentally rejects present legislation as being oppressive and discriminatory. Explaining the opposition of SAAWU to registration, Njikelana said registration meant swearing an oath of allegiance to racially discriminatory laws with which the workers did not agree. He also said '. . . if we were to register into the institutionalised labour system we would be acknowledging support for the present labour laws. This we cannot do because the workers do not want to'.[9] Because there is such a gut feeling against registration there appears to be no careful analysis by members and officials of the controls or opportunities that registration might bring.

SAAWU takes up a position on political matters more overtly and explicitly than other independent trade unions. It has demanded that black workers be granted political rights. At its third annual congress' in Durban in May 1981 it demanded universal franchise in South Africa as well as the abolition of pass laws and the migrant labour system. At a conference the preceding year it also called for the abolition of the Group Areas Act and the Separate Amenities Act.

Ciskeian independence has been very strongly opposed by SAAWU. Some of the harshest criticisms by union officials were reserved for the Ciskei, its independence and authorities. The essence of SAAWU's reasons for opposing the Ciskei and its independence were that Ciskeian workers would lose their South African rights in an independent state and that the Ciskei government was being used by the South African government to oppress Africans.[10] After the funerals of his mother, uncle and close friend, Gqweta issued his strongest statement yet against the Ciskeian authorities: 'A ship of fools will never escape its revolutionary destiny — this is what the illegitimate son of Pretoria called Ciskei is driving people to. The leaders of Ciskei are political fanatics.'[11]

Practices
a) Organisational methods and structures
SAAWU's organisational focus is the work-place because it believes

that is where its strength lies. Only after more than sixty percent membership has been achieved at a plant does a workers' committee get elected there under the auspices of the union. The workers' committee is composed of a Central Executive Committee elected from the whole factory plus shop stewards who are elected from each department. Only the Central Executive Committee negotiates with management while shop stewards are 'feelers' in the work-place. They filter grievances through to the Central Executive and report back to workers. Union officials hold regular meetings with the workers' committee over industrial training.

The next level of organisation in the union is the Branch Committee. Each region has a branch committee that is composed of the Branch Executive Committee, and the chairman and secretary from each of the companies organised in the region. The East London Branch Executive Committee (B.E.C.) in December 1981 had five posts. All the members of the B.E.C., with the exception of the treasurer, were union organisers. Likewise the overarching controlling body of SAAWU, the National Executive Committee, contained a majority of organisers, namely T. Gqweta (president), S. Njikelana (vice-president), S. Kikine (general secretary), plus an under-secretary and treasurer. There is therefore formally no workers' control in the two top-most structures of SAAWU, but the officials claim that all decisions are referred to workers at each branch.

SAAWU has relied heavily in the past on mass meetings to refer decisions taken by the Branch Committee to workers. Mass meetings were used not only to ratify Branch Committee decisions, but also to maintain the solidarity of workers and sustain support for the union. For instance, union meetings in September and October 1980 to discuss strikes were attended by at least 2 000 workers each. In December 1981 a thousand workers met at the East London city hall to condemn the detention of SAAWU officials.

However the Ciskeian and South African authorities have sought to undermine SAAWU organisation by blocking venues used for meetings by the union. The pressure even extended to the office space rented by SAAWU and at the end of December 1981 it faced its second eviction from premises it was renting.

A way in which contact is maintained between union members and officials is by officials encouraging members to visit the union office and they stress that every member knows where the office is. SAAWU also has novel ways of organising and building up popular support.

Union officials board buses and encourage workers to sing union songs.

It is relevant to ask whether all these organisational practices of SAAWU effectively express a mass participatory democracy or not. In other words, is SAAWU putting its principle of mass participatory democracy into practice? When probing this issue with a member of the East London Branch Committee he maintained that it was democratic to take issues raised by the Branch Committee back to workers through workers' committees, but it was also democractic and preferable for workers to participate at mass meetings because it was easy for a worker who did not understand anything to ask.

The system of referral of decisions by the Branch Committee or a higher body down to the workers through the workers' committee is more akin to a system of representative democracy. This is more clear when considering the Branch Executive and National Executive Committees. Both these committees have majorities of union officials, not workers, who take decisions that are only subsequently ratified by members. These decisions also have to be passed through several levels of organisation before they reach shop-floor members.

On the other hand participation at mass meetings clearly has its limits. At a meeting of 2 000 or even 200 members very few of them can actually get an opportunity to speak especially when officials give lengthy speeches as happened at some meetings. Certain sensitive union work such as the drafting and hammering out of an agreement cannot be done at a mass meeting either. A final agreement can virtually only be ratified or rejected at a mass meeting. It seems as if SAAWU officials did not properly inform workers of the content of the Johnson and Johnson agreement before signing it, a factor which was responsible for weakening the workers' position considerably during the subsequent strike.[12] Too much reliance had been placed in the past on the union's leaders for many of its activities.

The key question to ask about SAAWU is whether the mass of workers control and participate in union policy and activities. The lack of worker majorities in the highest committees constitutes a problem at the upper level while the rather inferior role for shop stewards vis-a-vis the Central Executive Committee presents another problem at the grassroots level. Frequent holding of mass meetings, whenever possible, could counteract the exclusion of workers and their representatives from key committees, but the attendance of mass meetings does not imply mass participation and control. Mass meetings cannot be equated with mass participatory democracy. The union is however committed to achieving workers' participation and control and an awareness exists of the shortcomings and obstacles that inhibit such a process in the union.

What are SAAWU's organisational strengths and weaknesses? By the end of 1981 its two strongest factories were Chloride and K.S.M. while Johnson and Johnson, Parker Pen and Nairn Industries (carpets) were the next strongest. It had formal recognition at three companies and some form of *de facto* recognition at a further seven. It is in these ten factories that SAAWU's greatest immediate industrial strength lies. As a rough estimate its membership could be in the vicinity of 2 500 at these companies. While the union certainly has membership and organisation at many other factories, it would be unwise to take SAAWU's claimed membership figures as an indication of its strength. In July 1981 membership in the East London area was stipulated at 20 000 and growing rapidly.[13] As far as paid-up membership is concerned, it would have been a maximum of 5 000 during the latter half of the year judged by the subscriptions collected.[14]

On the other hand strikes which were not entered into judiciously enough weakened the union by precipitating the mass dismissal of workers. By selective re-employment management was able to eliminate the strong SAAWU members thereby giving union organisation and membership at such factories blows which have been hard to recover from. Membership has to be painfully built up again and the union can be faced by workers who are reluctant to get involved in union affairs again. Companies at which this happened include S.A.T.V., Raylite, Furniture Industries, Berkshire, Everite and Dunlop Flooring. The outcome of the Wilson-Rowntree strike is still awaited, hence its name may not yet be added to the above list.

SAAWU's strength does not lie exclusively in shop-floor organisation. It also lies in the popular support it receives from East London's African workers.

b) Community involvement
SAAWU's involvement in black communities has thus far exclusively taken the form of expressing support for community issues and making overt political demands for blacks. SAAWU leaders have frequently appeared on public platforms with community organisations and expressed solidarity with their objectives. For instance in May 1981 Njikelana took part in anti-Republic rallies on the Wit-

watersrand and called for a 'People's Republic' at one protest meeting.[15] He also made an explicit call for solidarity in order to achieve political liberation at a Wilson-Rowntree boycott mass rally in Cape Town when he called on people to unite: 'Genuine cooperation will bring the progressive movement closer together for the liberation of the oppressed and exploited people of South Africa.'[16]

The public support for community issues and political demands makes SAAWU popular with the black community and could also raise the community's expectations that SAAWU should play an active role in support of their demands. It is not clear that SAAWU leaders would be comfortable with such a role, but while it is the only viable independent black organisation in East London such expectations could persist.

The other side of the coin of SAAWU's overt political demands, is that it has become highly unpopular with the South African and Ciskeian states. This accounts considerably for the fact that they, together with many Border employers, have seriously attempted to destroy SAAWU.

Onslaught against SAAWU

The fundamental reason why the South African and Ciskeian states have launched an assault against SAAWU is because it constitutes an ideological, political and economic threat to the policy of separate development and to the Ciskei. Ideologically SAAWU is nonracial, believing in participatory democracy and its leadership has called for a government based on workers' interests. As such it challenges the racial and bourgeois foundations of the whole system. Politically it opposes the very existence of the Ciskei, not only its independence. Its outspoken opposition, as well as its widespread popular support amongst African workers in the Border region, are threats to the legitimacy of the Ciskeian authorities' who have to resort to force and violence to retain control. Economically SAAWU challenges the Ciskei authorities' desire to supply the Border employers with a cheap and docile labour force.

As a result there is an orchestrated onslaught on the part of the South African and Ciskeian states in cooperation with many regional employers to repress SAAWU. The union has been subject to police baton-charges, frequent detentions of members and officials of the union, repeated charges under the Riotous Assemblies Act, direct interventions by Major General Charles Sebe and his department, the C.C.I.S., and of the South African security police in industrial disputes and the affairs of the union. In addition to this a document written by an officer in the Security Branch of the South African Police on how to break the power of SAAWU was circulated to companies in East London in the second half of 1980.[17] The security police document proposed long-term and short-term solutions to break SAAWU's power. The long-term solutions put forward were either to force black unions to register as industrial unions or to encourage TUCSA to become more active in recruiting and organising workers in East London. The short-term solutions included a strike-breaking strategy of encouraging firms to keep records of unemployed workers with whom they could immediately replace striking workers. A labour reserve list would help firms 'not to give in to ridiculous demands' and make it easier for them 'not to give in to pressure from the workers if they demand that SAAWU be recognised as a union'. Another short-term plan rested on the claim that chairmen of the Chambers of Industry and Commerce as well as the Afrikaanse Sakekamer were 'attending meetings where the aims of SAAWU are being explained to them as well as the necessity of uniform action by industry in East London against SAAWU', and that these chairmen would call meetings of representatives of different industries where 'they would press for uniform action of all industries'.[18]

The security police document on how to break the power of SAAWU received even greater significance when the Minister of Police, L. le Grange, placed his seal of approval on it in parliament when he answered that the security policeman concerned 'acted in good faith towards the maintenance of law and order as provided in section five of the Police Act, 1958'.[19] He also said that no action would be taken against the officer concerned. Steven Friedman, labour reporter of the *Rand Daily Mail*, commented that Minister le Grange seemed to be saying that in certain circumstances it was legitimate for policemen to 'break' legal organisations — in this case SAAWU, an unregistered trade union.[20] The attempted destruction by the security police of an unregistered trade union that did not conform to the government's desired policy thus received overt support from the Minister of Police. This raises the question whether the executive of government — through the principle of joint cabinet responsibility — approves of the attempt on the part of the security police to break the legal, but unregistered and independent, trade union.

Maybe the most remarkable aspect of the onslaught against SAAWU on the part of the South African and Ciskeian states is the fact that SAAWU has thus far survived it. The major reasons that account for its survival are firstly the fact that SAAWU does seem to have popular support from its members at the work-place. Secondly the organisation's leaders have shown a remarkable resilience and commitment to their members. When Njikelana was released after his fourth detention, he said 'detentions only harden us and make us more determined to strive for justice and democracy in this land . . . . My detention has only made me more resolute about carrying on. We have a duty to our members not to let things like this interfere with our work.'[21] Thirdly, SAAWU appears to have a fair depth of leadership and organisational ability. Therefore the detention of leaders had not stopped union organisation from carrying on although it has disrupted it quite severely.

The detentions have the unforeseen advantage of forcing the union to face up to the fact that it had placed too much reliance on its leaders in the past. It has therefore been forced into organising in a way that shares responsibilities more widely.

Fourthly, some employers had broken ranks by recognising SAAWU thereby undermining the attempted strategy of other employers and the security police. Finally the South African state has thus far restricted its onslaught to a low level attrition on SAAWU. It has not banned the organisation nor any of its leaders outright because it is most probably trying to persuade the international community that freedom of association exists in South Africa.

Conclusion

The emergence of SAAWU in the East London area over the past three years is of immense significance politically. Unlike the independent trade unions that emerged in the early 1970s there were no former trade unionists or white intellectuals involved in the formation or leadership of the union. The African leaders of SAAWU were relatively young men in their mid-twenties without any former trade union experience when the union commenced. Nonetheless they established a viable worker organisation that severely challenged arbitrary managerial rule over black workers in factories that sparked off intensive industrial conflict in the region over the past two years. They were also soon perceived as a threat to the system by the South African and Ciskeian states.

When SAAWU is viewed in the context of the South African political economy, it is only to be expected that the lack of political rights for black workers would make the workers want to use the organisation to attain their political rights. Its overt political role had generated a great deal of popular support. This has simultaneously been a source of great potential strength and of great danger to the organisation as it unleashed a repressive onslaught by two states on SAAWU. The struggle between SAAWU on the one hand and the South African and Ciskeian states on the other hand has been characterised by the immense inequality between the two sides. Whereas the only weapon at the disposal of SAAWU has been the ability of workers to withhold their labour power, the states have used a wide range of repressive measures at their disposal. These have included baton charges, detentions, court cases, the Riotous Assemblies Act and other repressive laws, and, more recently, shooting. Security police interventions to try and break the power of SAAWU occurred continuously and included an attempt to organise a united front against SAAWU on the part of East London employers. Many employers have cooperated, but some have broken ranks and decided to recognise SAAWU as the representative trade union at their factories. It is therefore in work-place organisation that SAAWU has made its greatest gains and entrenched itself most thoroughly in the East London region.

Notes

1 Minutes of the National Conference of Black Allied Workers' Union (South Africa), 23-25 March 1979.
2 *Rand Daily Mail (R.D.M.)*, 31 October, 1980.
3 *R.D.M.*, 24 August, 1980.
4 See the article on Wilson-Rowntree by Mike Morris in *S.A.L.B.*, VII, 4 and 5 (February, 1982), pp. 18-27.
5 See the article, 'East London and Labour: 1981, a Summary', *S.A.L.B.*, VII, 4 and 5 (February, 1982), pp. 28-33.

6 *Daily Dispatch (D.D.)*, 10 November, 1981.
7 *D.D.*, 17 October, 1981.
8 Interviews, SAAWU East London offices, 14 December, 1981.
9 *D.D.*, 22 January, 1981.
10 *R.D.M.*, 31 July 1981.
11 *Sunday Express*, 15 November, 1981.
12 See 'East London and Labour: 1981, a Summary' p. 32.
13 *R.D.M.*, 31 July 1981.
14 Interview with Mzuzwana (Yure) Mdyogolo, 14 December, 1981.
15 *Sowetan*, 29 May 1981.
16 *Cape Times*, 7 September, 1981.
17 *Hansard*, 7 August, 1981, Col. 23.
18 Document: 'Labour Situation — East London', *S.A.L.B.*, VI, 8 (July, 1981), p. 17.
19 *Hansard*, 19 August, 1981, Col. 92-3.
20 *R.D.M.*, 24 August, 1981.
21 *Sowetan* and *D.D.*, 11 August, 1981.

Reading 4. (1982)

Growth of a New Worker Organ — the Germiston Shop Stewards' Council*

Jeremy Baskin

'People work all the time now. We are like preachers, only it is the Church of Union now.' (Shop stewards' council member.)

A crowd of about 500 workers make up the audience at the D.H. Williams Hall in Katlehong. It is mid-April. Every three months the Germiston Local of FOSATU holds a general meeting for all members in the area. The mood is positive and militant in this, one of the fastest growing areas for FOSATU. The chairman opens the meeting with a brief speech. The struggle has come a long way, he says. But we should remember that we are not fighting only for a twenty cents wage increase, but for our rights and for our country. Workers in the audience shout their approval.

Then the organisers' reports begin. Moses Mayekiso of Metal and Allied Workers' Union reports that MAWU membership in the area is now about 10 000. Factory after factory gets reported. The details of various strikes are given. Since the beginning of the year over thirty factories have struck for wage increases.

Then Ephraim Tshabalala rises to report on the Chemical Workers' Industrial Union (C.W.I.U.). The union is active in

---

* First published in a more extended form in *S.A.L.B.*, VII, 8 (July, 1982), pp. 42-53.

eleven factories in Wadeville and has 2 900 members. One story he tells makes the audience angry.

The Glass and Allied Workers' Union (GAWU), with a local membership of about 800, gives its report. A Carlton Paper shop steward gives the report on the Paper Wood and Allied Workers' Union (PWAWU). He reports only on a recent strike following dismissals at Nampak. The union organises in three factories and has about 600 members.

The time for comments and questions from the audience has come. The problems of strikes are the main concern. The speeches are all different. Most are militant, but some are cautious. But overall the message from the different speakers is very much the same. The strike is our only weapon. We are fighting for our rights and we need strong organisation and we need to move in the right direction.

The rest of the day is spent talking about FOSATU policies, an education lecture is given and there is information on the Henkel boycott in support of striking workers in Durban.

The area

The Germiston Local in FOSATU covers mainly factories in Wadeville (Germiston) but also includes workers from the nearby Alrode (Alberton) industrial area. The area is known for its concentration of metal and engineering factories, which is why MAWU predominates in the local. The workers mostly live in the nearby townships of Natalspruit, Katlehong and Vosloorus. FOSATU has its offices conveniently located on the edge of Katlehong. Known as Morena Stores, it consists of one large empty room at the back of a garage and shop.

FOSATU is new to the area as a properly organised force. One or two other unions are active in the area but not to a very large extent. The General and Allied Workers' Union, hard-hit by recent detentions, has a small presence. There are also CUSA-affiliated unions which appear to have been losing membership to FOSATU affiliates over the past year. In the area, particularly Wadeville, FOSATU is easily the major union grouping.

The shop stewards' council was formed in April 1981 at a time when there were only three unionised factories in the area and of these only one (Henred Fruehauf) could claim to be properly organised. The aim, according to one of the organisers, was simply 'to organise the other factories'. The intention was to give shop stewards an organising role not only in their own factory but in other factories as well. Three office-bearers (all working locally) were elected at the time. The three original office-bearers all came from MAWU factories. Since the new elections (for four office-bearers) only two come from MAWU, whilst the other two work at glass factories.

The council is open to all shop stewards of FOSATU affiliates in the area. Four affiliates are active at present — MAWU, GAWU, C.W.I.U. and PWAWU. The procedures of the council are not always strictly adhered to, but in general a planning meeting alternates with the shop stewards' council every week.

The planning meeting is open to the chairpersons of the shop steward committees at different factories. It discusses how organising is going and the points to be put to the full shop stewards' council. 'At the planning meeting we just collect what's happening', one participant told me. All points have to be ratified and decided on by the full council, not by the planning meeting. The planning meeting is allowed to make emergency decisions, but these too have to be ratified later.

The shop stewards' council meets every second Wednesday after work (about 5.30 p.m.). There is no set method for sending representatives. Any factory where there are members, can be represented. In practice, well organised factories send a whole group, whilst others send perhaps one or two representatives. In addition, not all organised factories participate in the council. The committee says that usual attendance at council meetings is 'good' with between eighty and ninety shop stewards present. A council meeting I attended in mid-April had only 35 workers present, whilst another in early May attracted about 100 shop stewards.

One organiser explained the purpose of the council: 'The shop stewards' council is not to solve individual factory problems like dismissal . . . . At the council we discuss disputes like strikes. Let's say there's a strike in a certain factory, how can we help those workers? . . . Also it discusses about organising the local to be tight . . . educating the local . . . the stewards and all that.'

The main aim of the council, and the reason why it was formed, was to involve the shop stewards in organisational work. The problem was, and still is, that one of the fastest growing union areas in the country still has only one full-time organiser, a MAWU employee. At least two other unions send organisers on a regular basis, but they also have responsibilities in other areas. The practical problems, of having only one organiser, are therefore enormous. 'The organiser can't go to all the factories', it was explained. 'So we sat down and thought; let's change our strategy and give the job, the onus to the shop stewards. So they are doing the organising.'

Factories have been allocated to different shop stewards who now 'handle' them. They are also in the office on Saturdays and in the afternoons 'just like organisers'.

Every three months the council holds a general meeting for all FOSATU members in the area. But this sometimes doesn't materialise because of other FOSATU meetings scheduled for the same date. For example, the meeting of the Germiston local described at the beginning of this article was almost cancelled because it clashed with a FOSATU regional executive meeting. Some organisers were keen to cancel the general meeting, but the shop stewards' council was insistent that it should go ahead.

An emergency/special meeting of the council is held from time to time. The organiser, together with the secretary and the chairman of the council can convene a special meeting if this is felt to be important. This was done following the strike at Litemaster, and also earlier this year during the wave of strikes in the area. On that occasion, explained one of the organisers, 'there were discussions about how to keep those people solid, united, and stewards were visiting those factories on strike . . . encouraging them, explaining to them how to keep themselves united and how to push management. I think that's why we won in factories like McKechnie and T.M.F.'

Advantages and difficulties

Presently, the shop stewards' council is characterised by its militancy, mutual support of one group of workers for another and strong grassroots organisation.

All of this is made possible by strong *local* organisation. Workers in the area share many problems. They use the same buses and trains, they live in the same areas and they know other workers in neighbouring factories. The common conditions which workers face at a local level become a major spur to militancy, once organisation gets started.

The shop stewards' council ensures that problems and demands are shared by all the organised workers. This is of course what any union (industrial or general) tries to do. However, a strong local structure means that demands spread more rapidly and in a more grass-roots manner. Many of the strikes this year have revolved around wage demands. Workers' demands in one factory will be noticed by workers in a neighbouring factory, who have similar grievances. Most wage strikes this year concerned demands not simply for increases against inflation, but for a 'new wage'. This demand 'caught fire' in the area and spread rapidly, particularly in Wadeville. The fact that workers began presenting common demands generally strengthened their position in the area.

Only a few of the wage strikes were successful, the most notable victories being at T.M.F. and McKechnie Brothers. In most cases the employers refused to negotiate wages outside of the industrial council, a strategy in keeping with SEIFSA guidelines. 'But even in factories where we didn't acquire material success', comments one organiser, 'the important gain is that the workers learned that they have to struggle hard against the power of the employers to get what they want. And the employers learned that the workers are no longer prepared to sit back whilst the employers are making decisions for them.'

This working class offensive in the Germiston area is reflected in the structure of the shop stewards' council. It encourages unity between workers across union lines. Although workers' problems may differ from factory to factory, and from industry to industry, in most respects (and especially at a local level) they face the same problems. One executive member of the council explained that FOSATU's policy was for industrial unions. 'But to put the workers together in the locals', he continued, 'we must have a FOSATU local like the shop stewards' councils to bring the workers together, to make common decisions and to control what's happening in that certain area'. Workers are encouraged to see beyond their own union to the struggles of the workers as a whole.

The council has taken up a number of struggles and made them into battles for the Germiston workers as a whole. For example, it decided to act on the dismissal of 22 workers at Litemaster late last year. It was decided to support them financially and R2 000 was collected from Germiston workers to help the 22 for the three months they were out.

In the factory itself, the remaining workers instituted a ban on overtime. Then it was decided to take management to court on the grounds
that they had committed an 'unfair labour practice'. Workers were
also expected to pressurise their own managements to get Litemaster
to re-employ those dismissed. The issue was seen as an important one
for the area. Litemaster was regarded as a union stronghold and defeat
would have been a set back for the workers. For this reason the council decided that if all else failed (i.e. the overtime ban, the legal action
and pressure on other managements), then they 'have to support them
by all stopping . . . an hour or half hour whatever . . .'. The decisions over Litemaster were the result of an emergency meeting of the
shop stewards' council. In the end, a brief general strike was not needed because management backed down and re-employed the twenty
two. Perhaps it was the threat of strikes in the area, the risk of losing
the court case or possibly the pressure on management from their
German head-office, which led to the back down.

The issue of retrenchments is a burning one in Germiston area. On
21 April the shop stewards' council met and stewards from 72 factories
announced their determination to fight retrenchments. Employers
were accused of enforcing overtime while retrenching workers. The
council called for retrenchments to be negotiated with shop stewards
and union officials. 'Workers are the only ones to suffer when the
economy runs into trouble' said one organiser. The council wanted
employers to lay off workers for two or three months rather than
retrench them. Other action demanded by the council was that
workers should consider refusing overtime work and ask for a
shortening of working hours or days.

The council also united in opposition to the industrial council
system and SEIFSA. No wage increases were granted in late-April,
although these are usually granted at this time of year. This was a
result of the deadlock in industrial council negotiations, and
SEIFSA's refusal to negotiate wages outside this body. Opposition to
the system has been frequently expressed, most recently during wage
strikes at Haggie Rand (Jupiter) and SCAW Metals (Wadeville).
SCAW is regarded by workers as the 'pillar' of SEIFSA.

In recent months, management has frequently followed a policy of
dismissing all strikers and then attempting to re-employ selectively.
The shop stewards' council decided to take up this issue following the
dismissal of 380 workers at National Spring.

The dispute had arisen after management unfairly, in the workers' opinion, dismissed one of their colleagues. All 380 workers then downed tools in protest. Management then dismissed them all. The council decided to adopt a three-pronged strategy. Firstly, it would try to persuade township workers not to 'scab' by taking up the vacant jobs. Secondly, it would get shop stewards to approach their own managements to ask them to persuade National Spring to rehire totally, and not selectively as planned. Thirdly, it would approach the motor unions and ask them not to handle the company's products. This last tactic is a potentially very powerful form of boycott. It is not yet a well-developed tactic in this country and is only known to have been tried once previously, during the Firestone strike in the eastern Cape in 1981.

The council is therefore a body which allows workers to share their demands and to increase their power through common action and decisions. It has enabled the working class in the Germiston area to make major strides forward and achieve victories not only in one factory, but in the area as a whole. South African trade union history, from the I.C.U. to the present, is full of examples of extremely militant, fast growing workers' organisation which has subsequently collapsed. Usually this has occurred as a result of repressive state action as well as internal problems in the unions concerned.

The Germiston local shop stewards' council needs to consolidate itself if it is to survive. This is clearly perceived by the organisers and the council leadership. The dilemma is how to expand and grow whilst consolidating at the same time. In trying to resolve this dilemma the council has a number of advantages on which it can draw, as well as problems which it needs to face. Some of these problems are of a general organisational nature which most unions experience, whilst others are specific to the council.

One of the biggest advantages of the council is that it forces the shop stewards to be active. A shop steward at Henred Fruehauf, for example, cannot only worry about problems in his factory. He must also concern himself with the problems of the area as a whole. The most important way in which this occurs is by making the shop stewards' council responsible for organising. It is a widespread practice in trade unionism that workers will join after being approached by workers who are already members. People talk at lunch break or on the train home.

But the council expects more from at least some of its members. Once workers have joined they still require proper organisation.

'We're trying to make a move', explained one council executive member, 'that shop stewards should not rely on organisers. They should group themselves and go out and organise difficult factories'. This active participation in organising increases the experience and strength of the local. The fact that it emerged because of the shortage of organisers means that very real problems still remain. A part-time organiser cannot do everything done by a full-time organiser. But much of the load is taken off the full-time organisers.

The shop stewards who assist with organising still have to work and so cannot immediately deal with such things as strikes which break out during the day, a frequent occurrence in Wadeville. Newly organised factories also tend to rely too much on the union officials.

Shortage of full-time organisers has combined with enormous membership growth in the area, especially in the last twelve months. This has led to major problems such as workers having 'joined' but waiting up to two months to be properly signed-up and get dues receipted. Negotiations at certain factories (such as T.M.F.) have also fallen behind.[1]

'We're still expanding, too fast. We can't cope', one official admits. What has happened frequently is that a relatively small percentage of workers in a factory will join the union. Then there will be a strike, other strikes having been seen all around, and the workers will come to the union to join up and ask for help. The problem becomes how to capture the spontaneous militancy of the workers, but at the same time build solid organisation.

Mayekiso, a MAWU organiser, admits to delays in organising and dealing with problems. 'The workers, if they join, want everything done *now*', he explains, 'whether they are organised or not. Well, we believe that you can't just join the workers today and then tomorrow you approach management and you solve their problems. You have to organise them and to train them and to give them a spirit of unity. Then you approach management about recognition and solving their problems. Because if you approach management before they become united, then they'll be victimised and you won't be able to solve their problems. They don't accept that fully. When they join the union they've got burning issues.'

An advantage of the council is that it puts power into the hands of shop-floor leaders. The representatives on the council are directly elected by the workers in their factory. Therefore, there is direct representation on the body that decides most of the important issues in the area. In theory it is the executive committees of the various unions that set policy and determine action. In practice, in Germiston, it is the shop stewards' council that is the power at the local level. This was felt to be 'not a problem' by the council executive. All the local executive committees of the various unions support the council. Often a decision is taken at the shop stewards' council and the executive committees must go along with it.

The lack of structure in the council is felt by some to be a problem. In particular there are no rules for ensuring that whenever decisions are taken, those present represent the majority of the area's organised workers. There is fairly strict policy concerning what the planning meeting can discuss and ensuring that the full council has the final say. But on the question of representatives there is no clear policy. Shop stewards from any factory may attend, whether that factory has majority union membership or not. In practice some organised factories will neglect to come whilst unorganised factories may be represented.

The council executive doesn't feel that it is necessary to make the structure more formal, and it doesn't see the need for a constitution. This would overlap with existing decision-making bodies, the regional executives and branch executives of the union. 'It's all right if we write down our objectives', said one member, 'but it shouldn't be called a constitution'. There appears to be an unwillingness to change the present system because although the meetings may lack structure, they are also informal and not bureaucratic.[2]

The council is planning to discuss the adoption of objectives. 'We talk of unity', it was explained. 'What kind of unity and how far should we go as a local? What sort of help, what sort of things we should do, and the disciplinary procedures. Because if we are to be united we have to have disciplinary procedures and some clear objectives . . . . As workers, then, we are involved in political issues, so we have to be clear on how to react to such things . . . . Problems like rent have come up . . . . We have to do some things outside the factory.'

A problem as mentioned earlier, which does emerge from time to time is when another FOSATU meeting is scheduled for the same time as a meeting of the council or a general meeting of the local. This is sometimes resolved by the chairman of the council and a number of others going to the Regional Executive Committee meeting. This unfortunately gives a bad impression to the people according to one shop steward.

A number of problems emerge from the meetings of the council itself. Participation in discussions is often very small with the result that a handful of strong shop stewards do a lot of talking. Participation is not always low however and some issues will lead to widespread discussion and contributions from large numbers of those present at the council meeting.

Possibly related to this is the fact that some organised factories do not attend meetings of the council. Representatives from SCAW Metals have difficulty in coming sometimes because they work on the three shift system. Consol Glass representatives face similar problems and other factories may also be affected by this problem.

Some factories don't yet see the need to have shop stewards attend the council. One problem here is that because the area is MAWU dominated, non-MAWU shop stewards have felt that discussions excluded them. This is a problem that smaller unions often face. But if one of the aims of the council is to promote inter-union solidarity, then it is a problem which needs to be overcome. Of the eleven most active factories on the council, only one (Plate Glass) is not in MAWU.

Conclusion

Despite the problems and difficulties which face unions and the shop stewards' council, the developments in the Germiston area are positive. The shop stewards' council has emerged as a body capable of directly expressing the demands of the workers. It has been a practical and very creative response to the upsurge of militancy and organisation in the area. Only time will tell how the council develops. Much will depend on whether it can continue to respond to the mass militancy in the area and, at the same time, consolidate and give disciplined organisation to the workers.

One member discussed the problems the council faces. 'We are faced with the problem of building solidarity amongst us. When we face a problem then they (the workers) must know it's a struggle, not an insurance that I just come, and I am helped. It's a long struggle. Then, to give them that understanding — that they are a certain class . . . that they have to fight . . . so that they know when they fight in factories, whom they fight and they distinguish themselves.'

May 1982

Thanks to the workers, shop stewards and officials in Germiston (especially Moss) for their cooperation and assistance. The responsibility for errors of fact or interpretation is of course mine.

1 Negotiating recognition agreements is a time-consuming business. MAWU has already signed agreements with three companies — Dresser S.A. and two branches of Henred Fruehauf. Final recognition is close to hand at three other companies — SCAW Metals, Reliable Products and Litemaster. About half a dozen companies are still busy negotiating with MAWU. All in all, about fifteen MAWU factories are 'well-organised' with shop stewards being recognised and taking up issues with management.

2 The nearby FOSATU shop stewards' council in Springs, formed on 15 August 1981, has been discussing the adoption of rules and objectives. Its proposed aims include 'building solidarity' and 'counteracting sectional union interests among workers and their representatives'; organising workers into FOSATU; assisting workers and unions by 'solidarity actions, publicity and financial support'; and making 'links with community organisations to encourage solidarity between the community and the workers' struggle'.

In Springs the aim is for the council to meet only 'once a year', and for its work to be carried out by sub-committees; a managing committee, an organising committee, a financial committee and a publicity committee. The aim seems to be to combine the council and the Branch Executive Committees in the area. It is proposed that the managing committee consist of the office-bearers of the three committees as well as the office-bearers and secretary of each FOSATU affiliate operating within the local.

Part II

Overview: Strikes and the Independent Trade Unions

*Phil Bonner**

The re-awakening of strike activity after the 1973 Durban strikes has reflected a growing confidence by workers in their own capacity to transform their situation. Given the repressive situation which has prevailed, the undeniable gains of the workers' movement over the last decade necessitated frequent resort to the strike weapon. While it is difficult to generalise about strikes, some broad historical patterns do emerge. The readings here have been selected because they reflect these broad patterns within the pages of the *South African Labour Bulletin*.

The 1960s were clearly the doldrums so far as worker organisation and strike activity were concerned. The harsh repression of the Congress movement and SACTU initiated a long period of quiescence. Nevertheless beneath this calm surface a number of contradictory trends were in motion which would lead to a new burst of worker organisation and successive waves of strikes.

One of the most notable features of the 1960s was the massive infusion of foreign investment into South Africa and the rapid growth of the manufacturing sector as industrial townships mushroomed. Massive new factories were erected and the industrial working class both grew and changed in composition. A much larger proportion of black workers moved into semi-skilled positions, and were thrown together in larger and larger units of production. The potential leverage of the working class was correspondingly enhanced.

* Dave Kaplan assisted with the preparation and editing of Part Two.

At the same time a range of state initiatives were undertaken which partly offset this trend. The 1960s, while witnessing a great expansion in the industrial working class, also saw much more systematic efforts to implant within it deep structural divisions. Influx control was tightened up, the contract labour system was refashioned to prevent migrant workers acquiring permanent urban rights, and the provision of new family housing in the African townships largely dried up. The impact of these policies should not be underestimated. Migrant workers were rendered far more vulnerable to state or employer intimidation, and were in certain important respects isolated from the permanently urbanised African working class. The potential for division and conflict was great.

Conversely, however, these very initiatives which were aimed at entrenching material and cultural divisions among workers were breeding contradictions which would ultimately drive the two groups together. As more and more workers were forced to base themselves and their families in the 'homelands', the rural economies of these areas began to experience accelerated collapse. The solution to mounting poverty centred increasingly on securing improved material conditions in urban employment.

The 1973 Durban strikes were the first visible intimation of this trend. They also brought together urban and migrant workers in the first concerted attack on declining standards of living to be seen since the early 1960s. A similar upsurge, though on a much smaller scale took place on the Rand, among transport workers in 1972/1973.

In both areas these spontaneous explosions of anger engendered a new sense of self-confidence, and triggered an ongoing series of strikes, so that by 1974 the number of recorded strikes reached a record 374. Among employers and the state this unanticipated upsurge engendered a mood of apprehension. The government continued its attempt, started twenty years before in 1953, to provide plant-based liaison committees and works committees to act as channels of communication to management. The intention, stated quite bluntly, was to provide alternative structures to trade unions by depriving African trade unions 'of their life's blood' so that they would 'die a natural death'. (See overview to Part III and Horner, Reading Nine).

Employers and the state were not the only groups to sit up and take note of the 1973 strikes. Intellectuals and activists outside of the working class also saw in these developments opportunities for a new phase of worker organisation and with their assistance new groups of trade unions were formed in Natal, on the Rand, and in Cape Town. In their formative phases (up to 1979), the demands of these unions concentrated overwhelmingly on trade union recognition. Frequently this led to strikes as employers, with rare exceptions, presented a united front against trade union recognition.

The struggles of the workers and unions were waged under extremely adverse constraints: workers had continually to confront police and labour department intervention, punitive action under influx control regulation, disguised or overt victimisation of militants on the shopfloor, and the pressure applied by employer federations on individual managements not to break ranks. The limits of even a legal strike were vividly illustrated in a dispute from September to November 1976 at Armourplate Safety Glass. Although the strike called by the unregistered Glass and Allied Workers' Union was legal, employers and the state combined in crushing the workers who held out for no less than eight weeks.[1]

The independent unions devised certain strategies at that time. They focused their attention on multinational companies who were susceptible to disinvestment campaigns and to pressure from the international trade unions and other groups. They accordingly forged links with the international trade union movement. In addition workers sought to utilise the works committee system, which afforded limited leverage if controlled by union shop stewards, to secure advances for their members. This in turn reinforced one of the other distinctive features of African trade union organisations in this period — the emphasis on strong, self-reliant shop steward committees, which would have to work largely without wider trade union support within works committees and more generally on the factory floor.

The Heinemann Electric dispute (Reading Five) in some ways illustrates the problems facing trade unions at their extreme. The Metal and Allied Workers' Union (MAWU) members in the plant were confronted by an obdurate refusal on the part of management to negotiate with the union. This was done by means of victimisation, by intervention of the powerful employers' federation in the engineering industry, SEIFSA, and ultimately by brutal police repression. Yet in some ways the Heinemann strike marks the ending of this phase of worker organisation. Barlows, a major shareholder, was deeply embarrassed by the handling of the dispute and this almost certainly contributed to a re-assessment of this conglomerate's position on trade unions. Workers displayed remarkable solidarity, and even after the police attack they were not broken or bowed.

For many employers this was seen as a taste of things to come. In addition, within a few months of the strike, the Soweto school children's rebellion had begun. Following this a new spirit of militancy and a younger generation of factory floor leaders schooled in this environment began to emerge. Consequently the state began to think out a new strategy of containment and reform, which, in the case of workers, was to reach fruition in the Wiehahn Commission Report. (See the overview of Part III and Reading Ten.)

A dispute that straddled this period of re-appraisal and contained an innovative strategy in strengthening the workers' demands took place between the Food and Canning Workers' Union, and Fatti's and Moni's over a seven month period in 1979. In the wake of the 1976 disturbances, the union was able to capitalise on a new mood of defiance which was spreading through the main urban centres, and to revive a tactic which had fallen into disuse since the late 1950s — the consumer boycott. In the end it was the massive support of the boycott from the community which forced the company to cave in, and to accord recognition to the union.[2]

Within a few months of the Fatti's and Moni's dispute the Wiehahn Commission's findings were published and this transformed the terrain upon which trade unions had been operating. Although deep divisions emerged among the major trade union groupings as to the precise implications of the Wiehahn inspired legislation or as to the appropriate response, what is clear is that it opened up considerable space for trade unions, and engendered considerable confusion among employers.

The Johannesburg municipal workers' strike (Reading Six) indicates the manner in which the new legislation spurred municipal worker militants into organising the Black Municipal Workers' Union (B.M.W.U.). The strike which followed also dramatically illustrated the arrival of a new and pugnatious combatant in the industrial relations arena — the contract worker. What is perhaps most remarkable about the municipal workers' strike is the extent to which it widened itself to the largely migrant municipal work-force from its initial flashpoint at the Orlando Power Station. At the peak of the strike 10 000 African workers were out on strike. For the first time since the 1946 African mineworkers' strike a largely migrant work-force had flexed its muscles on such a large scale in a labour dispute. The strike reflected the growing squeeze being applied to migrants by deteriorating conditions in the reserves. The Johannesburg municipal workers were among the first to react because of the exceptionally bad conditions and low wages of their municipality. Increasingly, however, the same forces were to spur other migrant workers into action as was evidenced in the east Rand strike wave of the following year. (See Reading Seven).

The Johannesburg municipal workers' strike graphically illustrates the new opportunities and problems presented by this development. The collective misery and the hostel-based solidarity of migrants provided fertile ground for union organisation. It also produced a highly volatile constituency which was liable to explode at the first sign of organisation. The municipal workers' strike consequently broke out before the B.M.W.U. had had a chance to establish even the rudiments of organisation. This, combined with the migrant workers' vulnerability to repression (deportation and being sealed off in their hostels), allowed the strike to be broken.

The municipal workers' strike also foreshadowed the kinds of problems that unions would encounter when dealing with any state linked employer. Municipal work is deemed an essential service and the Johannesburg municipality was controlled by National Party supporters. This ensured an especially uncompromising and brutal response to the strike. Other independent unions dealing with state linked employers would confront similar problems in the following years. For instance, in September 1982 the state owned South African Transport Services fired 400 African dockworkers in Port Elizabeth for utilising the go-slow as a last resort in a long drawn-out struggle for recognition of their union, the General Workers' Union. The state was to show its iron fist again during the two-day stayaway in November 1984 by anything from 300 000 to 800 000 black workers when the public corporation, SASOL, was the only company to dismiss all 6 000 of its employees who stayed away.

The east Rand strike wave (Reading Seven) indicates a number of similar dynamics at work, but in the context of somewhat more mature and stable organisations. Again contract workers took a leading role, sixty percent of the membership of the main union involved being migrants. Again the strikes spread rapidly, after a mood of collective confrontation had been created by the Colgate dispute, and the widely supported boycott of Colgate products. In this case however the unions had sufficient organisation to assume a directing and supporting role. Consequently, while stretched to the limit, they were often able to secure gains for their members, and there were relatively few cases of factory organisation being broken.

Two things stand out from this wave of strikes and were to become established features of the industrial relations scene. Firstly, workers provisionally won a de facto right to strike. There were almost no prosecutions for illegally striking (all of these strikes were illegal), and employers generally acceded to negotiations without summarily firing their workers (this right was subsequently formally written into a number of recognition agreements). Secondly, a large number of strikes centred on issues of management control and affronts to personal dignity. The previously hallowed area of management's right to manage, was coming under assault, introducing a new dimension into the workers' struggle in South Africa.

By 1981 the balance of power between employers and workers had therefore decisively shifted. Strikes which had been persistently lost in the 1970s were now being fought on more equal terms. Employers still generally retained the upper hand, and the protracted strikes which forced employers to their knees were still uncommon (the Volkswagen strike of 1980 in which the National Automobile and Allied Workers' Union forced the company to concede to a R2.00 per hour wage demand, was a rare exception). Still to make its appearance was an industry-wide strike, since hardly any unions had attained a dominant position in one industry.

However, the Dunlop strike in 1984 (Reading Eight) took on the form of a national strike at one company as MAWU mobilised workers at Dunlop plants round the country in support of the striking Durban workers. The strike displayed other remarkable features. It developed into a trial of strength between MAWU and Dunlop and lasted for no less than four weeks. It also demonstrated the union's ability to maintain a strike over a lengthy period of time. To sustain a strike of such dimensions requires a union organised nationally and with powerful and well-disciplined shop-floor organisation. MAWU had achieved both these by 1984, as had a number of other independent unions. The Dunlop strike thus symbolizes a new era in the struggles of the independent unions to advance working class interests at the work-place.

February 1985

Notes

1 Glass and Allied Workers' Union, 'Report on the Strike at Armourplate Safety Glass, 6 September 1976 to 1 November, being the First Legal Strike by Black Workers in South Africa', *S.A.L.B.*, III, 7 (June-July, 1977), pp. 60-72.
2 See Liz McGregor, 'The Fatti's and Moni's Dispute', *S.A.L.B.*, V, 6 and 7 (March, 1980), pp. 122-31, for details of the strike and boycott.

Reading 5. (1977)

Workers Under the Baton: The Labour Dispute at Heinemann Electric Company*

Metal and Allied Workers' Union

In March 1976 the members of the Metal and Allied Workers' Union (MAWU) demanded recognition by the management of Heinemann Electric, a company based in Elandsfontein, near Johannesburg. The reaction to this demand was a possible lockout by the factory management and a subsequent baton charge by the South African Police.

The background to the dispute

There had been a liaison committee at Heinemann for some time. The committee ceased to exist in early January 1976 when the majority of its members resigned on the grounds that it was an ineffective body.

Heinemann workers began joining MAWU in October 1975. By the end of January 1976 more than 75% of the work-force — 484 out of 606 — had joined the union. A shop steward committee was elected which met once a week. In addition regular factory meetings were held to discuss union and factory affairs. Some of the shop stewards were elected to the union executive. It can thus be

* First published in *S.A.L.B.*, III, 7 (June-July, 1977), pp. 49-59.

seen that Heinemann was a highly organised factory in which workers participated continuously and at all levels in the running of union affairs.

The widespread support by the workers for the union as their preferred form of organisation and representation was clearly shown by the almost unanimous boycott of management instituted liaison committee elections on 26 January.

Heinemann workers had several times instructed their union officials to open negotiations with management. Union officials met with the managing director, Wolfgang Wilckens on 20 February. They presented him with a petition signed by 480 workers calling for a recognition of MAWU. They also informed Wilckens of a number of grievances among the workers. According to union officials a cordial discussion on the nature of trade unions was held on this occasion. Wilckens said that he was not unsympathethic towards unions and was prepared to discuss ways in which the union could operate within the factory.

Immediately after his meeting with union officials, Wilckens addressed ex-members of the liaison committee. He strongly criticised Heinemann workers for joining MAWU and according to those who were at that meeting, condemned union intervention in company affairs. He maintained that grievances within Heinemann could be sorted out without the participation of a union.

On 3 March a letter was sent to Wilckens by the union. It contained an article by B. Godsell (*S.A.L.B.*, II, 6) of the Anglo American Corporation outlining the inadequacies of the in-factory committee system which was not complemented by an industry wide trade union. The letter also noted the concern felt by workers for the recent dismissal of a female employee. On the same day, Wilckens phoned the union officials to inform them that he had met with a group of forty workers. Although unelected, he claimed that this group was 'representative' of the factory. According to Wilckens this group was not against having a liaison committee. They were going to consult with other workers on this issue and report back to him on the following Monday.

Union officials brought this phone conversation up at a factory meeting on 6 March. The workers felt that Wilckens had misrepresented their position and decided to elect an ad hoc group of sixteen to meet with Wilckens. It is important to note that the workers decided that the whole shop steward committee should not go to this meeting for they felt the possibility of victimisation very keenly and were unwilling to expose all the shop stewards. Events were, once more, to prove the workers right.

At a meeting between Wilckens and the ad hoc group of sixteen, Wilckens was informed that workers did not want a liaison committee. He was asked to accept this as a democratically arrived at decision of the workers in this factory. He was also asked to stop trying to force a liaison committee on the workers. At this point Wilckens introduced representatives of the Steel and Engineering Industries Federation of South Africa (SEIFSA). SEIFSA's anti-union stance is well known, and their intervention in local factory disputes has been frequent. The SEIFSA representatives addressed the meeting and attempted to persuade the workers that they should accept a liaison committee. They also denigrated the union officials.

After this meeting Wilckens told the workers that he would be calling a general factory meeting on 10 March. The union executive instructed its officials to request permission from Wilckens to be present at this meeting. Wilckens refused and said that he would have no further contact with the union. The meeting turned out to be a statement by Wilckens on the virtues of the liaison committee.

The build-up to the confrontation

On 11 March, Wilckens instructed the ad hoc committee to meet with him. He again stressed the advantages of a liaison committee, this time calling it a 'management-worker committee'. The ad hoc committee rejected the proposal once more. Wilckens ignored this rejection and instructed them to distribute pamphlets outlining the committee system proposed by the Heinemann management.

At the same time as these meetings were taking place, a systematic offensive against union organisation within the factory occurred. Shop stewards were moved out of their departments and isolated from other workers. Some foremen attempted to prevent workers speaking to each other in the factory. There was also an attempt to introduce disunity along racial lines within the work-force. The workers however were not taken in by these attempts at splitting their ranks and maintained solidarity throughout the period.

On 13 March the workers held a factory meeting. They decided to dissolve the ad hoc committee of sixteen since it was obvious that Wilckens was attempting to use it for his own ends. On 15 March Wilckens was informed that this committee was no longer considered representative of the work-force. On the same day workers observed policemen inside the factory.

On 17 March elections for a 'management-worker committee' were held. This was seen by workers for what it was — a disguised form of a liaison committee. The election failed. Three out of 606 workers voted in the elections. On 18 March, management circulated a memorandum stating that there would be no committee at all in Heinemann.

On Friday, 19 March, workers decided on a memorandum requesting fresh negotiations between MAWU and Wilckens. It was immediately drawn up and circulated for signature by all workers. This initiative was simply ignored by Wilckens. The management of Heinemann had obviously decided on more aggressive action in the factory.

Between Monday 22 March and Thursday 25 March, police were present on the factory premises. Their presence, and rumours spread by foremen that action against union members was imminent, only increased the tension within the factory. Several shop stewards were pointed out by foremen during work and accused of being the 'poison in the department'. On Wednesday 24 and Thursday 25 several new workers were hired. With one exception they were people who had not worked at the factory before. On Thursday 25 twenty union members, including three leading shop stewards, were fired. They were notified of their dismissal five minutes before the factory closed for the night. They were also told that the reason they were being fired was 'a general reduction in the work-force'.

The confrontation begins

Events now moved to a climax. The management of Heinemann and of its parent company, Barlow Rand, have presented the events after 26 March as a strike by workers. They have claimed that it was necessary to call in the police to protect workers from intimidation. The facts contradict this picture.

The evidence in one of the trials following the baton charge revealed further behind-the-scenes activities on the part of the management of Heinemann. Under cross examination Wilckens admitted that the possibility of dismissing the whole work-force and employing them on condition they accepted the firm's policy of working through a liaison committee had been discussed. This strategy was discussed, according to the court evidence, with the labour officer of SEIFSA. In his judgement, the magistrate noted:

> There is also evidence to show that the complainant firm was not blameless in the march of events, and there must be more than a sus- picion that the events were in fact engineered by the firm in order to reach a show-down with their workers.

Just before 7.30 a.m. on Friday the work-force gathered outside the gates. They were told that they had all been dismissed and that they could re-apply for their jobs on the following Monday. Workers requested that they be allowed to discuss this with Wilckens. When he did not turn up, the workers decided to return on the Monday. They hoped then to be able to meet with Wilckens.

The workers arrived on Monday 28 to keep their meeting with Wilckens. They found the gates locked once more, and a large force of police armed with pick handles, batons and dogs present. The workers and union officials asked to see Wilckens only to be told that he would arrive at 9.30 a.m. Wilckens had not arrived by this time, and the workers were told by Van Lieres, the factory manager, to collect their leave pay, and U.I.F. cards by 10.00 a.m. If they did not do so by that stipulated time, they would have to go to the industrial council offices to do so. By 9.55 a.m. he told them they had four minutes left to collect their pay and cards. Only a few workers did this, the rest were waiting to discuss the matter with Wilckens.

The baton charge

At 10.00 a.m. a policeman told the workers to disperse within half an hour. Police pick-up trucks began to arrive, and police dogs were brought out from inside the factory. The tension began to rise dramatically. At about 10.20 a.m. the secretary of MAWU, Sipho Kubheka appealed to the workers to leave. He noted that there was no point in them being arrested. Workers agreed with him and began to move off singing.

Independent eye witnesses maintain that the police charged at least five minutes before the appointed time. In addition it would seem that workers were already moving off when the police attacked. A large number of workers were badly beaten, including pregnant women. Twenty four were taken to Natalspruit hospital in two ambulances. Four others were treated at other hospitals. One union official, Gavin Andersson, was detained in hospital where he was treated for a broken arm.

The magistrate in the trial of Andersson and Khubeka noted '... it has not been proved that the accused engineered the beginning of the strike; and that being so it appears to me that events would have taken much the same course even had the accused played no role'. The fact is that those who will not recognise the legitimate aspirations of workers in their attempt to gain meaningful negotiation rights cannot but resort to punitive action and repression. The Heinemann incident reveals this inherent tendency in South Africa's industrial legislation in its starkest form.

The aftermath

As a result of the Heinemann affair two union officials, Sipho Kubheka, the secretary, and Gavin Andersson, an organiser, were charged with inciting a strike and with obstructing the police in their duty. These were charges in terms of the Bantu Labour Relations Act, the Riotous Assemblies Act and the Police Act. Four Heinemann workers were arrested at Elandsfontein station and charged under the Riotous Assemblies Act, the Bantu Labour Regulations Act and the Industrial Conciliation Act. These workers were twice refused bail, and it was only after an appeal to the supreme court that bail was permitted to them. They have been found not guilty and discharged.

In the case of Kubheka and Andersson, they were found guilty of instigating employees to strike. Kubheka was sentenced to a fine of R45 or thirty days gaol, while Andersson was sentenced to R90 or 45 days. Both were acquitted of the charges under the Riotous Assemblies Act and of obstructing the police.

Heinemann management has continued in its campaign to institute a liaison committee. It refused to give jobs to any of its dismissed workers unless they undertook to support a liaison committee. As a result it had to hire more than 300 new workers. Management then forced workers to participate in a liaison committee election. It took photographs of some workers who reluctantly accepted management nomination for the liaison committee. Workers were then forced to put a disc in a box underneath each picture, thus indicating which candidate they wished to vote for.

The problem reflected by Heinemann

The Heinemann dispute thus speaks volumes about the inadequate nature of South Africa's industrial legislation. Until such time as employers and government are prepared to heed workers' demands for meaningful participation in the system of industrial bargaining through independent trade unions, incidents like Heinemann will continue to scar industrial relations in South Africa. Workers have recognised the deficiencies of the in-factory committee system. Management's only response to workers' rejection of the system has been pious and inaccurate statements concerning their inability to go beyond government policy in this regard. One such statement was made by Barlow Rand, Heinemann's parent company, following the March events. A Barlow Rand statement said that the group would not recognise unregistered African trade unions.

> We feel obliged to negotiate within the framework created by law and cannot opt out of industrial agreements which apply to the whole industry. This does not imply that we are happy with the existing industrial relations legislation. We believe it needs drastic revision (R.D.M., 3 April, 1976).

The fact is that employers can recognise trade unions. Barlow Rand and Heinemann must realise that it is they who make the choice. In almost every incident noted in this article, it is Heinemann management who have been the antagonistic and provocative party. The workers and their recognised representatives have always attempted to negotiate over the issues involved. Even in the face of police presence, workers and union officials attempted to avoid a confrontation. Employers and the state must realise that insistence on the in-factory committee system leads logically to workers under the baton.

Reading 6. (1981)

Migrants Awake — the 1980 Johannesburg Municipal Workers' Strike*

Jeremy Keenan

On 24 July 1980 about 600 black employees at the Johannesburg municipality's Orlando power station in Soweto stopped work as a result of a pay dispute. By Tuesday 29 July they had been joined by 10 000 black workers from almost every one of the municipality's departments. It was the largest strike ever faced by a single employer in the history of South Africa. By the end of the week it had been ruthlessly smashed: over a thousand workers were deported to their 'homelands' (Bantustans) and the union's leaders were taken into detention to be charged under the sabotage clause of the General Laws Amendment Act which carries a maximum penalty of the death sentence.

An 'in-house' union (U.J.M.W.) vs. a representative union (B.M.W.U.)

The strategy of the Johannesburg City Council (J.C.C.) to counter its black employees' awareness of their rights and their desire to organise themselves, was to try and form an 'in-house' union by

* First published in much more extensive form in *S.A.L.B.*, VI, 7 (May, 1981), pp. 4 — 60.

turning the existing liaison committees into a 'union' — the Union of Johannesburg Municipality Workers (U.J.M.W.).

Members of the transport department's works committee began discussing the possibility of an alternative union that would be genuinely representative of and concerned with the interests of the municipality's black employees. The initiative for this attempt came primarily from Philip Dlamini, a bus driver and chairman of the works committee. In November 1979, Dlamini called a meeting of the transport workers (running staff — drivers and conductors) at the Avenue Road bus depot. Its purpose was to discuss the possibility of forming an alternative union to the Council's U.J.M.W.

There was a general consensus on the need for a broadly based union that would embrace all the council's black employees. But the question was whether, even if there was substantial support from the non-migrant workers, it would be possible to educate and gain the support of the migrant workers who made up about 12 000 of the J.C.C.'s 14 000 or so black workers.

The inaugural meeting of the Black Municipal Workers' Union (B.M.W.U.) was held in the Selbourne Hall on 23 June, 1980. The hall had to be hired from the council at the cost of R107. About 300 attended the meeting. Here thirteen members of the steering committee were elected to the union's executive committee.

The initial core that was to provide the leadership in B.M.W.U. consisted of Dlamini, Joseph Mavi, and Gatsby Mazwi, all of the transport department.

Mavi, the eldest of the three, had had a considerable amount of experience in both labour and civic organisations. In 1970 he went to work as a long distance truck driver. He was first introduced to trade unionism after his colleagues voted him into the executive of the African Transport Workers' Union (A.T.W.U.). He was elected vice-president, and in 1975 he became president. In 1977 he rejoined the J.C.C. and was elected secretary of the transport department's works committee. Although Mavi's concern was for 'justice', he had never joined any black political party.

Control of the workers and barriers to organisation

The basis for the Johannesburg city council's control over the bulk of its work-force is the system of influx control, which, in effect, binds workers to their allocated jobs. The compound system is equally important as a mechanism of control. Once recruited to the council's employ, the worker's likely place of residence is a compound (referred to by the council as 'hostels'). The nineteen compounds used by the municipality to house its migrant work-force are geographically scattered and tightly controlled.

The Selby compound for example, is surrounded by a high wall topped with barbed wire. It has two entrances. One is through massive steel front gates which are flanked by a permanent police guard post. The other entrance is a well-guarded and easily controlled subway. Importantly, this makes it possible for the workers to be locked inside the compounds. Indeed, as we shall see below, the compounds provided the J.C.C. and the police with the means of easily dividing and controlling the workers during the 'strike'.

These forms of control and exploitation are, however, contradictory. In the case of the Johannesburg municipal 'strike', they enabled the council to pay exceptionally low wages to the bulk of its work-force and to keep them, for the most part, in appalling living conditions. They also provided the mechanisms for the containment and smashing of the 'strike'. But, on the other hand, it was the extremity of this control and exploitation which provided a ready and fertile basis for the organisation of the migrant work-force and which underlay the militancy of its response.

The strike at Orlando power station

The J.C.C. normally grants wage increases to its black workers on 1 July each year. When the weekly paid workers at Orlando received their increase on Thursday 3 July they found that the minimum wage had been increased from R30.36 to only R33.

The Orlando workers immediately called a meeting which was organised not by the B.M.W.U., but by the employees themselves at the Orlando compound. The immediate reaction of many of these workers was to call for a strike for a minimum wage of R58 a week (i.e. R25 increase).

Ntabozuko Somdake, a member of the B.M.W.U. executive, was at the meeting. He asked the employees who was going to represent the workers in their negotiations. They told him that the B.M.W.U. should do so.

At the meeting of the B.M.W.U. executive committee on 5 July, Somdake reported what had happened at the Orlando power station and said that the matter required urgent attention as the employees were threatening to strike if their demands were not met. The executive committee resolved to try and dissuade the employees from striking. Somdake was deputed to carry out this resolution. He informed the employees at the Orlando power station of the union's attitude and explained that it intended to approach the municipality and negotiate on their behalf. The workers agreed to a moratorium, but decided that if the matter was not resolved by 24 July, pay-day, they would strike. At this, the union gave Mavi a mandate to approach the municipality so as to negotiate.

The municipality, however refused this request, saying that it would not deal with an unregistered trade union. Mavi informed the union executive of the council's attitude, which was then conveyed by Somdake to the Orlando power station workers on 16 July. They adopted the attitude that they would wait and see what they were paid on 24 July; if this was unsatisfactory, they would strike.

The demands of the Orlando workers were not met. Nor had the question of the 'equalisation principle', which had been causing dissatisfaction among sixty black electricians been resolved.

The labourers, on receiving their pay notices, refused to work. They were joined in sympathy by the black electricians and trainee electricians. About 640 workers downed tools. The work stoppage was reported to the Department of Manpower Utilisation shortly after 8.00 a.m.

By midday at least 600 workers had been dismissed and/or locked out of the Orlando compound. Most of them initially went no further than the open veld outside the compound. There, they were confronted by armed police who had arrived earlier in the morning and who told them that their 'meeting' was illegal. Some moved off into Soweto where they found shelter with friends. Others made their way to Selby where some of them were locked in and then discharged, while yet others had to sleep outside the compound.

The J.C.C.'s response to the Orlando strike

The J.C.C.'s response to the Orlando power station 'strike' was:
1) A refusal to meet the workers' demands.
2) A refusal to negotiate with the B.M.W.U.
   The J.C.C. consistently held to this position on the grounds that 'there would be no negotiation with any union before it was registered'.[1]
   In addition to the fact that the B.M.W.U. was not registered, senior council officials said that an audience could not be given to the B.M.W.U. as:
   — all municipal workers, under the Industrial Conciliation Act, are regarded as essential workers and as such are forbidden to strike,
   — the worker militancy was politically motivated by a small handful of agitators,
   — the workers themselves refused to negotiate, saying only that they wanted more money.
   With regard to the second of these claims, it is true that the B.M.W.U., adopted a more political approach to labour issues. But, the council's claim that the workers refused to negotiate is simply untrue. Workers made it quite clear that they wanted to negotiate, but that negotiations were to be conducted with their representative, the B.M.W.U.
3) The dismissal of the work-force.
4) The replacement of the work-force with scab labour. Scab labour took three forms:
   a) white council employees worked double shift,
   b) workers were drafted in from other departments,
   c) new workers were immediately recruited from Venda.
The drafting in of workers from other departments was one of the major factors in encouraging the spread of the strike. Two hundred and eighty new workers were immediately recruited in Venda, with the first eighty arriving on the Tuesday following the stoppage. This action incensed workers, and Mavi warned that bringing in replacement workers could lead to fights between the 'strikers' and the new workers.

The immediate replacement of the Orlando power station workers generated what became one of the major issues of the strike — namely, the breaking open of the workers' lockers.

The Orlando compound, unlike most compounds, has lockers which lock. Workers consequently used them as a place of security in which to keep not only their own possessions and money, but also those of friends and colleagues who did not have access to such security. When the workers were dismissed, few of them were allowed to collect their belongings from their lockers. Many of them had several hundred rands in cash in the lockers. On Sunday Mavi publicly expressed the anxiety of these workers when he said to the Sunday Post — 'What if the money and belongings of these workers gets lost?'

The workers' anxiety was not ill-founded. Their lockers were opened and their possessions removed. There seems to be no doubt as to who was responsible for this. Oberholzer, chairman of the management committee, told the Sunday Express that: 'We went there to their lockers which were numbered and put their clothes in municipal bags which were numbered'. The question is where did these possessions go?

The strike spreads

On the Friday morning (25 July) about 800 electricity workers at the Van Beek compound in Doornfontein, both labourers and office staff, went on strike in support of their 550 Orlando colleagues who had been dismissed on the previous day. The Van Beek workers refused to board the council trucks taking them to their respective places of work, and continued to linger in the compound. Watched by police, they declined to appoint representatives to discuss their grievances with council officials for fear of victimization and because, as they said, the council should negotiate with their union, the B.M.W.U. They also rejected attempts by a Department of Manpower Utilisation official to intervene on their behalf, insisting only that the minimum wage be raised from R33 to R58 a week.

By Friday night the number of workers fired and/or on strike was:
— 550 electricity workers at the Orlando power station,
— 800 electricity workers at the Van Beek compound,
— 300 workers from the transport department (security guards, artisan assistants and general maintenance workers),
— fifty to sixty workers from the city engineer's Goch St. workshop.
About fifty of the Orlando workers ('who had nowhere to go') appear

to have been taken back by Friday night, thus leaving a total of 1 600 to 1 700 strikers.

Within the council itself the Progressive Federal Party councillors warned that there could be a labour crisis if other municipal workers came out in sympathy. Oberholzer, however, commented that the strike would not spread, saying that 'They are confined to certain groups of people. We are taking certain steps to ensure that they do not spread.'² He refused to elaborate. The management committee called a special meeting on Friday and endorsed the town clerk's decision to reject the workers' demands.

As the news of the J.C.C.'s hard line attitude spread, the anger of the work-force increased. The mood of the workers grew even more defiant when they heard that the J.C.C. had refused to provide train tickets to the Orlando workers who had been paid off on Friday afternoon. On Saturday another 400 transport department workers, mainly technical staff, joined the strike, bringing the total number of strikers to about 2 000.

The events of Thursday and Friday placed the B.M.W.U. in a difficult position. The union had only been in existence for a month. Although it claimed 9 000 members at the start of the strike, the union's paid-up membership was only about 900. Most of the others had either made applications or given verbal willingness to make applications. As many of them were illiterate, the translation from verbal intention to completed applications and paid-up membership took time.

It seems quite clear that the union did not want a strike at that particular stage of its development. Not only were its efforts being directed towards consolidating its organisation and building up membership, but, as one member of the executive pointed out, July is probably the worst time of the year for municipal workers to strike from a purely strategic point of view. In the cold weather months refuse does not rot so quickly thus creating an immediate health hazard, while workers evicted from their residences are subjected to the freezing winter nights.

There is, in fact, a considerable amount of evidence to indicate that the union initially tried to avert such a strike. At its executive meeting on 5 July it was reported that the Orlando power station workers were threatening to strike as a result of their low wages. Most of the executive members came out strongly against striking and members of the executive were sent to Orlando to cool tempers. Again, at the executive meetings on 12 and 15 July it was resolved that the Orlando workers should be dissuaded from striking.

The B.M.W.U. thus found itself with a strike 'on its hands'. However, as the weekend progressed and the union leaders were able to meet with the workers and ascertain their feelings, it became clear that the bulk of the work-force was in an extremely militant and defiant mood. Workers were demanding increases in their minimum wage, improved working conditions, the reinstatement of their colleagues and the recognition of the B.M.W.U.

Faced with this situation, the union was hardly in a position to dissuade workers from striking. Indeed, many workers made it quite clear that they would come out in sympathy with their colleagues on Monday, regardless of the position or advice of the union. The B.M.W.U. therefore saw that its role was to organise the strike 'responsibly' in terms of the interests of the bulk of the work-force. It accordingly issued instructions that firemen and ambulance men should stay at their posts so as not to endanger life, and instructed the remainder of its 9 000 or so members to report for work on Monday morning but not to start work.

The weekend was also marked by the government's first direct comment on the situation. On Saturday the Minister of Commerce and Consumer Affairs, Dr S.W. van der Merwe issued a statement warning that the strikes, and others in Natal, the eastern Cape and Cape Town, were being deliberately orchestrated by South Africa's enemies to secure a reduction in the overall standard of living.'Our enemies', said Dr van der Merwe, 'want economic chaos. They want relations between our people to deteriorate'.[3]

On Sunday the black staff at four of the city's five cleansing depots, namely Selby, Norwood, Nancefield and City Deep, and comprising most of the cleansing section's staff of 1 800, downed tools as from 6.00 p.m. The Antea compound workers serving the industrial areas of Croesus, Langlaagte and Industria were expected to down tools on Monday.

The council attempts to break the strike

The council for its part, did not spend the weekend idly. On Saturday a paymaster visited the Van Beek compound to pay off the strikers, and buses were organised to take them home. None of the strikers, however, came forward.

On Sunday the council tried in earnest to get the strikers back to work and focused its attention mainly on the Van Beek compound. The 'terms' put to the Van Beek workers in the compound on Sunday illustrate the deceitful and underhand attitude which characterised the J.C.C.'s management of its black work-force. The compound was sealed. No one except the municipal compound police and a few 'trustees' were allowed to pass through the gates.

The officials told the workers that if they did not go back on Monday morning, they would lose their various benefits, would be put on buses and deported and would be replaced by new contract workers as had already happened at Orlando, where, the officials said, the strikers had already all been replaced. This was quite untrue. The first eighty Venda replacements did not arrive at Orlando until Tuesday.

On Monday the situation was further confused by press reports on the state of the strike. The council had stated that as far as the electricity department was concerned by Monday evening all the Van Beek workers were back at their jobs and that only 300 of the 550 Orlando power station workers were still on strike. This was reported unquestioningly by the press, thus giving the impression that the strike was beginning to collapse in certain departments and compounds.

What happened on Monday was rather different. About 75 — 80 percent of the Van Beek workers were taken from the compound to their places of work under armed escourt. The trucks took roundabout routes trying specifically to avoid the Selby compound area which would have given the lie to the council's stories. Unfortunately for the council, workers from other compounds such as Antea, City Deep and elsewhere were converging on Selby. Some of these, as well as other colleagues who were in the streets and quite clearly not working, were seen by the Van Beek workers. Messages that Mavi and Somdake had got into the Van Beek compound were being confirmed and most of the Van Beek workers, on reaching their work-places, immediately downed tools and joined their colleagues.

The Council's first attempts to smash the strike had failed.

The strike peaks: Monday to Wednesday, 28 — 30 July

Monday began with 3 000 — 4 000 workers meeting at the Selby compound. These included workers from other compounds as well as those who had come in from Soweto. The majority, about 2 000 workers were from the cleansing department. The streets around the area were cordoned off by armed police after reports of stoning. Workers themselves turned away all traffic trying to enter the compound. A traffic official, Makolla, who drove a bakkie into the compound was dragged down from the vehicle, stabbed in the thigh and beaten. This, and an attack on a bus inspector, were the only two incidents of violence by strikers reported during the strike.

Later in the morning the strikers at Selby were joined by about 600 workers who had marched fifteen kilometres into Johannesburg along the Soweto highway from the Orlando power station. The chanting crowd, stretching more than two kilometres down the road, was cheered as it marched into the compound.

As the crowd swelled onto the pavement, the police baton charged, clearing the pavement and forcing the crowd back into the compound. The gates were locked, and police reinforcements, armed with machine guns, shotguns, short riding crops, and equipped with gas masks were brought onto the scene. The divisional commissioner for the Witwatersrand, Brigadier Gert Kruger told the press that the police were keeping a 'low profile'.

Soon thereafter armed police, accompanied by white officials, entered the Selby compound. Wilsnach, director of the J.C.C.'s housing department, addressed the crowd saying that not one of them had lost their jobs and that they were free to go back to work. His address was met with jeers and a chant of 'Who are you?' He told the crowd to 'think over' the July increases of between R11.45 and R15.25 per month, and the annual bonus of between R143 and R198 that would be paid out in October.

Wilsnach's address was brushed aside by the crowd, which continued to mill around until 4.30 p.m. when Mazwi, the union leader who had managed to become resident in Selby, told them that negotiations with the municipality were continuing; that they should disperse until the next day, and that they would not give in until their demands were met. Mazwi also asked the strikers to help find accommodation for the workers sacked and ejected from Orlando. 'Either we find beds for our brothers, or all of us must spend the night sleeping in the streets together,' he said.

Workers in the other main compounds had also refused to work. By Monday night the number of workers on strike had risen to more than

5 000. In addition to the electricity and transport workers, and 2 000 to 3 000 in the cleansing section, about 450 men in the gas department, 200 men in the traffic department, and 400 men in the sewerage department had joined the strike.

Striking workers again converged on Selby early the following day, and armed police rode shotgun on the buses.

At 7.30 a.m. the police stopped strikers who had arrived at Selby from other compounds from going into the Selby compound and joining the crowd of about 3 500. The police announcement was met by a rain of missiles from the men locked inside the gates. The police baton charged the crowd, restored a degree of calm, and then agreed to allow the men to enter the compound.

Early newspaper reports put the number of men on strike at between 5 500 and 6 000. Reports coming in from various departments varied slightly. However, towards the end of the day, when the city engineer confirmed that 8 500 of the 9 000 men in his department had downed tools, it became clear that at least 10 000 had joined the strike.

Early on Wednesday police moved in to cordon off the compounds housing the striking workers, thus preventing them from leaving to congregate again at Selby. Only those workers who could prove their identity and residency in a compound were allowed to enter.

Council officials planned to tour the compound in what was to be a final effort at persuading the strikers to return to work. Most of the workers came from the Transkei, Venda and Bophuthatswana. The council's strategy, in its attempt to by-pass the B.M.W.U. was to bring in envoys of these three 'homelands' to persuade the strikers to return to work and to elect compound representatives who would 'negotiate' with the council. The scheme collapsed. Boyang, the Bophuthatswana 'vice-consul' said he would not speak to workers unless this is what they wanted. Venda and Transkei representatives were not available for comment. But Baldwin Mudau, leader of the opposition Venda Independence Party, said that workers were unlikely to respond to 'homeland' representatives.

Senior council officials therefore toured the compounds without the 'homeland' representatives. Gerrit Bornman stressed that the outcome of the tour of the compounds by officials would be decisive in whether the council gave effect to the ultimatum that workers return the following day or face dismissal. The council team went from compound to compound telling workers that they would be paid for the day (Wednesday) if they returned to work. The workers were also told that they would not receive any further wage increases and that those who did not return would discharge themselves.

The determination and solidarity of the workers was demonstrated at the end of the day when the police opened the Selby compound gates. Management had arranged for a fleet of buses to be at the compound to take striking workers home. Police, armed with shotguns, machine guns and dogs stood by the gates and alongside the buses. Not a single person boarded the waiting buses.

Thursday 31 July — the strike smashed

By about midday on Thursday, Council officials were claiming that the number of striking workers had dropped to about 2 500 and that they had broken the back of the week-long strike.

Workers in each compound were questioned individually by a council clerk in the presence of armed police. They were asked if they were prepared to go back to work. As one employee said, 'We were intimidated by the police and did not want to say no, so we told them that we wanted to work, but wanted more money. Many of the workers said this.' Through this sort of intimidation many of the workers were effectively forced onto trucks taking them to their workplaces, although many later jumped off the trucks and returned to their compounds.

As far as the leaders were concerned, Mavi, Dlamini, Mazwi, Sere and Somdake had all been dismissed. They could no longer set foot on Council property without fear of being arrested for trespass. They were also wanted by the security police who were hunting for them and could therefore not return to their homes where police were waiting for them. They lived and moved around town in hiding, meeting in the streets, parks and other public places. Mavi himself spent much of his time hiding amongst the busy crowds at Park station.

Many of the workers interviewed since the strike claim that they were told that if they did not go back to work, they would be deported immediately to their 'homelands'. Oberholzer, however, denied that any such threats had been made. 'The workers', he said, 'all returned to work willingly, and those who wanted to go home were paid off'.[4]

At about 9.00 a.m. the crowd in Selby was addressed by a S.A.P.

official employed by the J.C.C. Those workers who said they were prepared to work were ordered to one side and loaded onto trucks, which then left for the work areas. The remainder, numbering at least 1000, which included many who expressed a willingness to work, but at higher wages, had been kept on one side under guard by S.A.P. and municipal police.

Many of the workers who came into Selby during the course of the day were given no such 'choice'. As they entered the compound the police inspected their reference books, stamped these with a 72 hour endorsement to leave the area, and confiscated others. Some of these workers also claim to have been assaulted by armed police. The men were forced into a queue and made to file past either an open pay truck or the administrative manager's office. They were told that they would receive their full entitlement from the municipality. Most of them, however, appear to have been quite considerably underpaid, and none appear to have received their pro rata share of leave pay or pension benefits. It is very difficult to envisage how these workers could have been paid off correctly as pay records appear not to have been prepared in most cases. Furthermore, the council had no idea which workers had come into Selby that morning. Several workers, some of whom had not even been on strike, but who happened to have been in Selby were herded into the queue, had their reference books endorsed out, despite some of them having Section Ten rights, and were handed a sum of money which in most cases bore no relationship to what was due to them. Indeed, some workers were paid nothing.

After the workers had collected their pay they were held as a group by the police. Some of those who asked to relieve themselves were prevented from doing so, others were taken to the toilet under police escort.

The group was held until 4.00 p.m. when about five PUTCO buses arrived. The workers were then driven to the old disused City Deep compound. This went on late into the night until all 1 200 to 1 300 employees had been moved. At about 8.30 a.m. on Friday the men were loaded onto PUTCO buses to be taken to their 'homelands'.

The moving of workers to City Deep was clearly an attempt to contain and isolate resistance before deporting them, along with some of the council's alleged 'agitators and intimidators', to the 'homelands'. However, there was speculation in legal circles that the workers were moved to 'neutral territory' to circumvent the possibility of a restraining order prohibiting eviction. Lawyers, quoted in the *Star*, pointed out that the workers were legal tenants in the municipal compounds where they were housed, and as such were protected from summary eviction.[5]

The union did not hear about what it considered to be the unlawful arrest, detention and assaults on its members until about 4.00 p.m. that day. The information received at that stage was largely in the form of rumour. Some time was spent in ascertaining whether the rumours were substantiated by facts. When the situation had been clarified, the B.M.W.U. and its attorneys sought an urgent application for an interdict seeking to restrain the J.C.C. and the minister of police from wrongfully and unlawfully detaining and assaulting members of the union; and from wrongfully and unlawfully depriving them of their possessions and personal effects contained in their lockers and in the dormitories of the compounds in which they were residing.

Mavi had to come out from hiding. Late on Thursday night, as he waited, with other union executive members and their attorneys, in the corridor of the supreme court, while the union lawyers and the J.C.C. sought to reach an agreement, he was seized and taken into detention under Section 22 of the General Laws Amendment Act.

By midday Friday, 1 August, the buses had left and the eight-day strike had been effectively crushed. From early in the morning workers at the Selby compound were escorted on their way to city cleaning duties by police in riot uniform. Police were inside the compound in two cars.[6] By 8.00 a.m. the compound was quiet.

Strike leaders charged and acquitted

The contradiction between the state's reformist pretensions and its determination to prevent the emergence of democratic worker representation was highlighted in the smashing of the strike. This was further evidenced in the lengths to which the state was prepared to go after the strike in pressing charges against the strike leaders and its assistance to the city council through WRAB (West Rand Administration Board) in victimizing the strikers.

These attacks on the workers after the strike were intensified by the detention and arrest of the union leaders. Whatever organisational resources the B.M.W.U. could muster up at this stage were directed towards the crisis facing the leadership. The many municipal workers who suffered at the hands of the J.C.C. and the state were thus not in a position to confront their problems collectively under the organisation of the union. When Joseph Mavi was seized in the corridors of the supreme court on the night of Thursday 31 July, he was detained under section 22 of the General Law Amendment Act which meant that he could be held incommunicado for fourteen days.

On Thursday, 7 August, the security police raided the offices of the B.M.W.U. in Sauer Street and seized several documents.[7] A week later Mavi and Dlamini were charged in court under the 'Sabotage Act', which carries a minimum five year jail sentence and a maximum penalty of death. Those convicted under the Act 'are liable to the penalties provided for by law for the offence of treason'.

The hearing itself was postponed three times within a two month period from August to October. The fact that the state kept postponing the hearing clearly suggests that it was finding great difficulty in collecting sufficient evidence to substantiate such serious charges in court. This was borne out when, on 19 October the state withdrew the sabotage charges and replaced these with charges under the Black Labour Relations Regulation Act.[8] This was a significant back-down by the state. The act carries no mandatory minimum sentence, and the accused could receive a suspended sentence or even a fine if found guilty. The case was set for February 16 — 20, 1981.

The trial centred around the state's attempts to prove that the accused unlawfully instigated a strike and incited other employees to continue the strike. The initial charges had rested on such sweeping allegations that the defence was forced to ask for further particulars in order to prepare its argument. However, the state was unable to provide further details with reference to the strike as a whole; all the details came down to the role of the accused with reference to the 'strike' in the transport department. As a result, the accused were acquitted.

The trial reflects the serious light in which the strike was held by the state. That it was unable to resolve the situation within the framework of its industrial relations system is a telling comment on the contradictory position in which the state finds itself when the migrants awake.

Acknowledgements

This article was written with considerable assistance from members of the B.M.W.U. executive, Slauzy Maruma, Priscilla Jana and Associates, Councillor Janet Levine, the Black Sash Advice Office, the Industrial Aid Society, members of the J.C.C. Staff Board, Emelia Portenza and above all, several hundred black employees of the J.C.C. Thanks are also given to the editors of S.A.L.B. for helpful comment and advice.

Notes

1 Chairman of the staff board, J.C. de Villiers. *Star,* 25 July, 1980.
2 *Star,* 26 July, 1980.
3 *Sunday Times,* 27 July, 1980.
4 *Star,* 1 August, 1980.
5 *Star,* 4 August, 1980.
6 *Star,* 1 August, 1980.
7 *Rand Daily Mail,* 8 August, 1980.
8 Most press reports stated incorrectly that they had been charged under the Riotous Assemblies Act.

Reading 7. (1982)

The 1981 East Rand Strike Wave*

Jeremy Baskin

In the five months July to November 1981, the east Rand was the scene of more than fifty strikes involving almost 25 000 workers. It is one of the areas in the country where unionism has grown fastest.

Roughly half the strikes involved workers organised by the FOSATU affiliated Metal and Allied Workers' Union (MAWU). Other FOSATU unions, in the chemical, food, textile, paper and transport sectors, were also involved to a much lesser extent. CUSA-affiliated unions in the chemical and construction industries were connected with three strikes. The independent commercial workers' union (CCAWUSA) was linked with one stoppage, whilst the African Food and Canning Workers' Union (A.F.C.W.U.) had members come out in two major stoppages. In addition, a few of the recorded strikes occurred in places with no known union presence.

On the east Rand workers come from different areas. The white employees mostly live in the residential parts of town or on mine property. Black workers are housed in a number of townships which fall under the East Rand Administration Board (ERAB). A significant proportion of the workers, especially in heavy and dangerous metal jobs, are contract workers who are mostly housed in hostels in townships like Vosloorus and Tembisa.

* First published in more extended from in *S.A.L.B.*, VII, 8 (July, 1982), pp. 21-37.

General causes

The east Rand strikes were the result of general as much as particular workers' grievances. These will be dealt with in turn.

Generally inflation was exerting pressure on workers' wages. Massive price increases, particularly of basic foodstuffs, came into effect during the year. There were also widespread rent increases in the twelve months preceding the strike wave. It has been estimated that the level of inflation which the lower income groups experience is *twice* as high as the official Consumer Price Index (C.P.I.).[1] The result was that east Rand workers were feeling the financial squeeze keenly and they needed substantial pay increases simply in order to keep up with inflation.

Contract workers, who account for approximately thirty percent of east Rand workers[2] were being especially squeezed. On the one hand, the small rural subsistence base which they still possess was being further eroded, particularly in KwaZulu which was experiencing the worst drought in memory, and which suffers from massive and growing unemployment. A high proportion of workers from the strike-hit metal industry come from remote and drought devastated areas of KwaZulu.[3]

On the other hand, migrants are being increasingly squeezed from the cities by the influx control laws and their especially rigid application by the ERAB. With more and more people coming onto the labour market, contract workers are confronted with ERAB clamping down on 'illegal' workers, cutting down on the proportion of jobs available to contract workers, and no longer allowing them to transfer or take up contracts in urban areas.

It is not surprising that migrants adopted a particularly militant attitude during the strike wave. Webster and Sitas have estimated that sixty percent of workers involved in these strikes which occurred in the metal industry (approximately half of the total) were contract workers.[4]

Another background cause which can be identified is the growth of the independent trade union movement. On the east Rand alone the Metal and Allied Workers' Union (MAWU), a significant organisational force in the area, claims a membership increase of fifty percent during 1981 with a total of 25 000 members signed up by the end of that year. One unionist said that the workers organise themselves and come to the union offices. 'We don't have to go to factories to recruit these days.' Similarly, the significant growth of the A.F.C.W.U. in the area, has been a phenomenon of the last two years. The growth of the unions should be seen as both a cause and a consequence of a growing worker militancy and self-confidence.

The general political climate is also an important consideration. In the Transvaal, particularly, 1981 was a year of heightened militancy. The political climate of 1981 was an important background factor not only because of the high level of militancy but also because, for the first time in many years, a 'progressive' trade union movement was complemented by the hegemony of a 'progressive' political ideology.

Immediate causes

The factors outlined above made the east Rand situation volatile. But it caught ablaze for more specific reasons. In well over half of the known strikes the central demands concerned questions of management control: the unfair dismissal of fellow workers or shop stewards; the arbitrary actions of certain foremen; the demand that worker representatives who had been 'bought' be removed; and changes in the work-load required by management. About one-third of the strikes revolved around wages or related issues, whilst about ten percent concerned demands that management recognise a particular trade union. The significance of these figures is that they reflect the increasingly sophisticated strike action which black workers are now undertaking. Struggle is occurring over issues which were previously the undisputed prerogative of management. It is worth examining more carefully the specific cause of grievances which sparked off the strikes.

Wages
Many of the demands centred around calls for a 'living wage' of R2 per hour. However, in no case was this demand won. Instead it was common for workers to return to work after having been granted either a small increase in hourly rates or an attendance bonus. In some

factories management responded with no concession. At Triomf Fertilizer (Chloorkop), workers stopped work demanding a 35% pay increase. Management refused to talk to the strikers and all 500 were immediately dismissed.

Many of the wage strikes occurred in the immediate aftermath of the new industrial council agreement for the metal industry, which came into effect at the beginning of July. The agreement set a new minimum rate of R1.13 per hour, and granted most black workers 20 — 23% increases over the agreement of the previous year.[5] Inflation between these two agreements ran officially at 14,6%, but if we remember that Keenan's estimates put the level for workers at *twice* that, then it becomes obvious that the agreement was totally inadequate.[6]

Union recognition

Although only about ten percent of the strikes revolved around questions of union recognition, the dispute over this issue was of great importance at one factory in particular, Colgate-Palmolive. The Chemical Workers' Industrial Union (C.W.I.U.), affiliated to FOSATU, first approached management for recognition in early 1980. Management finally agreed to recognise the union in August 1981 after a protracted dispute involving a lengthy exchange of correspondence, discussions between the union and the company, the threat of a legal strike, a boycott of Colgate products and finally, a two day strike.[7]

What concerns us here is not simply that a recognition agreement was signed, since this is becoming increasingly common. Rather what is important is the quality of recognition. The Colgate workers defeated a determined effort by management to force them onto the industrial council as a prerequisite for recognition. The fact that only twenty Colgate employees were covered by the agreement was relevant. More important was the workers' objection to the whole industrial council system as undemocratic, bureaucratic and an attempt to circumvent meaningful plant-level bargaining. Management continued to delay and bring up new problems after having agreed to negotiate and after C.W.I.U. had called off its boycott and its threatened strike. The workers then came out on a two day strike. The workers were strong and organised enough to compel management to recognise the union on their own terms. An agreement was finally signed in August 1981.

A contrast was provided by two strikes at Johnson Tiles during late September and early October which revealed the dangers of weak organisation. Some 300 workers struck demanding recognition of the CUSA affiliated Building, Construction and Allied Workers' Union (B.C.A.W.U.). The union represented only 365 of the 860 workers at the firm and was therefore in a weak position. Management decided to dismiss some of the strikers and to re-employ selectively. The B.C.A.W.U. suffered a defeat.

Management control

The fact that the majority of strikes challenge management control is an indication that the labour movement has grown not only in size but also in quality. The range of issues which workers are prepared to take up has widened and the weapons at their disposal have increased. An example of the militancy which emerged was seen at Harvey Tiles, where a number of brief stoppages occurred. The workers made far-reaching demands on their own accord, and achieved some radical changes in the shop-floor power structure. One successful demand was that supervisors be reduced to the ranks of ordinary workers. In addition, all proposed changes in production had first to be discussed at a general meeting of the workers. However, they eventually pushed too far, too fast and instead of consolidating their gains they were all dismissed following a dispute during December 1981 and January 1982.

In early July, a strike in the relay adjusting department of the Telephone Manufacturers of South Africa (T.M.S.A.) occurred because workers felt production demands were too extensive. Management conceded. A similar incident occurred at Mine Steel Products in Boksburg when workers were dismissed after refusing to carry an extra heavy load. The remaining workers staged a brief strike and management backed down.

SCAW Metals, an Anglo-American owned factory, was the scene of a stoppage in October when six workers refused to join the closed shop Iron Moulders' Society (I.M.S.). Challenging an old established 'craft' union in favour of the industrial union, MAWU, they were all reinstated without joining the I.M.S. By asserting their right to join the union of their choice, they were indirectly challenging managerial power and confronting an undemocratic measure on the shop-floor.

Arbitrary dismissals were one of the major causes of strikes. About 25 of the known stoppages during the strike wave concerned objections to dismissals. More than half of these stoppages resulted in reinstatements. Sometimes workers struck because of the dismissal of their leadership, as happened at Boksburg Foundry. At other times strikes broke out in order to challenge the unfair dismissal of fellow workers. The origins of the T.M.S.A. strike in October lay in an incident where three workers who had already knocked-off were dismissed for playing cards.

The reason for the large proportion of strikes contesting dismissal is not because there were more unfair dismissals than before, but because workers were prepared to challenge them. This can be seen as a function of their organisation on the one hand, and of the militant and self-confident mood engendered by the strike wave, on the other.

In a variation of the above theme, workers struck on a number of occasions to demand the dismissal of someone. Some strikes revolved around the demand that foremen be dismissed, and T.M. Foundries saw a successful strike along these lines in September. In at least three cases (at Vaal Metals, Boksburg Foundry and Nickel Chrome) workers successfully demanded the dismissal of worker representatives whom they believed had been 'bought-off' by management.[8] Webster and Sitas believe that managements were confronted with an increasingly powerful MAWU and resorted to attempts at coopting leadership, in some cases by offering promotion to the chairman of the shop stewards' committee or giving access to training schemes provided by the firm.[9] However, a well-organised and aware work-force is quite capable of seeing through and responding to managements' more sophisticated industrial manoeuvres.

A significant feature of the strike wave was the resistance shown by workers to racist abuse from white foremen. The racial division of labour in South Africa has meant that conflicts between supervisors and workers have assumed the form of black-white clashes. Mostly the clashes are verbal, but at times they become physical. On a number of occasions strikes were the direct result of such clashes.

At SCAW Metals a fight between a black worker and a white foreman led to the worker being dismissed. As a result, 2 000 workers came out for four days demanding the reinstatement of their fellow worker. Management eventually conceded this and reinstated the worker, explaining that the employer association told them they could 'no longer get away with dismissing a black worker when he assaulted a foreman who called him a kaffir'.[10]

But not all actions were collective. One worker at Colgate was so angry at being called 'kaffir', that he took matters into his own hands and threw acid in the offender's face. As a Colgate shop steward explained, 'We want to be treated as people not as commodities.' Workers at that factory are continually confronted with racist supervisors (even death threats) and underhand attempts at keeping facilities segregated in what is claimed to be a nonracial company.

Extreme racist attitudes and actions can be found at all levels in most companies. Racism is not simply to be found amongst white workers and foremen. However the racism of white workers is notorious. It appears to be increasing in areas like the east Rand because they are feeling threatened by the growth of black worker militancy and assertiveness. White workers are also finding their privileges undermined by some of the reforms the state has been introducing in recent years. For example, blacks are now moving into a number of jobs that were previously guaranteed for whites. Also where there exist established grievance procedures and strong shop steward committees the arbitrary control that the supervisor once had over his 'boys' has diminished. Often the shop steward will go over his head and appeal against an official warning or a dismissal. The material and psychological effects of such action is significant. A number of white workers have responded in a narrow fashion by joining ultra-rightwing groups.

What the east Rand strikes show is that black workers are no longer prepared to let racist insults pass by pretending not to notice them. This is largely the intrusion of growing political awareness from the community into the factory. The way in which community, political and shop-floor issues affect each other highlights any attempt at placing barriers between these spheres, as unrealistic. Workers have combined a growing dignity with strong organisation and the self-confidence to take a stand against racist supervisors.

How the strikes spread

There were rumblings of discontent in June. Boksburg saw 600 workers at a local dairy strike over a dismissal and at Springs there was conflict at Stag Packaging. Two issues were to prove of major importance. Firstly, events at Colgate had been brewing for some months. The boycott was being launched and FOSATU-organised workers in the area were seeing the looming battle as important for the region as a whole. Anger at Colgate management's instransigence was growing. Secondly, the inadequate increases which the new metal agreement introduced in July, affected large numbers of workers in the metal-dominated east Rand.

Workers at Colgate-Palmolive struck on 14 July. 'People saw a victorious strike', one shop steward said, 'and they were inspired'. This tendency for strikes to spread by example as well as geographically was most noticeable at the outset. A strike of 2 000 workers over wages occurred at the MAWU organised Salcast A.M.F. factory in the week preceding Colgate. The days following the Colgate strike saw workers striking at the nearby factories of Hendler and Hendler, Bisonboard, Langeberg Co-op and Vaal Metals. A major strike by about 4 000 workers protesting against inadequate wages and a new death benefit scheme occurred amongst workers at the Boksburg E.R.P.M. gold mine. A similar geographical spread of strikes occurred later at Wadeville.

At Bisonboard workers demanded a wage increase of R1 per hour, not because negotiations were due but because of developments in neighbouring factories — Langeberg Co-op and Hendler and Hendler are situated across the road. The 'imitation effect' was not limited to unionised workers. One MAWU organiser recalls Actonville workers from a non-unionised printing factory coming into the office and saying they were on strike because of other strikes in the area.

The mood in the Boksburg/Benoni area was especially tense and exciting for workers at this time. As a factor it should not be underestimated. The psychological burden of oppression is an immense one and the feeling of being 'on the march' was an enervating force for workers. The tension was not reduced when unknown arsonists destroyed the Benoni offices of FOSATU in July. The subsequent continuation of the strike wave shows that the fire had no intimidatory effect.

A further significant factor in the spread of the strikes was the hostels. There was, according to many sources, a general feeling in the Vosloorus hostels that it was time for an increase. In Tembisa and other hostels the mood was similar. For union organisation the hostels are complex institutions. They are overcrowded, uncomfortable and sometimes tightly controlled places where liquor and the frustrations of a single-sex existence take their toll. But at the same time they bring large numbers of workers together in a single place and encourage a common awareness of life in the factories, in the cities and in the rural area. One union organiser explained how 'strikes would get discussed in the hostels over supper' and how whenever union members met in the hostels other hostel-dwellers were interested to know what was happening. Hostels can be difficult to organise, but once organised they can (and did) become pillars of the unions' strength.

The role of the unions

There were some who saw in the strike wave the work of agitators and subversives. Clearly, for these people, the unions were to blame. Doubtless some of the strikes were planned, but not by union officials. In most cases, workers took action and then contacted the unions. If anything the unions encouraged negotiation and a return to work.

The east Rand unions, by their very nature, brought workers from different factories in the same industry into contact with one another. This allowed issues such as the metal industrial council agreement to be opposed by similar demands in different factories. It brought into contact workers from Hendler and Hendler, Salcast and SCAW Metals etc. who could then compare their different situations.

Important too, given that the strike wave covered an entire region, were the meetings which different shop stewards' councils held. This FOSATU structure (and mostly FOSATU unions were involved in the strikes) brought together shop stewards from different industries. This allowed for unified action such as the spreading of the demand for R2 per hour. It also made solidarity action possible. The Colgate boycott was launched and popularised at shop stewards' council meetings on the east Rand. Workers in may factories started wearing boycott stickers on their overalls. The threatened success of the boycott was undoubtedly a factor which caused management to back down and recognise the union. Another solidarity action, which was ultimately thwarted, followed the T.M.S.A. strike in Springs. After the dismissal of all the strikers and the refusal of managements to talk, the Springs shop stewards' council met and decided that all shop stewards should pressurise their own managements to employ the T.M.S.A. workers. This happened at a number of Springs factories (notably Kellogg and Braitex), although without success. At the meeting it was also decided to call a general meeting for all Springs workers that Sunday. Possible solidarity action was on the agenda, but the meeting could not take place because it was banned. Thus the existence of unions was important for the structure they provided which enabled workers to keep in contact with one another.

Most of the strikes on the east Rand broke out spontaneously, or were initiated at the shop-floor level. The unions encouraged workers who came out to act in a disciplined and united manner. This strategy generally paid off. The unions discouraged protracted stoppages and encouraged workers to resume production once management had agreed to negotiate (as, for example, at Hendler and Hendler). At Colgate, the two day strike was aimed at stopping management delays in finalising a recognition agreement which they had already conceded in principle. Overall, the strikes were of short duration. Excluding those that were unresolved, the longest (e.g. Plant Protection, SCAW, Dorbyl, T.M.S.A.) lasted only four to ten days and were all unsuccessful, with the exception of SCAW Metals. Not all the shorter stoppages led to victories, but the tendency was for them to have a far greater success rate.[11]

The unions generally played a cautious and disciplining role. Particularly important were structures, such as the shop stewards' councils, which provided important arenas for workers from different factories to meet.

State involvement

Direct involvement by the state was a notable feature at a number of strikes. In this Boksburg was different. A legal case following assaults during the Rely Precision strike in 1980 resulted in a number of Boksburg policemen being required to pay large sums in damages. This seems to have exercised a cautioning influence on police in the Boksburg area, with the result that industrial conflict is usually left to management and the workers to sort out. This was not the case at Triomf Fertilizers where 500 workers struck in August at the Chloorkop plant, near Kempton Park. They were demanding pay increases of 35% and their stoppage came at a crucial time for farmers. Management insisted on negotiating through the liaison committee but workers wanted them to talk to their union, the CUSA affiliated South African Chemical Workers' Union (SACWU). During the strike, white schoolboys were used as scabs to maintain deliveries. According to the union, armed police and management arrived at the Tembisa hostels where the workers resided and forced them onto the lorries to return them to the plant. Some were re-employed whilst others were paid off and evicted from the hostels in a manner reminiscent of the Johannesburg municipal workers' strike. Company officials denied that this had occurred.

At Telephone Manufacturers of South Africa (T.M.S.A.), the largest factory in Springs, the state played a major role in defeating the strike. On Thursday 1 October, three workers in the moulding department (No. 26) were dismissed, allegedly for playing cards. Workers felt this was deliberate provocation and pointed out that the workers had already knocked off. The shop steward who took up the matter was told to return the following day. When workers returned the next day they found they had been locked-out. They were immediately supported by workers from department 27. Both departments were summarily dismissed at which point all other departments walked out singing. Riot police arrived. One worker representative claimed that he had asked to talk to management but was instead taken into an office by the riot police and allegedly assaulted.[12] A total of 1 600 to 1 700 stopped work, that is, over eighty percent of the African workers. Almost all of the 1 000 coloured workers remained at their posts.

That evening a meeting in KwaThema resolved not to return to work but to send representatives to negotiate with management. Management said they were only prepared to talk to two unions — the white-run Electrical and Allied Workers' Union and the TUCSA affiliated Radio, Television, Electronic and Allied Workers' Union (R.T.E.W.U.). They also refused to reinstate either the three originally dismissed workers or the whole of department 26. Regular attempts at negotiation during the course of the following week, saw management refusing to talk.

A week after the beginning of the strike, some workers started returning. This created a lot of animosity and the townships became tense and, at times, violent. A number of workers were arrested by the security police on assault charges. One participant expressed the view that 'the idea of an injury to one is an injury to all is gaining ground'. Amongst T.M.S.A. workers the call was growing for a general strike in the Springs region. A general workers' meeting to discuss this was prevented by a ban on meetings in Springs during the weekend of 10 — 11 October. In addition, a leading FOSATU official and Springs worker, Chris Dlamini, was prohibited from attending gatherings over that weekend.

The state action finally broke the back of the T.M.S.A. strike. Over the next few weeks strikers drifted back to work although not all were re-employed either because they were blacklisted or because management had decided 'to stabilise the African work-force at 1250 for business reasons'.[13]

The fact that major changes in the production process were impending at T.M.S.A. — changes which would ultimately involve the slashing of the work-force from 3 000 to 250 — may have been responsible for management's hardline attitude towards the strikers. They may have felt that this attitude would allow workers 'to dismiss themselves' and thus enable management to re-employ a reduced number excluding leadership elements in the process. A defeated work-force would be less likely to resist forthcoming retrenchments.

The striking workers wanted management to talk with MAWU. T.M.S.A. were only interested in R.T.E.W.U. MAWU claims that some of their members were also members of R.T.E.W.U. since they had been given forms in the factory to sign up. They were about to petition to end their membership at the time the strike occurred. Clearly management made use of the fact that there was another union, in order to avoid talking to the majority union MAWU.

The T.M.S.A. strike was defeated for a number of reasons including: firstly, the crucial intervention of the riot police and the prevention of union meetings; secondly, a totally inflexible management, possibly wanting to smash organisation prior to the introduction of more capital-intensive technology, and thirdly, and most importantly, the fact that the T.M.S.A. plant was not sufficiently well organised to sustain such a major confrontation with management. The workers had only recently been transferred from the FOSATU Workers' Project to MAWU. Only a few coloured workers in a factory where they formed an unusually large proportion participated in the strike. The fact that 1 300 workers remained at their posts, weakened the workers from the outset. Another factor, which may have contributed to the defeat, was insufficient follow-up attempts to get international support from the mother-plant.

The T.M.S.A. strike was not, however, a total setback for the Springs area as some had feared it would be. T.M.S.A. workers are still interested in organisation and total union membership in Springs at the beginning of 1982 stood at around 8 000.

Conclusion

This article has looked at some aspects of the east Rand strike wave of July to November 1981. Many other areas remain to be explored such as the details relating to management's responses, or the role which SEIFSA played. The creative role of the shop stewards' councils also deserves to be examined in more depth.

Hopefully this article provides some basis for an assessment of the strikes which have been occurring lately on the east Rand, particularly in the Germiston area. These strikes, in contrast to those addressed by this article, have been largely over wages. For all the differences, however, what the current strike wave indicates (and there have been at least twenty strikes), is that last year's strike wave was no isolated occurrence and that worker organisation in the area has 'taken off', beginning a period of rapid growth.

Notes

This article is based largely on interviews and discussions with shop stewards, union officials, workers and management, as well as discussions with a number of people who are knowledgeable about the east Rand.

1 See 'Inflation and the Working Class', *Work in Progress,* 17 (1981), pp.26-28.
2 Administration Board figures.
3 It is estimated that sixty percent of east Rand contract workers come from Lebowa and south Ndebele. The remainder come from a variety of areas including the northern parts of KwaZulu. The more remote the 'home' area, the more likely it is that the worker will occupy the least attractive jobs. Contract workers are concentrated in certain industries/jobs such as foundries, municipalities, and construction, where the work is dangerous, exceptionally heavy, and generally the most poorly paid.

4 E. Webster and A. Sitas (1982), 'Stoppages in East Rand Metal Factories', FOSATU *Occasional Publication* No. 3, p.7.

5 See Government Gazette No. 7562, 1 May 1981, R879 & R880.

6 See *WIP* 17, already cited.

7 See Chemical Workers' Industrial Union, · 1981, 'Workers Struggle at Colgate', *S.A.L.B*, VI, 8, (July, 1981), pp.18-33,for earlier details.

8 At Boksburg Foundry workers struck in August for the reinstatement of a dismissed shop steward. In October they struck for a full two days to remove the *same* shop steward who they believed had been 'bought'. Both strikes were successful.

9 E. Webster and A. Sitas — 'Stoppages' p.4.

10 E. Webster and A. Sitas — 'Stoppages ...' p.4.

11 Richard Hyman has distinguished between lengthy strikes ('trials of strength') and 'demonstration stoppages' whose chief purpose is to 'to call attention to workers' feelings of grievance' and in which strikers are usually willing to return to work to allow for negotions '... even before concrete concession have been offered' *(Strikes* [Fontana, Glasgow, 1977], second edition p.24). There is also the very short stoppage where workers wish to draw immediate attention to a grievance, whilst they remain on the premises. A number of these extremely short and successful stoppages occurred at factories such as Harvey Tiles and Vaal Metals during the strike wave.

12 *Sowetan,* 12 October, 1981.

13 *Star,* 17 October, 1981.

Reading 8. (1984)

The Dunlop Strike: A Trial of Strength*

Ari Sitas

> Whilst walking, thinking about the workers' problems I saw a fist flying across Dunlop's cheek.
>
> A.T. Qabula

Prefigure of industrial relations to come

On 18 September 1984 the Dunlop strike ended with management agreeing to the unconditional reinstatement of all 1 200 workers. The strike lasted for four weeks. The workers, jubilant about their victory, poured out of St Anthony's Hall in Greyville to return to work, marching and chanting through Durban's busiest streets. Scenes of elation spilled over into the factory yard rounding off a trying period of conflict and discipline: a conflict which, in its strategies, duration and tone, might prefigure much of what industrial relations will be like in South Africa: a trial of strength between employers and strongly organised workers.

Such confrontations have been a rarity in South Africa's history, given scant trade union resources, black workers' meagre savings and adverse legislation proscribing such actions. Natal's history in particular is marked by hundreds of outbursts, volatile demonstration strikes, all of short duration — the strike at Dunlop's appears as one of the few poignant exceptions.

* First published in more extended from in *S.A.L.B.*, X, 3 (December, 1984), pp.62-84.

Immediate causes of the strike

According to Dunlop's industrial relations manager, G. Sutton, all workers were dismissed for unlawful industrial action. The dismissal followed stoppages on 9, 15, and 17 August. For management the issue was clearcut: 'In spite of the workers and the union being informed that any further industrial action would lead to dismissal, the shifts refused to work and were dismissed.'

The first stoppage occurred on 9 August as a response to the suspension of three MAWU shop stewards. Management suspended the stewards because they had allegedly breached the disciplinary procedures agreed to in the recognition agreement with the union. The shop stewards refused to sign the disciplinary warnings of workers who refused to work overtime. They felt that they could not be a party to such disciplinary measures since it was within the rights of workers to refuse overtime. The union argued strongly in support of its shop stewards. Management agreed then to resolve the dispute the following week at a meeting with the trade union and the shop stewards. On hearing this, workers agreed to return to work.

The second stoppage occurred on Wednesday, the fifteenth, when workers discovered they were being short paid. They stopped work and asked management to justify and rectify the problem. Management argued that the pay was short because the first stoppage wasted a day's work. The workers retorted that it was management that closed the factory on that day despite their willingness to return to work. Management closed the factory again and called for a special meeting with the shop stewards and the trade union. It was at this meeting that the shop stewards articulated the four issues which were at the bottom of the workers' discontent: (1) that management had suspended their shop stewards wrongfully; (2) that management had short paid them; (3) that they were being abused and ill-treated by a manager and his foreman; and (4) that management was systematically preventing an 'unfair labour practice' case of four dismissed MAWU members from coming to the courts by blocking MAWU's conciliation board application. Management articulated strong objection to the way workers were 'forcing' the issues through stoppages. Yet at the same time they were ready to rectify the issues if the workers returned to work. The union agreed.

On Thursday, the sixteenth, workers returned to work. That afternoon a meeting was held between the shop stewards, the union and management. A deadlock developed and management refused to rectify any of the four issues tabled for discussion. The shop stewards said that management's intransigence would anger the workers. Management indicated that they did not care, but agreed that the shop stewards and the union would report to workers on Friday, the seventeenth. The mass meeting with the workers was to cause a dramatic turn in events. According to MAWU and its shop stewards the meeting decided to take legal action on the first three issues, but hold a secret ballot for a lawful strike on their fourth grievance. There was overwhelming majority support. Management though, an hour after the announcement of the result of the ballot, advised all 1 200 Sydney Road tyre workers that they were dismissed for unlawful action.

Over the course of the following week the strike began to escalate: the Benoni, Ladysmith and the Durban sports and commercial plants of Dunlop held their own strike ballots in support of the Sydney Road workers. The votes indicated a majority support for solidarity strike action. In other words, all Dunlop's workers in South Africa — save the Eastern Province factories — were ready to flex their muscles behind their Durban brothers. In Natal, all these workers were MAWU members. In the Transvaal (Benoni) they were members of the Chemical Workers' Industrial Union (C.W.I.U.) also an affiliate of FOSATU. The strike was taking on national proportions.

On the twenty third, workers at the small sports factory in Durban came out on a sympathy strike and all 120 were dismissed, also for unlawful action. The commercial branch workers followed immediately after. As the Ladysmith and Benoni factories were gearing themselves for action too, Dunlop's management initiated a novel legal intervention: they appealed to the supreme court for an injunction prohibiting the secretary of MAWU and/or the organisation from inciting unlawful strike action. If won, this injunction was to sever the trade union from its rank and file, proscribing the strike as an affair between Dunlop's management and its workers.

From its first week then, the strike appeared to gain momentum and become a major, if not national, confrontation between management and labour. Yet, these immediate causes of confrontation hide a broader context which needs to be explained before the explosive dynamics of the strike can be elucidated. A few words then are necessary to introduce the protagonists of this industrial dispute.

The protagonists of the dispute

Dunlop South Africa has a reputation for being an efficient and profitable multi-national corporation. It sprawls all over South Africa: its Sydney Road, Congella factory is the largest and oldest (1 100 workers). Not as large, but of comparative importance are the Ladysmith (800 workers, car tyre), the Benoni (650 workers, industrial products), the East London (450 workers, mattress and pillows) factories, and a small plant in Jacobs, Durban (150 workers, sports goods). Dunlop S.A. is an industrial giant with assets exceeding R110 m. and planning a further R55 m. expansion programme to further modernise production facilities. Finally, despite the bleak economic environment, Dunlop has shown a remarkable degree of profitability.

The South African operation, however, contrasts radically with the performance of the mother company, Dunlop Holdings U.K. The British multinational has been for some time in a crippling state of depression and its attempts to reorganise its facilities on an internationally competitive scale has earned it amongst union circles the title of a 'union basher'. In the face of declining profits after the oil crisis of the early 1970s the company was caught in a vice whose ever tightening jaws spelt on the one hand, declining demand, on the other, a debt crisis arising from high interest short and long term loans from financial institutions. All this has precipitated an international reorganisation of its world empire.

This reorganisation has reached a dramatic intensity over the last five years: after its failed joint operations with Italian rubber multinational, Pirelli, it instituted a series of measures that caused turmoil amongst its workers in the U.K. It closed down its Merseyside factory affecting half of its 11 000 U.K. labour component. It squeezed forty percent productivity increases and reorganisation of its shift systems out of its Washington Durham workers, to compete with its German and Japanese operations. It transferred its golf-ball production to Georgia U.S.A. to take advantage of the changing relationship between the dollar and the pound. Through its associate company, Sumitomo, it internationalised its sportswear production in the Far East. Yet, the vice kept on squeezing, necessitating repayments of debts which in turn saw Dunlop selling its Malaysian rubber plantations and its New Zealand operations. Of late Dunlop Holdings U.K. is at the mercy of the banks that financed its internationalisation. They demand repayments of a crippling £800m. debt.

It is from this predicament that rumours arose that Dunlop S.A. is 'for sale' in order to make some of the repayments. Another rumour had it that pressures on Dunlop S.A. were increasing because its high profit runs were to be the lever through which Dunlop U.K. would buy its freedom from the banks. Whatever the case, whether Dunlop S.A. was to be the prize jewel, or the fairy godmother, the pressures on the local corporation's performance were escalating. Part of Dunlop's behaviour can be ascribed to this international pressure.

For its part, MAWU, is also propelled forward by issues wider than its relationship to Dunlop management. The union, formed in 1974 in Natal in the aftermath of the Durban strikes, has experienced in its first period both enthusiastic expansion, and decline. It is only since 1982 that the union has begun to experience a period of militant revival in Natal (as opposed to the revival in the late 1970s in the Transvaal): its membership has doubled between 1982 and 1983 to reach a paid-up membership of 8 000 workers. Its confidence has increased after a series of victories on wages, dismissals and recognition agreements.

As an affiliate of FOSATU it has been committed to strong grassroots organisation at the work-place through shop steward structures; and has been a hard bargainer for a 'living wage'. For MAWU Dunlop's management symbolised a traditionalist authoritarian management with a tough anti-union stand. They pointed out Dunlop's traditional hostility to trade unions and MAWU in particular, and its refusal to treat MAWU and its shop stewards as anything more than a 'glorified liaison committee'. But while MAWU is faced on the one hand by intransigent employers like Dunlop, it is also faced on the other hand with an acute militancy from its rank and file. All over Natal, the mood of workers has changed creating a volatile situation, or as one organiser put it, '... 1973 type conditions without the explosion like the Durban strikes ...'. It is these pressures that make MAWU's relationship to Dunlop unthinkable without the real actors of this conflict, Dunlop's workers.

Dunlop's workers

In the main, Dunlop's workers are second-generation urban residents with Section Ten rights. Despite this, many have active links with Natal's (KwaZulu's) countryside. A sprinkling of coloured and Indian workers are clustered in the more skilled jobs. One of the main features of the African labour force at Dunlop is its stability: the average years of service per worker approximates fourteen. There are a substantial number who have worked more than 25 (in one case, 37) years with the company. In many other industrial contexts this could mean unambigiously a high level of job satisfaction. Such an assumption in the context of Durban's industrialisation would make little sense. Part of the explanation has to do with the structure of Natal's labour market: Natal's industry relies on 'cheap' labour for its clothing, textile and food sectors, which are dominant. Dunlop, together with a few other chemical, metal and motor firms pay relatively high wages. In this way they attract workers with few other alternatives. But in all these 'high' paying factories, wages are lower than the national average. For instance, Natal Dunlop pays twenty to forty percent less than other rubber and tyre manufacturers in South Africa.

Furthermore, most workers are employed to work shifts as machine or process operators in a modern labour process which combines sophisticated chemical, moulding, mechanical and trimming operations. All these processes are highly rationalised and inter-connected, based on a system of mass production. Consequently, work is an unending drive towards high production targets, called 'scores'. Productivity and efficiency have been the twin imperatives at Dunlop. Workers do not see all this as either fulfilling or satisfying: in the mill department work is seen to be heavy and dangerous, and elsewhere exhausting.

The continuity of service amongst older workers at Dunlop ensures the continuity of a factory tradition informing both behaviour and expectations from management. There was a strong sense amongst these older workers that they had been around far longer than any of Dunlop's managers. Their memories spanning the 1940s to the present speak invariably of a 'thankless toil' sacrificing their years in return for nothing. The messages to the younger workers were also simple: they too should expect nothing from Dunlop. Whether particular events recounted were actually experienced or not, whether they were informed by rumour or exaggeration, expectations were coloured by their stories: Dunlop was not and is not the benevolent employer it sees itself to be.

Nevertheless, save for a few interpersonal skirmishes and a few mini-stoppages, Dunlop remained quiescent throughout the 1960s. It was only in 1973 during the strike wave engulfing Durban as a whole, that black workers downed tools demanding higher wages. What emerged in the 1970s as a source of new frustration was the liaison committee. In its career it gained very little in the form of wage increases, night shift allowances, improvement of facilities or benefits in the factory. Rather, Dunlop created its own industrial council for the tyre plant in Durban through which the in-company union adjusted wages. This left the liaison committee to deal with issues like canteen facilities and tea-breaks.

To sum up, Dunlop's senior workers were the suppliers of a tradition of frustrated expectations. Their experience over time solidified into a deeply felt grievance that informs new workers, distancing them from any trust relations with management. This distance and frustration was to be utilised by MAWU in organising drives of the 1980s.

Organising drives at Dunlop

MAWU began organising at Dunlop on a systematic basis in mid-1982. Initially, it proved difficult as workers were suspicious of such talk as joining unions: 'There is no such thing as a union. This is something which is going to eat our money...', 'Don't you think that the white (organiser) is going to rob us and doublecross us with other whites?', 'How do they know our problems, they don't work here.' But MAWU managed to secure the support of a disgruntled, informal leadership, frustrated by the failures of the liaison committee. These workers, some very old, long-service people and some young, militant and assertive, formed a steering committee to organise inside the factory. During this first phase, it was primarily the older workers who led the recruitment drives. Prominent among these was a worker with 37 years at Dunlop and who was a respected liaison committee member. Another, with more than 25 years had been politically active in the 1950s and early sixties, and was now an influential community leader in KwaMashu's Section Nine. They argued incessantly with everyone, persuaded and chastised. More than most they stood up as symbols of opposition. Being so close to retirement, with all their benefits to lose, they were standing up for the union. They were ready to become 'a black Jesus for the black nation' as one worker put it. Or according to another, 'They've got a home, they've got everything, instead of resting and letting their sons look after them, they are ready to stand firm for the union.' In the first month 200 had joined, by the second 400, and by the third 600, out of the 1 100 workers. With each gain for the union relationships between workers and Dunlop management deteriorated further.

The process of recruitment was difficult — not only due to the fear enunciated by workers. It was made difficult by the activation of recruitment by the in-company union inside the factory. Dunlop since the 1940s had established an in-company union — the Durban Rubber Workers' Union — to cater for its Indian and coloured workers. The 'union' opened up its scope to include African workers as a response to MAWU's recruitment drives. A black personnel officer began zealously organising workers against MAWU. This precipitated an escalation of conflict: in a short time workers had to decide to which 'impi' (regiment) they belonged. Conflict became personalised between two 'chiefs' of the impis: the personnel officer and one of the elders. The few workers who had joined the Rubber Workers' Union urged the others not to join a union of 'outsiders' who would steal their money; they should join a union recognised by management. MAWU was accused of wanting to break the company and lose everyone their jobs. The MAWU supporters accused the others of being 'bosses tools' and challenged them to show where their offices were; they taunted them that unlike in MAWU where they knew the workers ran the union, they were unsure of who ran the Durban Rubber Workers' Union. As the conflict was escalating and MAWU was winning vociferous support, management began to recruit hundreds of additional workers from the Labour Office — Dunlop feared a strike.

These factory conflicts, buttressed by Dunlop's refusal to recognise MAWU, enhanced the metal union's dominance in the factory. But the strike, which could have meant the defeat of MAWU, did not take place. Instead the steering committee members kept pile-driving pressure for recognition onto management. They also set about creating a play about work and life at Dunlop to publicise their grievances. The play in turn tightened the links between Dunlop workers and the rapidly expanding national union movement. Again, instead of resorting to strike action over recognition the workers instituted a canteen boycott which was supported by Benoni Dunlop workers. The steering committee finally, in numerous contingents, began travelling to Ladysmith to assist organisation of Dunlop workers there. In the midst of all this flurry of activity Dunlop decided to abolish the liaison committee, stop the Dunlop Rubber Workers' Union and finally recognise MAWU.

Recognition of the trade union was, at the same time, a signal to attempt to roll back the tide of militancy in the factory. According to shop stewards, there was an immediate clamp-down on discipline and a tightening of supervisory controls in the factory. The 'three warnings' system began to be implemented with zeal. Finally Dunlop's attitude to unilaterally changing scores and production bonuses, led to mini-stoppages and go-slows all over the plant. Both workers and management expected a major confrontation to break out. Alongside this escalating conflict MAWU and its shop stewards were trying to negotiate a wage agreement with Dunlop. (It was also at this time, October 1983, that four worker leaders were dismissed. It was over these leaders that workers were to strike in 1984.) The company and the union were seriously deadlocked over wages with management refusing to speak to the workers' representatives unless the go-slow and the factory turmoil ceased. Workers were pushing for a strike. Issues almost came to a chaotic climax during a mass meeting called by the union. There, the shop stewards argued for discipline on the factory floor and for following the procedure for a legal strike. On this there was instant division: workers attacked the shop stewards for avoiding the issues and demanded immediate strike action. At the end of the meeting during which the union and shop stewards came close to losing a substantial number of supporters, the arguments for a legal strike prevailed. The strike ballot on 16 November predictably showed over ninety percent support for the strike. Management responded by recruiting potential scab labour. On the evening of the fifteenth as the union was getting ready for the strike, the Minister of Manpower called for a conciliation board to resolve the dispute. This would have made the strike illegal. On the sixteenth the strike did not happen. Instead hundreds of unemployed potential scabs, having been promised jobs, crowded outside the factory gates. After hearing that there were no jobs to be had, they became angry and charged through the gates towards the factory demanding their jobs. In a twist of irony the police were called in to repulse the scab labourers. Conciliation meetings in November and December failed to resolve the deadlock. The factory closed down for Christmas with a strike looming in the new year.

The workers returned 'cold' from their Christmas break. Many had accumulated more debts during the festive season, others needed money urgently because relatives in the countryside had borrowed heavily to offset the effects of droughts and most were feeling uncertain about a lengthy confrontation. The shop stewards were urged to settle and accept management's offer.

After the failure of the wage negotiations, both the work-force and the union experienced internal problems and harassment. The shop stewards were feeling that the workers were turning against them. Accusations of selling out echoed within the shop steward structures, acrimony developed between shop stewards and workers. Enemies of the union climbed onto the bandwagon. A series of death threats were sent to most shop stewards' home addresses. The union felt a severe weakening of its presence in the factory and the shop stewards witnessed unity in the factory collapsing. At that stage it was difficult to assess where the challenge to union authority was coming from. One challenge was coming from a younger and militant stratum of workers who were accusing the leadership of not being tough enough. By the time of the 1984 shop steward elections there was a feeling that a good number of shop stewards were too 'soft' and too accommodating of Dunlop's management.

The elected shop stewards included some of the old but also brought into the limelight a new stratum of leaders. All of them were now seen as legitimate representatives, pulling the union out of a crisis in the factory. MAWU was saved from disintegrating into factional disputes through its strict allegiance to factory elections and democracy.

It is to the credit of the shop stewards that the factory was united again through endless meetings and consultations with workers. Furthermore, closer ties were developed with all the other Dunlop factories' shop stewards. Finally, they conducted themselves with a missionary zeal to air grievances and seek out problems in the factory — given the wage agreement which was binding for the year.

The year rolled on with a vengeance for the majority of black workers in South Africa. Pressures — economic and political — were becoming suffocating at work, at home and in travelling between the two. Conflict over bus fares was brewing and General Sales Tax (G.S.T.) was increased. Then came the increase on hire purchase and credit. Alongside this came township-bound political turbulence affecting all the residents of the free-hold locations: Lamontville, Claremont and Chesterville. Finally, the new political reforms — such as the tricameral parliament — were furiously debated. To quote facets of this mood: '... the government is stealing from us with G.S.T. They then use the money and press us down more and get the Indians on their side...', '...Dunlop's like the government. Sometimes they confuse me.... Is Dunlop the government and the government our exploiter...', 'I sometimes don't know whether I need to fight for my rights or to fight to protect my rights...it's all the same: Dunlop says this is how many tyres to make the score, *they* decide. The government says, "this is the score: Indians in and kaffirs out", *they* decide.' By the middle of the year the political register among black workers at Dunlop spelt new mood.

A few weeks before the strike, a worker died on the job, crushed by a moulding machine. The event struck a political chord amongst the workers. He was immediately seen to have died in the struggle on the 'machine'. He was give a hero's funeral at Lamontville during the peak of the U.D.F. and Inkatha conflict. If anything this death enhanced the political feelings of the work-force. Perched on top of this mounting discontent the shop stewards at Dunlop felt that a 'disaster' was coming. As one of them said, 'Our relationship with Dunlop has been a disaster waiting for a time to happen. That it began on 16 August is irrelevant. Dunlop was uncompromising since MAWU entered the factory. With such an attitude the suspicion of our brothers was the last insult. From then on it was a conflict over dignity.'

Rather then describing the experience of the strike, its day to day drama, it is imperative now to draw out the main features of the strike.

Main features of the strike

Nine features characterised the four weeks of conflict and perserverence: (1) the dismissal of all hourly paid workers by Dunlop; (2) the discipline of the strikers; (3) the creation of a single channel of information by the shop stewards; (4) the leadership offered by the shop stewards; (5) the national nature of the strike; (6) Dunlop's legal strategy; (7) the strike's nonracial nature; (8) the challenge to Dunlop's black foremen; (9) the workers' hardened resolve to continue until they won their demands.

1. Dunlop dismissed all hourly paid workers for 'unlawful strike action'. Although this seems heavy-handed at first glance and an attempt by Dunlop to show its toughness as a company, it is an action which created a situation of strength out of fundamental weakness. By dismissing all workers, Dunlop covered itself from any retort by MAWU through the industrial court for an unfair labour practice or an unfair dismissal. But this was also a source of vulnerability. By dismissing all the workers, skilled and semi-skilled, its 'obedient' and 'opposing' workers, it allowed the union to begin the strike with the production lines dead and all the workers out behind it. Provided the strikers did not break ranks, management would be in a very difficult position. The strike, then, from its first moment took on the features of a total confrontation.

2. The total dismissal of workers gave the union and the shop stewards an opportunity which they turned to their favour. The second feature of the strike was the remarkable discipline achieved by the striking workers: every day from 7 o'clock in the morning to 1 o'clock at lunchtime, all workers had to 'clock in and out' of St Anthony's Hall. Registers would be taken and anyone late or absent had to stand on stage and explain himself. If he showed disrespect for the strike, if he gave superficial excuses or lies, he would be found guilty by the body of workers and fined. The fines were contributions to the strike fund. Preferable to the workers was that leave of absence should be granted the day before. This discipline buttressed by volunteer groups ensured that all workers were present, together, every day of the strike. 'Once we voted for a strike', stated a shop steward, 'we were on strike and not on holiday. We all have families, a lot of us in the countryside, we all have problems at home but this is not the time to go visiting. The weekend Saturday and Sunday are sufficient ...'. The discipline of the

strike endorsed by the majority of workers ensured that the strength of the strike remained undiminished throughout.

3. Through this disciplined participation, a single channel of communication and information was achieved, neutralising attempts to weaken the workers' resolve. The shop stewards were aware that Dunlop would begin to try and attract some workers back through fear of losing their job, through spreading false reports about the situation of the strike. After discussion with the workers it was argued that all news of the strike was to be channelled through the meeting. All rumours, news, offers and counter-offers were to be raised at each meeting and discussed. This again ensured that confusion and conflicting reports, the usual outcome of a strike situation, were avoided.

4. A fourth feature of the strike was the effective leadership given by the shop stewards themselves. For half the period the union was overwhelmed by the trend to legal struggle and the escalating nature of the strike. The stewards would meet again in the afternoon, preparing agendas for the next day; counting and worrying over the day's strike contribution; rushing to other factory meetings to explain their situation; travelling great distances to liaise with other striking Dunlop workers; fundraising and preparing for a boycott of Dunlop sports products. Throughout the strike they provided both leadership and clarity to the volatile mood of the majority of the workers. Important too was the contribution of Dunlop's cultural wing led by oral poet/writer Qabula, who mobilised new performances for the strikers, new plays, poems and workshops. Invariably lots of strike time was taken over by such events which entertained, and highlighted the issues of the strike.

5. The first four features ensured the strength of the strike at the Sydney Road factory while the fifth feature concerns the national escalation of the strike. Having grown as a national industrial union and being an affiliate of FOSATU, MAWU has created effective links amongst Dunlop workers throughout the country. The close ties between Durban shop stewards and those from Benoni and Ladysmith allowed for a broadening of the strike effort. Within a week all Durban plants were on strike. This was carried over to Ladysmith and Benoni workers who struck in solidarity. Dunlop was faced with a near general strike unless it resolved the dispute with MAWU.

6. From this escalation flowed Dunlop's novel legal strategy: instead of attempting to charge workers for unlawful strike action, it pressed the supreme court to grant an urgent injunction prohibiting the branch

secretary of MAWU inciting workers to unlawful action. Presenting its case, Dunlop stressed the urgency of the situation, as it was losing R229 000 per strike day at its tyre plant in Durban. The judge found, on the basis of the papers submitted to him, that there was evidence of incitement. He also found that this strike was illegal but deferred his decision because no oral evidence was led. In essence then, the strike continued but leaving the union and the workers worried about the implications of the judgement. The implications were never tested and the judgement dissolved in the face of a stubborn strike which refused to budge.

7. A seventh feature of the strike is that it broke the existing divisions between coloured, Indian and African workers. The reluctance of the former two to join the trade union, their fears as a minority group in the midst of a mass of militant African workers, changed through the days of the strike. Here again, the factory leadership stressed the nonracial character of the union and the strike, and the bonds between Dunlop's workers increased. In the context of Natal's divided working class history, this was no small achievement.

8. A crucial development in the course of the strike (in the third week) was the challenge presented by the the striking workers to black foremen at Dunlop who continued to work. These foremen, part of Dunlop's black advancement policy, were asked to come as a group to St Anthony's Hall and discuss with the workers where they stood in relation to the strike. The foremen argued that their sympathies were with the striking workers. But, being salaried staff they faced unique problems at Dunlop which separated them from hourly paid workers. After a lively debate they were asked to leave in order to caucus and present the workers with a clear position: if with the workers they should join the strike, if not, then they should go back to work. The workers' wanted them on strike. After all, they would have been the people to train any new labour force, crucial to the breaking of the strike. The foremen knew that if the workers went back to the factory, victorious or not, they would have to work together and this would make things difficult for them if they did not join the strike. The foremen present at that meeting decided to join the strike which strengthened the strike's effectiveness immensely. Some foremen, however, broke ranks after the decision, which was to create chaos when the workers returned to work.

9. The last feature of the strike was the victory of the workers over what one of them called the 'three temptations'. Firstly, to give in

because of the pressures at home as resources declined — the fear passed on by kin and friends that through the strike everything could be lost — security, home, children's schooling, money. Secondly the temptation to give in because of the pressures inside oneself: fears that one will fail politically, that the strike will bring trouble, that nothing good will come of this. Finally, the temptation to give in because of the company's messages: newspaper advertisements for a new labour force, the sight of scabs outside the factory gates, messages from 'Bantu Radio'. These temptations had to be struggled with daily. It was remarkable the degree of determination shown by Dunlop workers to sustain such a trial of strength and to be ready to extend it.

On 15 September Dunlop agreed to the unconditional reinstatement of all workers.

Hard road to industrial democracy

It becomes clear as one unravels the threads of the dispute that: (a) a new level of conflict has been reached in South Africa through the strong national organisation of workers. The escalation of solidarity action in support of the Sydney Road workers is certainly an index of an increasing sophistication in strike activity; (b) an old theme still persists, through a variety of causes, that black workers are ready to sacrifice everything over issues that are seen as legitimate or just, over defence or acquisition of rights in the factory; (c) another theme persists — to gain even a little ground, black workers have to risk all in confrontations, like in the one described. If the road to political democracy is hard, the road to some semblence of industrial democracy is harder.

Postscript

Since the workers returned to the factory, after an initial period of chaos (with workers venting their frustration on foremen and managerial personnel who either broke rank with them or maltreated them in the past) relations at Dunlop have improved. The issue of dismissals which sparked the strike, has been referred to advisory mediation. The other grievances listed by the workers have been settled. According to MAWU the managerial climate at Dunlop has begun to change.

Notes

The quotation at the head of the article is from A.T. Qabula's 'Praise Poem for FOSATU', *Fosatu Workers News* and *Staffrider* VI, 3 (1986).

The material in this article was reconstructed in the following way: all the material as regards workers' experiences, attitudes, etc. was collected through interviews with workers and shop stewards during 1983 and 1984. This was greatly aided by A.T. Qabula's prose piece, 'Cruel Life Beyond Belief' and an initial attempt by some of the shop stewards to write their own story of experiences at Dunlop. The events of the strike were reconstructed from *Daily News, Natal Mercury, Natal Witness* and *Rand Daily Mail* between 17 August and 25 September, 1984.

On the Dunlop workers' play see A. von Kotze, 'Workshop plays as Worker Education', *S.A.L.B.*, IX, 8 (1984), pp.95-111.

On Dunlop U.K., see the *Economist* (January 1973 to June 1984); *Financial Times* (January 1978 to December 1983). Also *Daily News, Sunday Tribune* and *Financial Mail*. For its history in Natal see: Natal University, *Regional Survey: Industry in Greater Durban, I and II* (Durban, 1950); ibid., *Regional Survey: The African Factory Worker* (Durban, 1946); and oral interviews with the Community and Labour Project of the Sociology Department, University of Natal, Durban, 'Class, Race and Industrialization in Natal'. Some of the issues were also raised in a collective paper, 'Monopoly Power and Poverty in Natal's Industries', Second Carnegie Commission (Cape Town, 1984).

On MAWU see L. Ensor, 'A Look at the Open Trade Unions', *South African Labour Bulletin* I, 7 (1975) and A. Sitas, 'MAWU in Natal', *South African Labour Bulletin* 9, 4 (1983).

Finally, I would like to thank MAWU for making available much of its documentary material and its time to help construct this article.

Overview: State Policy and Labour Legislation

Johann Maree and Debbie Budlender

Introduction: state and working class in South Africa

In South Africa the state regulates and controls the working class in a number of ways:
— it reinforces racial divisions within the working class by means of numerous discriminatory laws, especially ones that grant differential political rights — and hence power and wealth — to whites, coloureds and Indians, and Africans;
— it controls the movement of the African working class through the influx control laws;*
— it allocates the labour of the African working class by means of influx control aided by the labour bureau system;*
— it regulates and intervenes in industrial relations with effects on the working class as a whole; and,

---

* The pass laws were abolished on 1 July, 1986. While this removed the state's power to allocate African labour, it has retained influx control by other means.

— it controls, curtails and represses organisations of the working class deemed to be a threat, by means of security legislation and other measures.

Part III deals with the state's regulation and intervention in industrial relations, concentrating on how it has affected the African working class and the independent trade union movements. It also touches on the state's selective repression of the trade union movement.

Industrial relations up to 1979

The industrial relations system that prevailed in South Africa when the independent unions emerged in the 1970s was dualistic in character: one system existed for whites, coloureds and Indians another for Africans. White, coloured and Indian workers were granted trade union rights under the Industrial Conciliation Act, first passed in 1924, but substantially amended in 1956. They could form registered unions and had access to the principal industrial relations machinery such as industrial councils and conciliation boards. African workers, on the other hand, were denied these rights.

From the inception of the first labour laws at the beginning of the century African workers were strongly discouraged from forming trade unions. All African men and, subsequently, women as well were excluded from the definition of 'employee' in the Industrial Conciliation Act, thereby preventing them from belonging to registered trade unions and participating in industrial councils. Instead, African workers were supposed to direct any organisational energies or aspirations which they might have into a factory based system of statutory works committees. In Reading Nine Horner analyses the Native (later Bantu) Labour (Settlement of Disputes) Act of 1953 which made provision for the introduction of works committees.

At the time of the 1973 Durban strikes the works committee system proved itself totally ineffective as a channel for communicating workers' grievances. The response of the government was to try and breathe life into the committee system instead of granting Africans trade union rights. It amended the 1953 act to introduce plant-based liaison committees and upgrade the works committees. Liaison committees could be composed of up to fifty percent management nominees, but were denied rights of negotiation. Works committees on the other hand were wholly elected by African workers, but could only be established in enterprises where no liaison committee existed. The title of the act was also changed to the Bantu (later Black) Labour Relations Regulation Act of 1973.

Management, supported by the state, thereupon enthusiastically promoted liaison committees. But in the main African workers rejected the committee system and opted for trade unions instead. As a result independent African unions emerged throughout the country's major industrial centres. In cases where the independent unions made use of the works committees it was a temporary strategy in order to gain shop-floor representation and advance their organisational strength. The legal status of works committees and the anti-victimisation clauses in the act also helped to give African workers confidence and potential legal protection while the trade union movement was still weak.

By 1977, even though 2 503 liaison and 301 works committees had been set up, the failure of state policy was apparent. As a last ditch stand to forestall the development of full-blooded trade unions the government amended the Black Labour Relations Regulations Act in 1977 to grant liaison committees the right to negotiate in-plant agreements on wages and working conditions. But it offered too little too late. In spite of the still weak position of the independent unions at that time, African workers continued to demonstrate their strong support for these unions.

The state realised that more fundamental change was needed if it was to regain control, and appointed two commissions of inquiry into labour legislation: the commission of inquiry into Labour Legislation (the Wiehahn Commission), which was to make recommendations regarding labour relations and the utilisation of labour for laws administered by the Departments of Labour and Mines; and the Commission of Inquiry into Legislation Affecting the Utilisation of Manpower (the Riekert Commission), which was to examine the pass system with respect to the regulation of movement and employment of African workers.

There were also other forces at work that led to the appointment of the Wiehahn and Riekert Commissions. The most important were the high levels of industrial and political conflict that erupted in the 1970s; the shortage of skilled manpower that threatened to put a stranglehold on the generation of economic wealth reguired to ensure the survival of capitalism and white political domination; and international pressure against racial domination in South Africa with the possibility that it could disrupt investment and trade with South Africa.[1]

The Wiehahn Commission proposed that African workers should be allowed to belong to registered unions and that union membership should be open to workers of all population groups. The registration of African unions, the Wiehahn Commission argued, would bring them under the same regulation and control exercised by the state over other unions. These controls placed obligations on the union to provide the state with the names and addresses of office bearers and officials, union membership figures and audited financial statements of the union. In addition a registered union has to draw up its constitution in accordance with specifications laid down in the Industrial Conciliation Act. Other recommendations included the abolition of the legal reservation of specified occupations for whites only and the establishment of an industrial court that would interpret labour laws and adjudicate on issues such as unfair labour practices.

The government cautiously accepted the major recommendations of the Wiehahn Commission. It accordingly amended the Industrial Conciliation Act in 1979 to extend the definition of employee to include African workers with permanent urban resident rights. Contract workers, commuters and foreign Africans were still excluded from the definition of employee. However, after substantial criticism and solid opposition from the independent unions to register under such conditions, the definition was again amended in September 1979 to include all Africans except foreign workers from internationally recognised countries. Thus, for the first time in the country's history, the state recognised African trade unions by giving Africans the legal right to belong to registered unions and participate in the central industrial relations machinery.

The 1979 amendment act also made provision for an industrial court. Seen together with the establishment of a permanent advisory National Manpower Commission, this reflected the state's growing reliance on the role of 'experts', especially in the legal field. The National Manpower Commission was expected to provide much needed information while the industrial court was intended to defuse industrial conflict by removing its resolution from the work-place and replacing it with complex legal arguments beyond the reach of most workers.

In August 1979, a month before African migrant workers were

allowed to belong to registered unions, the editorial board of the *South African Labour Bulletin* published a substantial critique of the Wiehahn Commission as well as the amendments to the Industrial Conciliation Act that followed in its wake (Reading Ten). The editors argued that the new law attempted to re-establish the state's control over African trade unions and to divide the African working class between urban residents and migrant workers who would be excluded from trade union membership. The Riekert Commission recommendations, which suggested the cooption of urban African residents at the expense of rural based Africans, served to reinforce these conclusions. In retrospect the critique by the editorial board over-emphasised the element of control in the act by assuming that the state would be able to use the concessions made to African trade unions as mechanisms for controlling the unions.

Industrial relations in the 1980s

The independent trade unions' response to the 1979 act was not what the state intended or anticipated. Far from rushing headlong into registration, the independent unions viewed registration with suspicion and some of them entered into a heated dispute on whether or not to register. (See Part IV on the Registration Debate.)

Other developments forced the government into further reforms of labour legislation in the 1980s. These developments included the very rapid growth of both the unregistered and registered independent unions from 1980 onwards. New unregistered unions also emerged that were overtly more political. Furthermore, in defiance of the policies of employers' associations[2] the unregistered unions succeeded in signing a number of recognition agreements with companies. The agreements included the right to negotiate wages and working conditions at the company level outside the industrial councils. In 1980 there was also a resurgence of black worker militancy as the level of the strikes increased dramatically and carried on rising in 1981.

As a result of these developments the government amended the Industrial Conciliation Act again in 1981 and renamed it the Labour Relations Act. As Benjamin, Cheadle and Khoza show (Reading Eleven), the amendment extended the administrative controls previously imposed only on registered unions to unregistered unions and federations as well. In addition the restrictions with regards to political involvement and strikes already imposed on registered unions were tightened up and extended to unregistered unions. The editors of the *Labour Bulletin* also criticised this amendment.[3] They argued that it focused on the wrong aspect of strikes, namely the legality or illegality, instead of acknowledging that in collective bargaining the strike is a legitimate weapon of last resort for workers. Thus the legislature should rather have sought ways in which the balance of power between management and workers could have been made more equal.

To some extent the Labour Relations Amendment Act of 1981 was also a continuation of the reforms proposed by the Wiehahn Commission in 1981. It finally abolished the dual system of industrial relations in South Africa by deleting all reference to race in the act and repealing the Black Labour Relations Regulation Act.

Since 1981 the Labour Relations Act has been amended every year up to 1984, but none of the amendments constituted fundamental changes. In 1982 the power of the industrial court was increased: the restoration of the status quo at the work-place pending the resolution of certain kinds of disputes, which used to be dispensed by the Minister of Manpower, was transferred to the court. This led to a considerable increase in the use of the court by the unions. In 1983 unregistered unions were granted access to conciliation boards, but the following year a clumsy attempt was made to force unregistered unions to comply with the administrative controls required by the state: agreements signed by an unregistered union with companies would be null and void in a court of law if the unregistered union did not comply with the requirements specified in the act.[4]

Contrary to earlier expectations, the industrial court initially delivered numerous judgements that increased workers' rights at the work-place and thus strengthened trade unions in relation to management. It did so mainly by means of rulings on unfair labour practices.

In its first few years of existence the court delivered hard blows against victimisation of union members, arbitrary dismissals and retrenchments of workers, and the nonrecognition of representative trade unions, regardless of whether the unions were registered or not.[5]

These judgements were passed down by permanent members of the bench. However, subsequently some of the ad hoc members made rulings applying common law principles which contradicted earlier judgements and undermined collective rights won by the unions before. In addition, the Minister of Manpower at times blocked the independent union's access to the industrial court by refusing to appoint conciliation boards, the only route by which independent unions outside the industrial council system could get to the Industrial Court.[6]

The repressive arm of the state

The reforms in industrial relations introduced by the state since the Wiehahn Commission Report in 1979 have to be seen in the context of the state's security legislation and repressive powers. The state has a veritable arsenal of security legislation at its disposal which it can invoke at any time to curtail or even destroy organisations which it deems to be a threat to the capitalist system and to its own survival. The critique of the Wiehahn Commission (Reading Ten) summarises the major laws that have been used by the state against trade unions. In fact, it can be argued that the state liberalised the labour laws precisely because it was confident that the network of security laws and apparatuses at its disposal could contain working class organisations and their political aspirations within narrowly defined boundaries. Trade unions that stepped out of line could be dealt with by the state's security apparatuses.

State repression of the independent unions carried on throughout the 1970s and 1980s. However, the state concentrated its most harsh repression against the independent unions that assumed a confrontationist stance towards it. SAAWU was hit the hardest because of its challenge to the Ciskei as a separate and independent ethnic state. It consequently had to bear the brunt of an onslaught from two states (if we are to accord the 'independent homelands' their juridical status).[7]

A disturbing development in all but one of the 'homelands' has been the adoption of labour and security legislation as well as state action even more repressive than that of the central South African state. With the exception of KwaZulu, unions are either forbidden or very circumscribed as is the case in Bophuthatswana. The 'homeland' labour laws are generally akin to the repealed Black Labour Relations Regulation Act allowing only for a type of plant-based liaison committee.[8]

For people involved in the independent union movement the state is always present in a very physical form. The security police are never far away. There is also always the threat of more repressive 'political' measures being used against them and the insecurity this brings with it. In order to demonstrate what this means in real life we publish an update of the list of banned trade unionists (See Reading Ten). The original list was printed in August 1979 in the *South African Labour Bulletin*. In addition the names of trade unionists who died in detention over the ten years ending in 1984 is included.[9] It is a list of those about whom we know. There could be many more who have disappeared unrecorded and forgotten.

February 1985

Notes

1 See P. Bonner and E. Webster, 'Background' (to the Wiehahn Commission), *S.A.L.B.*, V, 2 (August, 1979), pp. 1 — 12.
2 See M. Morris, 'Capital's Responses to African Trade Unions post-Wiehahn,' *S.A.L.B.*, VII, 1 and 2 (September, 1981), pp. 75 — 76.
3 S.A.L.B. Editors, 'Critique of the Act', *S.A.L.B.*, VII, 1 and 2 (September, 1981), pp. 35 — 7.
4 See H. Cheadle, 'Labour Relations Amendment Act 51 of 1982,' and M. Brassey and H. Cheadle, 'Labour Relations Amendment Act 2 of 1983,' in *Industrial Law Journal,* IV, 1 (1983), pp. 31 — 37; also P. Benjamin, 'Labour Relations Bill,' *S.A.L.B.*, IX, 5 (March, 1984), pp. 24 — 27.
5 See C. Nupen, 'Unfair Labour Practices and the Industrial Court,' *S.A.L.B.*, VIII, 8 and IX, 1 (September/October, 1983), pp. 39 — 64, and 'Unfair Dismissals,' Carnegie Conference Paper No.117, University of Cape Town, (1984); and N. Haysom, 'The Industrial Court: Institutionalising Industrial Conflict,' in *South African Review II,* edited by South African Research Service (Ravan Press, 1984), pp. 108 — 124.
6 See C. Nupen, 'Labour Power and Procedure,' *Financial Mail,* 30 November 1984, p.52.
7 See J. Maree, 'SAAWU in the East London Area, 1979 — 1981', Reading Three, for the extent of repression it experienced and *S.A.L.B.* VIII, 6 (June, 1983), pp. 59 — 60, for SAAWU's challenge to President Sebe of Ciskei. For a more general overview of union repression, see 'Union Repression Escalates', in *S.A.L.B.*, VIII, 8 and IX, 1 (September/October, 1983), pp. 9 — 12.
8 On labour laws and trade unions in the 'homelands', see A Lawyer, 'Homelands Labour Relations Laws,' *S.A.L.B.*, VIII, 8 and IX, 1 (September/October, 1983), pp. 65 — 78; C. Cooper, 'Bantustan Attitudes to Trade Unions,' in *South African Review II,* pp. 165 — 184; and N. Haysom and M. Khoza, 'Trade Unions in the Homelands', *Carnegie Conference Paper* No. 110, University of Cape Town, 1984.
9 We wish to thank Carole Cooper for her assistance in updating the list.

Reading 9. (1976)

African Labour Representation up to 1975*

Dudley Horner

In South Africa the authorities have, for many decades, regarded the organisation of African workers in trade unions with suspicion. A wave of strikes by African workers principally in early 1973 but continuing into 1974 and 1975 brought this issue forcibly to the fore. Existing legislation was amended in 1973 and further changes are mooted for 1976. These are, perhaps, best considered in the light of past experience.

The Industrial Legislation Commission

In 1948 the Industrial Legislation Commission (commonly known as the Botha Commission) was appointed to report on:
(a) 'the desirability or otherwise of having separate trade unions and employers' organisations for Europeans, Coloureds, and Asiatics ...
(b) the functioning of existing trade unions or similar organisations composed of Natives, and the desirability, or otherwise of regulating such organisations ...

* First published in more extended form in *S.A.L.B.*, II, 9 and 10 (May/June, 1976), pp. 11 — 39.

(c) the setting up of machinery for the prevention and settlement of industrial disputes involving Natives ....'

The commission sat for some three years and presented its report in 1951. Among its more important recommendations were:

(a) existing trade unions and employers' associations with a mixed racial membership should be separated on a racial basis, and further, in the case of mixed trade unions, this division should be into separate unions or into separate branches with white executive committees.

(b) African trade unions should be recognised in terms of separate legislation, subjected to a measure of reasonable control, and given sympathetic guidance.

The first recommendation was accepted by the government of the day and was later incorporated in the revised Industrial Conciliation Act (No. 28 of 1956). This led to the break-up of many formerly mixed unions into separate white and coloured unions or into separate branches of the same union. However, a large number of trade unions with mixed membership continued to exist at the discretion of the Minister of Labour who was granted powers to exempt them from the provisions of the act.[1] At the end of 1973, for instance, there were 41 unions of this sort with a combined membership of about 176 000 workers, of whom three-quarters were coloured.[2]

The second recommendation was rejected by the government which introduced alternative machinery in the guise of the Native (later Bantu) Labour (Settlement of Disputes) Bill which was presented to parliament in 1953. (Official terminology used to describe Africans changed from 'Native' to 'Bantu' in the fifties.) The reason for rejecting the commission's recommendation on African trade unions was plainly put by the Minister of Labour of the day when he commented that 'whatever form of control is introduced you will not be able to prevent them being used as a political weapon'.[3] Another goal mentioned by the minister was that if this system was 'effective and successful, the Natives will have no interest in trade unions, and trade unions will probably die a natural death'.

Clearly in the mid-fifties the National Party determined that labour relations in South Africa would be regulated by a dual system of controls: trade unions engaged in collective bargaining through the industrial council system would be the proper instrument for white, coloured and Asian workers while African workers would be provided for in a different way. It should be noted, however, that African trade unions were never outlawed, the authorities taking a somewhat cynical stance in this connection. For example, even after the wave of strikes by African workers in 1973 the Minister of Labour, Marais Viljoen, addressed the House of Assembly in the following terms: 'If we had wanted to prohibit these trade unions, Minister Schoeman would already have done so in 1953. This has never been done; we felt that they could simply struggle on like that. I think the establishment of these works committees will really deprive those Bantus trade unions of their life's blood and any necessity for existence. I therefore think that such a prohibition is unnecessary.'[4]

The Native Labour (Settlement of Disputes) Act (No. 48 of 1953)

The government having set its face resolutely against trade union rights for Africans, translated its policy into legislation in the form of the three-tier system contained in the Native Labour (Settlement of Disputes) Act. This redefined 'employee' in the Industrial Conciliation Act, to exclude *all* African workers, and aimed to provide for the regulation of conditions of employment for African employees and the settlement of disputes between these workers and their employers. Previously, under legislation passed in 1924, only 'pass bearing' or recruited African workers were excluded from the definition of 'employee'.

Essentially it provided for a works committee to be elected by the African employees of an establishment employing twenty or more workers; for regional Native Labour Committees appointed by the Minister of Labour from Africans (not necessarily workers) in the local community with a white Native Labour Officer in the chair; and a Central Native Labour Board consisting of white officials appointed by the minister. The machinery thus created allowed a very limited measure of direct representation to African workers and a larger measure of indirect bureaucratic representation.

The works committee was intended to be a frontline communication channel between African workers on the one hand and their employer on the other. It would be the first recourse if a dispute arose. It seems clear that neither African workers nor their employers, nor, perhaps, the labour authorities set any great store by this system of representation during the twenty years of its existence. For example, only seven such *statutory* committees had been established by the beginning of 1957, ten by May 1960, nineteen by 1961[5], twenty-four by 1969[6] and by January 1973, when a wave of industrial unrest broke out, there were still only twenty-four of these committees in existence.[7]

At that time there were some 21 036 registered factories employing 818 012 Africans in the Republic.[8] There were, it is true, a number of nonstatutory workers' committees in existence as well, but numbers were few. The authorities then took steps to overhaul the legislation.

The Regional Native (later Bantu) Labour Committees constituted the second tier and consisted of Africans appointed by the minister from the local community in each region sitting under the chairmanship of the white Native Labour Officer for that area. Among the duties of a committee were:

(a) to maintain contact with employees with a view to keeping itself informed of conditions of employment of employees in its area generally and in particular trades;
(b) to submit from time to time reports on any labour disputes which exist or are likely to arise; and,
(c) to assist in the settlement of disputes.

A regional Native or Bantu Labour Committee in any principal industrialised area was obviously burdened with a very onerous task.

A the time of the 1973 strikes, the only African member of the Johannesburg Regional Bantu Labour Committee who was an employee, rather than a self-employed or retired person, seriously questioned the efficacy of the system when he stated: 'very few workers know of the existence of the regional committees and fewer know that they have the right to form works committees. The only time we come in contact with workers is when there is already a dispute at a particular firm.'[9]

The upper tier provided by the machinery was the Central Native (later Bantu) Labour Board, consisting of white members appointed by the Minister of Labour after consultation with the regional committees. In early 1973 the board was comprised of four white members, one of whom was the chairman, an official on the fixed establishment of the Department of Labour. The other members were appointed on a contractual basis at an annual salary of R5 100. As a full-time body the board met daily.[10]

The board was to attempt to resolve disputes which had been

unsuccessfully dealt with by regional Bantu Labour Committees, but if it, too, was unsuccessful it had to report to the Minister of Labour stating whether it considered such a dispute should be referred to the wage board.

The act also provided for white Native (later Bantu) Labour Officers whose duties were:

(a) to acquaint themselves with the wishes, aspirations and requirements of African employees in their areas;

(b) to maintain close contact with the Native (Bantu) Commissioners and Inspectors of Labour;

(c) in collaboration with the Native (Bantu) Commissioners, to act as intermediaries between employers and African workers;

(d) to keep the Inspector of Labour and the Regional Native (Bantu) Labour Committees (and, where appropriate, industrial councils) informed of any labour disputes;

(e) in collaboration with the Inspectors of Labour, to try to settle any such disputes, with the assistance of the Regional Native (Bantu) Labour Committees; and,

(f) to chair such committees.[11]

In 1972 there were only seven white Bantu Labour Officers throughout the whole country but by 1975 this had increased to thirty.

It is hardly necessary to labour the point that until 1972 too much was expected of the seven Bantu Labour Officers. For their duties were not confined only to those described earlier, but they also attended, upon the instructions of the Central Bantu Labour Board, industrial council meetings and public sittings of the wage board. Since 1973 there has been an improvement and the numbers of Bantu Labour Officers have increased four-fold.

A member of the Central Bantu Labour Board or a designated Bantu Labour Officer was entitled to attend any meeting of an industrial council where conditions of employment which could affect African employees were to be determined. This they have done consistently over the years. The issues at stake are often complicated and these officers have, of necessity, to familiarise themselves with the structures of a wide variety of industries, trades and occupations, all of which imposes a yet heavier burden upon them. For example, in 1973 the board and/or its officers attended 188 industrial council meetings and also scrutinised 106 industrial council agreements and one conciliation board agreement.

Moreover, the board and/or its officers also submitted written representations in connection with thirteen investigations by the wage board and attended 44 of the public sittings in that year.

Finally, one of the principal objectives of the act was to settle disputes between African workers and their employers. Until 1973 all strikes by, or lock-outs of, African employees were prohibited as were the instigation or incitement of such strikes or lock-outs as well as sympathetic strikes or lock-outs. The maximum penalties for a contravention were severe and comprised a fine of R1 000 or three years' imprisonment, or three years's without the option of a fine, or a combination of both fine and imprisonment.

The act defined a labour dispute as one between an employer and two or more of his African employees in connection with employment, conditions of employment or a refusal to re-employ an African. In other words, a rather narrow definition.

In 1973 there were 47 labour disputes with no stoppage of work involving 3 846 African workers. These were usually settled by Bantu Labour Officers. A further 115 disputes, where work stopped, but which could not be regarded as strikes occurred and these involved 22 744 Africans. There were also 246 strikes in which 67 338 Africans took part.[12]

It would not be unfair to infer that the alternative system of labour relations imposed upon Africans by the state was inadequate and that when it was subjected to stress it cracked. African workers eschewed it, employers showed a marked reluctance to use it in a meaningful way, and even the state implemented it without vitality.

The Bantu Labour Relations Regulation Act (No. 70 of 1973)

During the 1973 labour unrest the government moved quickly to overhaul the system and published a draft bill embodying its aims in this regard. Its proposals, in the words of the Minister of Labour '... evoked wide interest, and comment as well as proposals for its improvement were received from most of the major employers' organisations, from trade unions, individual employers and other bodies'.[13] As a result the authorities altered the original bill and later introduced the Bantu Labour Relations Regulation Amendment Bill.[14]

The new machinery retained the three-tier system, which had operated for twenty years, with certain important differences.

The first tier

Instead of simply providing for the in-plant works committees at the lower end of the pyramid, a dual system of works and liaison committees was introduced. A liaison committee in any establishment consists of some members appointed by the employer and others elected from the ranks of his African employees. At least half the members of a liaison committee must be elected by the African employees but the chairman may be designated by the employer and need not be a member of the liaison committee, or may be appointed in a manner determined by the committee itself. As we shall see, employers have preferred the liaison committee and it is true that it takes precedence over the works committee in the act. The functions of a liaison committee are very simply defined. Its task is 'to consider matters which are of mutual interest to the employer and his employees and to make to the employer such recommendations concerning conditions of employment of such employees or any other matter affecting their interests ...'. The law does not limit the period of office of a liaison committee which would presumably be bound by the terms of its constitution.

The works committee, on the other hand, is a wholly elected body. In any establishment employing more than twenty African workers, *where no liaison committee exists,* such workers may elect a works committee consisting of no fewer than three or more than twenty persons. However representation is limited to a quarter of the total number of African workers in the establishment or section of the establishment at the time of the election. The bill extended representation in the sense that it allowed for more than one works committee in an establishment and in larger firms, therefore, sections of the African labour force can now elect their own works committees.

A meeting convened to elect a works committee is held under the chairmanship of the employer concerned or his authorised representative. Obviously where the employees and their employer enjoy a reasonably harmonious relationship dissension on this score is unlikely. However, where relations are cool or even hostile, where distrust exists on one or both sides, this particular arrangement is inadequate from resolving what may be a fundamental conflict of interests.

While the definition of a labour dispute is far wider than that contained in the 1953 legislation, and a Bantu Labour officer and/or Inspector, with or without the assistance of the Regional Bantu Labour Committee concerned, should intervene in an attempt to effect settlement there does seem to be a remarkable shortcoming in this connection. The act presumes that labour disputes are very largely concerned with wages and working conditions. This may be true in most instances but not in all.

A further difference between the liaison and the works committee is that the function of the former is 'to consider ... and to make ... recommendations', while that of the latter is 'to communicate the wishes, aspirations and requirements of the employees in the establishment or section of an establishment in respect of which it has been elected, to their employer and to represent the said employees in any negotiations with their employer concerning their conditions of employment or any other matter affecting their interests'. Evidently the legislature envisaged the liaison committee as a consultative body while the works committee was to enjoy negotiating rights limited to in-plant bargaining and thus falling short of collective bargaining as it is generally understood. The chairman of the works committee was to be the intermediary between the workers' elected representatives and the employer.

As the new system permitted the election of more than one works committee in an establishment, provision was made for a coordinating works committee consisting of the chairmen and the secretaries of each works committee where two or more such committees had been elected. The appointment of a coordinating committee was to be made after consultation with the employer concerned, and its duties were roughly the same as those of a single works committee.

Liaison and works committees in practice

There can be no doubt that generally employers have shown a marked preference for the liaison committee rather than the works committee. According to the *Financial Mail* there were 118 liaison committees in existence at the end of 1972.[15] In effect these were nonstatutory works committees which were covered later, by the new definition of 'liaison committee'. By the end of 1973 this had increased to 773.[16] By May 1975, 1 751 liaison committees had been registered.[17] This fifteen-fold increase does appear remarkable.

In mid-1974, Ryno Verster, of the Personnel Research Divison within the Department of Industrial Psychology at the University of the Orange Free State, conducted an investigation into the constitution and functioning of liaison and works committees.[18]

Among the most significant findings of the investigation were that in approximately 91% of the sample the initiative for establishing the liaison committee had been taken by management. In about nine percent of the sample the initiative had been taken by management and its African employees together.[19] Moreover, in determining African workers' needs for a liaison committee nearly 37% of the sample attributed the main factor to management's 'foresight', while some 24% had discussed the matter with African *supervisors* and obtained their views, and about eighteen percent had held general meetings of all their African employees. In only four percent of the organisations had African employees themselves brought the question of the establishment of a liaison committee to management's attention.

Rather surprisingly, African members of the liaison committee did not participate in selecting the chairman of their committee in 81,9% of the participating organisations. On the other hand, 79,1% of the respondents reported that African members of the liaison committee were elected rather than appointed by management. However, in only 16,6% of the firms could candidates be nominated without any restriction, for example, as to age or seniority.

Two hundred and eighty four companies responded to a question as to why they had preferred a liaison to a works committee. The majority of 147 (nearly 52%) gave as their reason that the liaison committee was an 'anti-polarisation' device conferring benefits such as better guidance by management and prompt solution of problems, thus serving both parties' interests and improving two-way communication.

One respondent advanced the reason that works committees resemble trade unions too closely. This is not quite correct for the differences between an in-plant committee and a trade union are more marked than the similarities. Nevertheless, it does encapsulate the fear of collective bargaining which exists perhaps more widely than the Verster survey indicates. Yet another respondent stated bluntly that liaison committees are consultative rather than negotiating bodies. This is, I believe, the crux of the matter. The disparity in the numbers of the liaison and works committees established since the 1973 labour unrest seems to indicate that management perceives its interests to be best served by a system of control through consultation. Whether this is the case remains to be seen.

We turn now to a consideration of works committees. In January 1973 there were only 24 statutorily-constituted works committees throughout the Republic[20] but by the end of March of that year these had increased to 31.[21] Later information put the number at 239 in May 1975, a ten fold increase in a little over two years.[22]

The Verster investigation collected less satisfactory data on these committees than it had on liaison committees. This was due in part to the fact that management is not represented on a works committee and in many instances was not able, therefore, to complete the questionnaire satisfactorily. In some cases, apparently, the works committee members viewed the questionnaire and its purpose with suspicion. Only 34 organisations employing 16 625 workers responded.

In fifteen of these (44%) management had taken the initiative for establishing the committee, while African employees had done this in five (15%), and management and employees together had taken the decision in fourteen (41%).

The most frequently mentioned reasons for choosing a works committee were that they were more effective than liaison committees, that they were more representative and acceptable to African workers, and that the workers preferred them.

In 1973 only three coordinating works committees had been established.[23]

The Verster investigation indicated that while the majority of participating organisations with liaison committees (56%) were opposed to the recognition of African trade unions, the majority of those with works committees (68%) were in favour of recognising them.[24]

The second tier
The second tier of the system, as we have seen, consists of the Regional Bantu Labour Committees. The 1973 act empowered the Minister of Labour to appoint to the regional committees members selected from liaison, coordinating works or works committees in their areas of jurisdiction. It also made it obligatory for a regional committee dealing with a dispute in any trade to coopt one or more African members from these subordinate committees in the relevant trade. Clearly, the 1973 legislation made a modest advance at this level towards more

direct participation by African workers in labour relations. However, the chairmen of these committees remain white officials.

The chairman of a regional committee was always entitled to attend any meeting of an industrial council where conditions of work affecting African employees were to be determined. The 1973 legislation enabled African members of his committee to accompany him and this included members of any liaison, coordinating or works committee in the trade coopted for this purpose. However, while these representatives of African workers may participate in the deliberations of the industrial council concerned, they have no voting rights. Their last resort if they have serious objections to proposals affecting their material interests is an appeal to the Minister of Labour. The latter is empowered to refuse his sanction to an industrial council agreement.

Wage orders
The 1973 act introduced, too, a new method of minimum wage fixing aimed at accelerating the regulation of minimum wages for African workers. The minister was empowered, after consultation with the wage board and the Central Bantu Labour Board, to accept, at any time, proposals concerning African wages or other conditions of employment in their trade and area from a *sufficiently representative group or association of employers* and to make an order embodying such proposals binding upon all employers and employees in the trade and area concerned. He was also entitled to extend the provisions of a wage determination or an order beyond the trade and area for which it was originally intended to other trades and/or areas. This approach clearly rests upon employer initiative and ministerial discretion. African workers do not participate in the process. Its only advantage for African employees is that laggardly employers can be induced by their confrères to increase minimum wages at fairly regular intervals.

Legislation of strikes
Whereas the 1953 legislation had outlawed all strikes, the 1973 act legalised strikes in certain circumstances. In effect, the definition of a strike in the Industrial Conciliation Act was adapted for the Bantu Labour Relations Regulation Act and the prohibition of certain strikes, too, was grafted onto the latter. This ignores the obvious difference between the two instruments: the former embracing the

concept of collective bargaining as it is generally understood, the latter providing grievance procedures, largely consultative machinery, and a method of settling disputes.

The following prohibitions on strikes and lock-outs of African workers remain (as they do in most respects for other workers covered by the I.C. Act):

(a) where a wage regulating measure or order is binding and where it has been in operation for less than one year;
(b) during the period of currency of any agreement, award or determination made under the Industrial Conciliation Act, 1956;
(c) where the African workers are employed by a local authority;
(d) where the African workers are employed in essential services providing light, power, water, sanitation, passenger transportation or a fire extinguishing service, within the area of a local authority;
(e) where they are employed in the supply, distribution and canning of perishable food-stuffs, or the supply and distribution of petrol and other fuels to local authorities or others engaged in providing essential services, if the minister has extended the prohibition on strikes to such industries;
(f) where the Central Bantu Labour Board has referred a proposed industrial council agreement which it finds unsatisfactory to the minister for a wage board recommendation;
(g) where the Central Bantu Labour Board has reported an unresolved dispute to the ministers for a wage board recommendation.

In *all* other instances a dispute must be referred to the liaison committee, coordinating works committee or works committee, as the case may be, which exists in the plant concerned. If the committee is unable to settle the dispute, or where no committee exists, a report must be made to the Bantu Labour Officer for the area concerned. After thirty days from the date of such a report have elapsed, a strike or lock-out may legally take place.

Finally, in 1973 a stronger provision prohibiting the victimization of African workers participating in the establishment, election or activities of liaison committees, coordinating works committees, or works committees was included.

The Verster investigation to which we have referred in the paper indicated that the majority of employers felt that the committee system was working well and was a useful means of communication in both directions. Nevertheless in 1974 there were 374 instances involving 57 656 African workers when work stopped.[25] In 1975 there were a further 119 strikes.[26]

Conclusion

The dilemma confronting the authorities is that in a period of marked instability in southern Africa their dual system of labour relations is overtly discriminatory. It depends ultimately for its effective implementation on acceptance by the African workers upon whom it is imposed. Whether an extensive committee system spread throughout thousands of factories, shops and offices will prove a successful technique for restoring industrial 'peace' seems doubtful.

Notes

1 Mixed means with white, coloured and/or Asian members. Africans were excluded.
2 Hansard Five, columns 359 — 368, 6 September 1974.
3 Minister Schoeman, Hansard Four, column 869, 1953.
4 Hansard Eighteen, column 8779, 11 June 1973.
5 Muriel Horrell, *South African Trade Unionism*. S.A.I.R.R. (Johannesburg, 1961), p.94.
6 Muriel Horrell, *South Africa's Workers*. S.A.I.R.R. (Johannesburg, 1969), p. 132.
7 Hansard Seven, columns 485 — 7, 20 March 1973.
8 Report of the Department of Labour for 1973 (R.P. 33/1975), p.24.
9 *Drum*, 9 June 1973.
10 Hansard Seven, columns 484 — 5, 20 March 1973.
11 Muriel Horrell, *South African Trade Unionism*, p.93.
12 Report of the Department of Labour for 1973 (R.P. 33/1975), p.13.
13 Hansard Seventeen, column 8390, 6 June 1973.
14 Some of the comment elicited by these bills is recorded in: Muriel Horrell and Dudley Horner, *A Survey of Race Relations in South Africa 1973*. S.A.I.R.R., (Johannesburg, 1974), pp. 276 — 281 and 286 — 291.
15 *Financial Mail*, 22 December 1972, p.1145. Cited in: R. Verster, *Liaison Committees in the South African Industry*, Bloemfontein, (U.O.F.S., 1974), p. 9.
16 Hansard Three, columns 160 — 161, 22 August 1974.
17 *Rand Daily Mail*, 22 May 1975. Cited in: Muriel Horrell and Tony Hodgson, *A Survey of Race Relations in South Africa, 1975*. S.A.I.R.R. (Johannesburg,1976), p. 212.
18 R. Verster, *Liaison Committees in the South African Industry*, pp. 14 — 16.

19 *Ibid.* p. 20.
20 Hansard Seven, columns 485 — 7, 20 March 1973.
21 Hansard Ten, columns 632 — 4, 10 April 1973.
22 *Rand Daily Mail,* 22 May 1975. Cited in: Muriel Horrell and Tony Hodgson, p. 212.
23 Hansard Three, columns 160 — 1, 22 August 1973.
24 R. Verster, *Liaison Committees in the South African Industry,* pp. 66—8, 108.
25 Hansard One, column 50, 7 February 1975.
26 Hansard One, column 18, 29 January 1976.

Reading 10. (1979)

Critique of the Wiehahn Commission and the 1979 Amendments to the Industrial Conciliation Act*

South African Labour Bulletin

Introduction

A persistent theme in the Wiehahn Commission report is that labour law and labour practice are 'drifting apart'. This the commissioners attribute to the movement of Africans into skilled and semi-skilled jobs alongside white, coloured and Asian workers (particularly since the late 1960s) on one hand, and the continuing 'dualism' in South Africa's industrial relations system, on the other. This means that employers have been put in the difficult position of having to negotiate with African workers through the committee system and with non-African workers, sometimes in the same factory and doing the same work, through the industrial council system.

At the same time, the commission is concerned at the increase in size and importance of unregistered (African) unions, particularly

* First published in more extended form in *S.A.L.B.*, V, 2 (August, 1979), pp. 53 — 79.

since the 1973 strikes. These unions, they consider, could undermine the statutory collective bargaining system and should be brought under the control (sometimes referred to as the 'protection') of the law.

Some employers have concluded agreements with unregistered unions. Furthermore, there is considerable pressure from outside the country, particularly through multinationals and the codes of conduct, and the commission while stating that it cannot be influenced by foreign demands considers that it would be naive to ignore foreign attempts to influence labour policy in South Africa.

In this context, it is useful to characterise the purpose of the commission, in broad outline, as the extension of control over unregistered unions, in a unitary system which can be sold abroad. At the same time, the commission's report appears to remove some of the formal power of white labour (although the material basis of the power in the industrial structure has probably already been eroded by job fragmentation and the deskilling process) while still providing some protection.

This critique examines the commission's report, the government white paper and the new legislation in terms of three inter-related questions: control, concession to foreign pressure, and the removal of formal restrictions on employment of a segment of the African labour force.

A new organ of state

One mechanism of control is the new National Manpower Commission (N.M.C.) created by statute.

The commission emphasises the principle of minimal state intervention in a 'tripartite' system (regulatory powers shared between the state, workers' organisations and employers' organisations). But it is clear that the state's role will shift to that of 'architect, designer, guide and initiator' (Wiehahn, para. 2.32). The state's functions are to become 'more dynamic', encompassing active intervention in the allocation and reallocation of labour and the 'preservation and promotion of industrial peace' (Wiehahn, para. 2.22).

The N.M.C. will be headed by a chairman appointed by the Minister of Labour. The chairman will be the only full-time member. Other members representing the interests of the state, employers and employees are to be appointed by the minister, who retains the right to determine their number and their tenure of office. Appointment will be open to all persons irrespective of race or sex.

The N.M.C. will be empowered to appoint specialist committees and will be supported by a strong professional secretariat.

The principal functions of the N.M.C. will be:
(a) to analyse the overall manpower situation by research into the design, planning and modernisation of manpower programmes;
(b) to keep a close watch over developments on the international labour front;
(c) continually to evaluate the application and effectiveness of labour legislation and practice.

It is to advise the government on all labour matters, including labour policy and administration (Wiehahn, para. 2.45.7; White Paper (W.P.), para. 5.2.3; Industrial Conciliation (I.C.) Bill, clause 2). However, the government has warned that the N.M.C. will have to guard against encroaching unduly on the preserve of the Department of Labour.

The power of the N.M.C. is evident in the specific primary tasks which it is to undertake immediately. It is to investigate the delineation of spheres of activity in labour matters between various organs of state and establish how liaison and cross representation are to be effected. Here it is to be linked specifically with the Defence Manpower Board (Wiehahn, paras. 2.41, 2.42 and 2.45.10) which advises the government on the use of manpower in times of peace and war to enable the defence force to carry out its task.

The N.M.C. has an antecedent in the informal Advisory Council of Labour, defunct since 1946. However, the N.M.C is to be a permanent statutory body with prescribed functions and powers, which the Advisory Council was not. The N.M.C. will have no executive powers, but its influence is likely to be pervasive. It will, in effect, prepare policy for the Minister of Labour to enable him to design and direct a highly legalistic industrial relations system. Its promptings will facilitate the Department of Labour's direct and speedy intervention on any matter which the state regards as undesirable.

Extending control of the unions

Thus in spite of its expressed commitment to minimal state control in employer-worker relations, the Wiehahn Commission's recommendations in practice involve exactly the reverse. The reasons emerge clearly from the commission's report. In the last few years, the commission notes, unregistered trade unions have grown and 'can only continue to grow in strength and importance'. Unregistered unions are enjoying financial and moral support 'on a broad front .... The fact that their existence is not prohibited, while at the same time they are not registrable and are therefore excluded from the machinery of the Industrial Conciliation Act, 1956, serves as an incentive to foreign labour and political organisations to aid them overtly and covertly. Added to this is the fact that other non-labour organisations regard these unions as vehicles for change, using them also in matters other than those of a purely labour character' (Wiehahn, para. 1.10).

This is particularly true since the 1973 strikes, the commission considers. Black trade unions outside the statutory industrial relations system could well 'bring extreme stress to bear on the existing statutory system — a development which could within a very short space of time pose a grave danger to industrial peace'. Furthermore, 'a very real danger exists that this development is in the process of creating ... an informal system which it might in the long run not be possible to dismantle or restructure even if registration were to be permitted at a later stage' (Wiehahn, para. 3.35.14).

The commission therefore concludes that the present situation cannot be maintained. It rejects the option of prohibiting black unions which would not only be discriminatory and remove existing rights, but would drive black unions underground and unite black workers 'not only against the authorities, but, more important, against the system of free enterprise in South Africa' (Wiehahn, para. 3.36.6).

The answer is to bring black unions under what the commission calls the 'protective and stabilising elements of the system' and 'its essential discipline and control' (Wiehahn, para. 3.35.5).

'Registered trade unions,' the Commission observes, 'are under certain statutory restrictions and obligations designed to protect and nurture a system that has proved its success in practice'. The report continues, 'The Industrial Conciliation Act, 1956, provides for matters such as the annual auditing of the trade unions' financial affairs; the maintenance of membership registers; the submission of annual reports, statements of income and expenditure and balance sheets to a meeting of members and to the Department of Labour; the strict control of constitutions and membership; and a prohibition on affiliation with any political party, or the granting of financial assistance to a political party, or to a candidate for election to a political party or to a candidate for election to parliament, a provincial council or any local authority' (Wiehahn, paras. 3.35.4 and 3.35.5).

However it seems clear that it was not the intention of the commission that large numbers of black workers should join registered unions, nor that all unregistered unions should achieve registration. On the contrary, the 'dualism' in the system is to be perpetuated but its racial element is to be softened and the working class is to be still further fragmented by the incorporation of some categories and the 'freezing out' of others. This disorganisation particularly of the unregistered trade union movement, is in itself a powerful instrument of control.

Unions with migrant or 'frontier commuter' members are to be excluded from the new labour dispensation. Although numbers of commentators and critics have contrasted the supposedly 'liberal' tenor of the Wiehahn Commission report with the government's subsequent white paper and draft legislation, on closer examination the distinction becomes less clear. In deference to foreign opinion and international standards the commission comes out against the legislative exclusion of migrant workers from registered unions, but a close reading of the report suggests that the commission expects migrants to be excluded by the unions themselves and even indicates what measures could be adopted to achieve this aim. (Wiehahn, para. 3.58. 1 — 3).

In considering registration or de-registration, the industrial registrar, in consultation with the National Manpower Commission, will take into account 'a wide spectrum of considerations', including 'the prevailing circumstances in the particular industry ... and the implications for the country as a whole in social, economic and political aspects' (Wiehahn, paras. 3.70 and 3.71). This confers a measure of discretion on the N.M.C. and the registrar which is extremely wide. Registration, de-registration and the regulation of unions will take place by administrative *fiat* from which there will be little room to appeal to the industrial court because the terms of reference of the registrar and the N.M.C. are so broad.

The commission recommended — and the draft legislation incorporates this recommendation — the establishment of a system of provisional registration to increase the registrar's flexibility in this matter (Wiehahn, paras. 3.87 to 3.89, I.C. Bill, clause 4).

In general, then, the message seems clear. Certain unions, probably weak parallel unions, will be incorporated into the official system and others will face difficulties. Unions with migrant labourers among their members will face problems in securing or retaining registration, or if they do secure registration on officially sanctioned terms will be condemned to impotence on the shop-floor because migrants working there are formally excluded. Finally in situations where an existing 'mixed union' needs to unionise migrants it might be encouraged to alter its constitution to maintain a bureaucratic leadership and exclude 'undesirables' from executive roles.

Further control on trade union activity will be achieved through the establishment of financial inspectors in the Department of Labour to inspect and analyse the financial affairs of industrial councils, employers' organisations and their federations, unions and their federations, works councils and works committees 'with a view to guarding against irregular or undesirable practices' (Wiehahn, para.3.157.7; W.P.para. 6.6).

The new industrial council provisions are also aimed at the disorganisation of the labour movement by splitting it up into unions contained by the formal system and those controlled outside it. At present industrial councils are constituted half by employer and half by employee representatives, individual unions being represented roughly according to size. Under the new dispensation this situation will change. Industrial councils, in the words of the commission, 'will have to contain safeguards and guarantees against a particular interest group dictating the process of decision making at the expense of other groups' (Wiehahn, para. 3.90). In practice this will involve 'the statutory requirement of strict parity in the representation of the various employee parties to the council' (Wiehahn, para. 3.92.1). No mention is made here of race, but it seems likely that race groups will be the main interest groups involved.

Following the commission's recommendations, further controls are to be instituted in industrial councils: all present parties to a council will have to agree in writing before new parties are admitted (I.C. Bill, clause 10). (It is true, however, that the draft legislation was amended in parliament to permit an appeal to the industrial court against the exercise of this veto. The court's decisions in this regard will be crucial for the direction which the labour movement takes). A two thirds majority of the council is required when matters are put to the vote, except in disputes concerning alleged 'unfair labour practices' where unanimity is required (I.C. Bill, clause 11). The definition of 'unfair labour practice' has been specifically included in the legislation to cover changes in 'traditional' labour practices (W.P. clause 1).

The industrial council is thus structured in such a way as to restrict severely the right of presently unregistered unions once registered to gain admission to industrial councils and, once admitted, to protect their interests on a variety of issues. Almost certainly the same preference for parallel unions will be exhibited when it comes to admission to industrial councils, and in the unlikely event of other unions being admitted their hands will be tied by the need to vote collectively with these parallel unions (in relation to whom they may well be a minority). The emasculation of the independent unions will thereby have been achieved.

The commission recommended strong restrictions on industrial relations training, accepted in the government white paper. Apart from employers, registered employers' organisations, registered trade unions and their federations, industrial councils and works councils and committees, and institutions within the system of formal education, all persons and institutions are to be prohibited from offering industrial relations training except at a centre approved by the Secretary for Labour. The Minister of Labour is empowered to grant exemption from this provision (Wiehahn, paras. 5.79.2 and 5.79.3; W.P. clause 8.2.2).

The provisions are expressly aimed at unregistered unions and training institutions. The commission considers that these organisations use material 'of uncertain origin and questionable ideological motivation' (Wiehahn, para. 5.58).

Freedom of association

The commission repeatedly refers to foreign pressure and the need to take account of it, and pays particular attention to the I.L.O. conventions. It makes great play with the principle of 'freedom of association'. As set out in article two of the I.L.O. convention 87 of 1948 this means that workers and employers, 'without distinction whatsoever, shall have the right to establish, and, subject only to the rule of the organisation concerned, to join, organisations of their own choosing without previous authorisation'.

On the face of it, this right is guaranteed in the Wiehahn Commission's report by the proposal that unions comprising any workers should be entitled to registration. However, not only are migrant workers expected to be excluded by the commission (and definitely excluded in the white paper and draft legislation) but closer scrutiny of the commission's suggested criteria for registration discloses further limitations on this right.

Thus the commission suggests the following criteria:

'3.87.1 The extent to which an organisation represents its eligible membership within the undertaking, industry, trade or occupation;

3.87.2 the degree of organisation existing within the undertaking, industry, trade or occupation and the extent to which the various interest groups (or population groups) are adequately represented;

3.87.3 whether or not the organisation is a *bona fide* union which in composition and objectives is relevant to the legitimate needs of the employer-employee relationship in the undertaking, industry, trade or occupation concerned;

3.87.4 the balance of representation of the various population groups within a mixed organisation;

3.87.5 economic activity and general conditions prevailing within the undertaking, industry, trade or occupation;

3.87.6 the viability, financial and otherwise, of the organisation seeking registration;

3.87.7 any other factor which would serve to maintain peace and harmony within the undertaking, industry, trade or occupation, and the national interest in general.'

A number of differences can immediately be noted between these and the criteria laid out in previous industrial conciliation legislation and, more generally, between these and the definition of the right of free association set out in I.L.O. Convention 87. To begin with, in place of the requirement that a trade union be able to *serve* the membership it represents is the requirement of *representativity* in the industry, whatever that may mean, which is obviously far more difficult to achieve. Further, the insistence on a balance of representation of the various interest groups in a mixed organisation seems to suggest parity along the lines of industrial councils whatever the respective strength of the race groups involved.

The draft legislation in fact prohibits the registration of new 'mixed' unions and restricts the geographic expansion of existing 'mixed' unions (I.C. Bill, clauses 3 and 5), unless the Minister of Labour sanctions such registration or expansion.

Finally, the two blanket provisions relating to 'economic conditions prevailing' within the industry, undertaking, etc. and 'any other factor which would serve to maintain peace and harmony ... and the national interest in general' allow the authorities to take almost any action.

Neither do these criteria allow for the registration of general unions, since unions will have to be based on an undertaking, industry, trade or occupation.

Clearly these criteria in no way secure the right of free association. The grounds for exclusion are so broad as to prevent registration of almost any trade union, and so vague as to make appeal to the industrial court in all probability fruitless. Furthermore, when read in conjunction with the Wiehahn Commission's implicit support for parallel unions and its negative attitude to migrant worker unionisation, these provisions seem to indicate an intention to register weak and pliable trade unions and a policy of attrition to those which remain outside the statutory system.

The obstacles in the criteria and procedures for registration are increased through the structure of the new industrial councils. Previously, once registered, a union was entitled to admission subject to the constitutional requirements of the industrial council concerned, provided a council existed in the industry. Under the Wiehahn recommendations this will no longer be the case. As has been noted, all existing parties to the council must agree before a new party is admitted. The implications of this veto when read in conjunction with the provisions on the closed shop are serious. In terms of the commission's recommendations and the white paper, closed shop agreements already in existence are to continue. This means that if a union is refused admission to the industrial council, the union's membership will be excluded from the closed shop and their only options will be joining a registered 'mixed' or parallel union or giving up their jobs. This is a travesty of the principle of free association.

So also is another consequence of non-registration. The chief means of incorporating the pliable unregistered unions and freezing out the others, apart from the closed shop provisions and possible administrative action, is the proscription of legally binding agreements between employers and unregistered unions. As a result of this the unregistered unions will be unable to continue with what was previously one of the main thrusts of their strategy — reaching legally binding agreements with employers on a plant by plant basis.

The expansion of the works/liaison committee system, recommended by the commission and accepted by the government, is likely to constitute further inroads on freedom of association and provide further mechanisms of control.

The major recommendations of the commission in this respect are: liaison committees should be renamed 'works councils', works committees and councils should be open to all races and their establishment should be actively encouraged. In the 'organised' sector, where an industrial council agreement is in force (or where a wage determination or other wage regulating measure exists) works committees and councils will not have statutory bargaining powers, but in other industries the committees and councils should be able to enter into agreements which are statutorily enforceable (Wiehahn, paras. 3.119 to 3.121).

The government has agreed that the autonomy of industrial councils must not be endangered, but considers that it is desirable that works councils or committees be permitted to negotiate 'on as many matters as possible' and to come to firm agreements with employers. Industrial councils should give these bodies 'as much latitude as possible' (W.P., para. 6.7.4).

Further, the National Manpower Commission is to give attention to the extension of the powers of works councils and committees to free them of restrictions so that in the foreseeable future 'they enjoy the same autonomy as industrial councils' (W.P., para. 6.7.4).

Regional works councils are to be established as an important link between the level of the industrial council and the level of the undertaking. These regional bodies are apparently to be actively encouraged in those industries where no industrial council exists because employer or workers' bodies are not sufficiently representative. This reinforces, or introduces a new form of dualism which will weaken the potential industrial council structure.

It is important to realise that the works council or committee is a factory or undertaking based unit without organisational links with other factories. Its worker representatives are employed by the company and therefore are at the mercy of management for their jobs. It has been fairly easy to victimise workers for actively furthering collective interests and there is no guarantee that the new system under the industrial court will be any different. In any case, the works council or committtee will have no independent officials who can negotiate strongly with management nor will it have a strike fund on which to draw should workers decide to go on strike.

The government's intention of encouraging works councils or committees to negotiate on as many matters as possible suggests an attempt to remove from the unions many of their traditional shop-floor functions. Employers have already been able to use works and particularly liaison committees to forestall the establishment and recognition of unions. The same is likely to be true of works councils. Once the works council is formally recognised management will have a powerful argument and institution with which to keep trade unions at bay.

Retention of the existing requirement that works committees and councils must be registered with the Department of Labour lends further support to this argument. In the past the Department of Labour has, on occasions, clearly indicated its preference for liaison committees over any form of worker organisation.

The Wiehahn Commission recommends that the works committees and councils be encouraged to attend wage board sittings 'in an effort to improve conditions of employment and to gain statutory protection'. The wage board procedure is not a collective bargaining process as no direct negotiation takes place between management and workers. Furthermore, under existing legislation African workers may not strike within twelve months of wage determination. The recommendation of the Wiehahn Commission is therefore contrary to collective bargaining procedures.

The relative status of unions and works committees or councils in the 'unorganised' sector where no industrial councils exist is not clear. The term 'unorganised' is inaccurate since trade unions do exist in many industries where no industrial council has been established. The government has not yet indicated whether in such cases works councils or committees are to be given statutory powers of whether the unions are to take preference.

Skilled shortages, training and job reservation

An important prong of the commission's argument is the need to continue and encourage the movement of blacks into semi-skilled and skilled jobs to counter the shortage of artisans which it identifies. This and the perceived need to move away from 'dualism' and race discrimination in employment led the commission to propose changes in work reservation, the closed shop and apprenticeship training.

The commission reports a shortage in April 1977 of 9 667 artisans (9 144 of them white) and 597 apprentices (485 of them white), mostly in the metal, electrical, motor and building industries. This supports the view, the commission says, that 'in the event of a continued upswing in the South African economy, serious shortages of skilled labour will result and that these shortages could become a distinct threat to the rate of recovery and the maintenance of a satisfactory rate of economic growth' (Wiehahn, paras. 5.14 and 5.15). Demand for black artisans in the 'white areas', the townships and the reserves is likely to increase, the commission considers. At the same time, the training of unemployed black youths as apprentices in the 'white areas' could alleviate unemployment and 'could also satisfy the aspirations of some of them' (Wiehahn, paras. 5.16 and 5.17).

Thus the commission concludes that it is 'absolutely essential' to allow the training of black apprentices in the 'white areas' and therefore recommends that indenturing be opened up (with suitable protection for group interests). The Apprenticeship Act as such does not exclude Africans but, the white paper points out, 'it has up to the present been the policy of the government not to allow the indenturing of blacks outside the black areas' (Wiehahn, paras. 5.16 and 5.32; W.P. para. 8.1.1).

The commission intends to cover the question of apprenticeship training more fully in a later part of its report; and this critique will therefore not go into detail on the matter of skilled labour and apprenticeship. However, a few points need to be made.

The significance of the reported shortage of artisans is not clear. The commission's interpretation of the shortages reported in the Manpower Survey is misleading; the survey in fact shows that the really serious shortages were reported not in the 'metal, electrical, motor and building industries', but in the categories 'government and provincial administrations' and 'South African Railways and Harbours' — 3 799 and 2 209 artisans respectively, out of a total reported shortage of 9 667 (Manpower Survey No. Twelve, Sector Groups, Department of Labour, 1977).

It is in fact probable that the movement of blacks into semi-skilled and skilled jobs (to which the commission repeatedly refers) conceals a process of 'de-skilling' of artisan work. Job dilution and fragmentation have probably already eroded the skill content in many 'skilled' jobs in South African manufacturing. The whole question of shortages of skilled labour barriers to black 'advancement' should be examined in this context.

In the same way, white worker resistance to changes in apprenticeship training, work reservation and the closed shop should be seen in terms of an attempt to protect remaining skills or at least the appearance of skills.

Following the commission's recommendations, the draft legislation repeals the work reservation provision (Section 77) of the Industrial Conciliation Act. The present five work reservation determinations are to stay in force but are to be 'phased out' by the Department of Labour in cooperation with the interested parties (Wiehahn, paras. 3.159.2, 3.159.4; I.C. Bill, clause 17).

In its recommendations on the closed shop the commission was split, with a majority of nine (including three of the four trade union members) supporting its retention, and five (three of whom were employers) recommending that further agreements be prohibited but existing agreements remain in force as long as the parties so desire. The government accepted the minority view (Wiehahn, paras. 3.157.19 and 3.158; W.P. para. 6.11).

Thus the new dispensation provides for continuation of the closed shop. Work reservation thus remains, albeit in a modified form (since some blacks will now be able to join registered unions), through controls over the admission of new parties to the industrial council. If a newly registered union were admitted on application to an industrial council it would automatically become a direct party to any closed shop agreement.

Work reservation through the closed shop could also be maintained by the control of black unions at the point of registration. For example, if a black union is refused registration its members and other black workers might look to already registered unions to represent their interests. This would give a great deal of power to a registered union where a closed shop is in operation.

Control via 'security' legislation

The Wiehahn Commission has ostensibly pursued a course of 'normalisation' of industrial relations to facilitate fuller expression of the principle of freedom of association. However, in spite of apparent differences between the commission's approach and the government's responses there is a common theme from which neither depart, namely the necessity to contain and control the labour movement.

To focus too narrowly on 'industrial legislation' in the strictest sense obscures many South African realities. Changes in the labour field are contained ultimately in the system of control to which the entire labour movement is subject.

Four acts dealing with 'national security' either have been or could be used to control union organisation and activity.

1. Internal Security Act

This act provides for the prohibition of publications, the prohibition of attendance at gatherings and the prohibition of persons being within or leaving defined areas — commonly known as banning — where, in the minister's opinion, they endanger the security of the state. Before 1976 the act was known as the Suppression of Communism Act.

Since its inception in 1950 the act has been used at crucial stages in the development of nonracial trade unionism as a means of destroying effective leadership. The first person to be banned under the Suppression of Communism Act was Solly Sachs, the very effective secretary of the 'mixed' Garment Workers' Union. By 1956 fifty six trade union officials had been forced to resign from their unions by the Minister of Justice through powers vested in him by the act. The Institute of Race Relations has calculated that between 1960 and 1978, 81 trade unionists had been banned or had their banning orders renewed. Certain industries have been more severely affected by bannings than others — the textile industry has had 27 trade unionists banned since 1950. More ominously, in October 1977 the first trade union organisation as such, the Union of Black Journalists, was banned.

The act is in breach of I.L.O. Convention No. 87, in particular paragraphs 3 and 4, where *inter alia* it is argued that 'public authorities shall not interfere and must provide necessary and appropriate measures so that workers can exercise the right to organise freely.' The minister acts on information derived from security police and this evidence has not been tested in a court of law. This lack of evidence can be illustrated by the case of Douwes Dekker and Tyack vs. Grobbelaar where Grobbelaar admitted, after being sued for libel, that there was no reason to believe that these banned people were engaged in activities that could endanger law and order (*S.A.L.B.* IV, 3, p.5).

2. The General Law Amendment Act of 1962

This act contains provisions concerning sabotage which is defined very widely. It has been argued that the pursuit of trade union rights could fall within this definition and the I.L.O., in Special Report No. Two argued that this was totally contradictory to the I.L.O.'s principles on freedom of association.

3. The Riotous Assemblies Act

This act, in particular Chapter II, has been used against picketing, as the description of the Armour Plate in 1976 would suggest. 'On 23 September striking workers began to picket at Armour Plate. Workers holding placards walked at intervals along the pavement up to the firm and back. The first to appear was management who took a close look and went into the factory. Shortly after, one policeman arrived by car. Later, police vans arrived and 27 workers were taken to the police station. Within a few hours they were in front of the magistrate and convicted under the Riotous Assemblies Act. They were each fined R50 or 75 days and detained in Modderbee Prison.' *(S.A.L.B.,* III, 7, p.65).

4. The Terrorism Act

In terms of the Terrorism Act a person is *prima facie* guilty of terrorism if — '1. with intent to endanger the maintenance of law and order in the Republic, he commits acts in the Republic or elsewhere, or attempts to commit such an act, or incites or organises its commission, or inspires others to bring it about, 2. he undergoes training in the Republic or elsewhere which could be of use to any person intending to endanger the maintenance of law and order, or attempts or consents to undergo such training or incites or advises any person to undertake it, 3. he possesses any explosives, ammunition, fire arm or weapon.'

Clearly this act does not affect trade union activity *per se* but the vagueness of the definition of terrorism is such that it could be used to charge people for trade union activities or strikes. In the case of the State vs Hoffmann, Parker and Jackson in Cape Town in 1977, the accused were charged under Section Two of the Terrorism Act for producing and distributing pamphlets during the 1976 stayaways, designed to undermine law and order. They were found not guilty. In 1976 in Pietermaritzburg ten men were charged with being members, or active supporters, of the A.N.C., and recruiting others to undergo training of a military or political nature outside South Africa to assist in the overthrow of the government by violence. The accused argued that the activities in which they were engaged dealt with trade unions and trade union training and not military training. But the court rejected their defence and found all but one of them guilty.

A preliminary list of people active in the labour movement who have been banned[1]

Name	Organisation	Date of banning
Abrahams, Elizabeth	SACTU	1964
★ Albertyn, Chris	Textile Workers' Industrial Union	1976 — 81
Alexander, Ray	Food and Canning Workers' Union	—
Altman, Phyllis	SACTU	1963
★ Andersson, Gavin	Metal and Allied Workers' Union	1976 — 81
Baard, Frances	SACTU	1962, 1971
★ Baskin, Jeremy	Wages Commission, U.C.T.	1976 — 81
Beck, Godfrey	—	1965
Bennie, Alvin	SACTU	1962
★ Bhengu, Moses	SACTU	1964 — 82
Blake, Margaret	National Union of Distributive Workers	—
★ Bloch, Graeme	Wages Commission, U.C.T.	1976 — 81

Name	Organisation	Date of banning
Bosch, Jonathon	—	1965
★ Budlender, Deborah	Western Province Workers' Advice Bureau	1976 — 81
Cheadle, Halton	Textile Workers' Industrial Union	1974 — 79
★ Cohen, Gideon	Wages Commission, Rhodes University	1977 — 81
Copelyn, John	Textile Workers' Industrial Union	1976 — 81
★ Cunningham (Murphy), Jeanette	Textile Workers' Industrial Union	1974 — 81
★ Curtis, Jeanette	Industrial Aid Society	1976 — 81
Davis, David	Trade Union Advisory and Co-ordinating Council	1974 — 79
Davoren, Edward	SACTU	—
Dlamini, Nontembi Lucy	SACTU	1963
Dlamini, Samuel	SACTU	—
★ Douwes-Dekker, Louis	Urban Training Project	1976 — 81
du Toit, Elizabeth	Food and Canning Worker's Union	1959
★ Favish, Judy	Western Province Literacy Bureau	1976 — 81
Ferris, John	SACTU	1964, 1969
Fletcher, Melville	SACTU	1961
Frankish, John	Western Province Workers' Advice Bureau	1977 — 79
Gaetsewe, John	SACTU	1964
Gomas, John	—	1965
Hashe, Viola	African Clothing Workers' Union	1963
Hemson, David	Trade Union Advisory and Co-ordinating Council	1974 — 79
★ Hofmeyr, William	Wages Commission U.C.T.	1976 — 81

Name	Organisation	Date of banning
Hollow, Mildred	Food and Canning Workers' Union	1960
★ Horn, Patricia	Institute for Industrial Education	1976 — 81
Lesia, Mildred	—	1965
★ Lewis, Jack	Wages Commission, Rhodes University	1976 — 81
Levy, Leon	SACTU	1962
Loza, Elijah	SACTU	1963, 1968, 1976 — 77 died in detention
Mabhida, Moses	SACTU	—
Makaringe, July	SACTU	1963
Malane, Lot	SACTU	—
Malindi, Zollic	SACTU	1960 — 73
Mamgobo Thoko	SACTU	1967
Mancoko, Livingstone	SACTU	1963, 1968
Marks, J.B.	SACTU	—
Mayekiso, Caleb	SACTU	1963, 1968
Mazibuko, David	SACTU	1965
Mbeo, Menziwe	Black Allied Workers' Union	1973
Mehoko, Emily	SACTU	1965
★ Mfeti, Phindile	Industrial Aid Society Metal and Allied Workers' Union	1977 — 82
Miacko, George	SACTU	—
Moeng, Patrick	—	1964
Mokgathla, Naboth	SACTU	—
Molepo, Nahab	SACTU	1965
★ Moodley, Mary	—	1963 — 83
★ Mthetwa, Alpheus	Metal and Allied Workers' Union	1976 — 81
Muller, Michael	—	—
★ Murphy, Michael	Transport and General Workers' Union	1976 — 81
Naidoo, Shanti	SACTU	1963, 1968
Nair, Billy	SACTU	1961
Ndhlovu, Muzuvikile	SACTU	1963

Name	Organisation	Date of banning
'Ndimande, Sibasiso	SACTU	1965
Ndzanga, Lawrence	SACTU	1963, 1968, 1975 died in detention
Ndzanga, Rita	—	1963
Ngcobo, Sikosidi	SACTU	1965
Nggunga, George	—	1963, 1968
Nxasana, Bekisisa	African Textiles Workers' Union Institute for Industrial Education	1967
Peters, Frederick	—	1976
Phillips, James	Garment Workers' Union	—
Poloto, Solomon	SACTU	1965, 1970
Poonen, Jengon	—	1963
Nanideen, Lutchman	—	1962
Routh, Gerald	—	1964
Rubin, Anne	—	—
Sachs, E.	Garment Workers' Union	1951
Schlachter, Rose	SACTU	1963
Selahle, Bonica	National Union of Distributive Workers	1964
Shope, M.W.	SACTU	1962
Sibeko, Archibald	SACTU	1960
Simkins, Charles	Institute for Industrial Education	1976 — 81
Sithole, Miriam	SACTU	1963, 1969
Tefu, S.	—	1951
Tloome, Daniel	SACTU	1963
Tole, Shadrack	SACTU	1963
★ Tyacke, Eric	Urban Training Project	1976 — 81
★ Tyacke, Jean	Urban Training Project	1976 — 81
★ Van Blerk, Wilma	Food and Canning Workers' Union	1976 — 81
Vogel, Piet	SACTU	—

1. This list is incomplete. Some orders have expired, others have been lifted, while yet others have been renewed.
★ Denotes currently banned (August, 1979).
— Denotes information not available.

Updated list of people active in the labour movement who have been banned or died in detention

Banned

Date	Name	Organisation
1978	Moroe, Isaac	Writers' Association of S.A.
1980	Badela, Sipho Mono	Writers' Association of S.A.
1981	Mtimkulu, Philip	MWASA
	Nqakula, Charles	MWASA
	Sisulu, Zwelakhe	MWASA
	Subramoney, Marimuthu	MWASA
	Thloloe, Joseph	MWASA
	Tsedu, Mathatha	MWASA
1982	Madlingoze, M.	MACWUSA
	Makhanda, D.	MACWUSA
	Mjuzawe, M.	MACWUSA
	Pityane, S.	MACWUSA

Died in detention

Date	Name	Organisation
1976	Mazwembe, Luke (Storey)	Western Province Workers' Advice Bureau
1977	Loza, Elijah	SACTU
	Ndzanga, Lawrence	SACTU
1982	Aggett, Neil	A.F.C.W.U.

November, 1984.

Reading 11. (1981)

A Guide to the Labour Relations Amendment Act of 1981*

Paul Benjamin, Halton Cheadle, Modise Khoza

The act amends the Industrial Conciliation Act 28 of 1956 which will now be known as the Labour Relations Act. The act follows the publication on 27 March 1981 of a draft amendment bill to which comment and criticism was invited.[1] This bill was overwhelmingly criticized by trade unions of all persuasions, as well as employer groupings. As a result, a much altered bill[2] and explanatory memorandum were tabled on 4 August 1981 and the act was passed on through parliament in August.

The amendments in the act that have drawn the most publicity are those which widen the scope of the controls placed on trade unions, or extend most controls already in the act to cover unregistered trade unions for the first time. Extensive controls have also been placed on trade union federations, whether registered or not. Other major amendments are the removal of all mention of racial discrimination from the act. The introduction of a system of works councils at plant level to replace liaison and works committees, and the alteration of the provisions regulating the granting of stop order facilities. These, and other amendments, will be dealt with by relating the amendment to the original section and by explaining its legal effect. Where the amendment was not included, or differs from that in the draft bill, or where proposed amend-

* First published in more extended form in *S.A.L.B.*, VII, 1 and 2 (September, 1981), pp. 18 — 28.

ments in the draft bill have been dropped, reference will be made to this in the footnotes.

Extension of controls over trade unions[3]

The Industrial Conciliation Act has previously contained a number of controls that registered unions have had to comply with. Only one direct control has previously been placed on the activities of unregistered trade unions.[4] This position has been altered. A number of new controls and additional sanctions have been placed on the activities of registered unions. All these new restrictions apply to unregistered unions as well; and the majority of those controls previously imposed on registered unions have now been extended to unregistered unions.

The type of organization that can be classified as a trade union, and therefore potentially hit by the extension of these controls, has been extended considerably. Previously a trade union was defined as an association of employees whose *primary* purpose was to regulate relations between employers and employees. The act has extended the definition to 'any association that involves itself in such activities at all' (Section One). This extension is presumably aimed at placing controls over those community organizations (such as PEBCO in Port Elizabeth) that have been involved in industrial relations in the past. As soon as such an organization intervenes in an industrial dispute, even if only on a single occasion, it will potentially be subject to all the controls placed on unregistered unions by the act.

Political activities
Prior to the 1981 act the political activities of registered trade unions were restricted. They were prohibited from affiliating to, or giving financial assistance to, a political party. A political party was defined as 'any association ... which has as its object ... the nomination of candidates for election to any legislative body ... or the influencing of public opinion to support or to oppose any such association or group' (Section 8(7)). These controls have been extended by outlawing further forms of political activity. The restrictions will now apply equally to

registered and unregistered unions and the latter will have one month after the act becoming law, to comply (Section 8(8)).

The restricted political activities have been extended beyond affiliation and financial assistance so as to include all activities aimed at influencing members with the object of giving assistance to political parties. Such 'assistance' (financial and influential), may now, in addition, not be utilized to assist persons seeking positions *within* a political party (Section 8(6)(d)). Previously, registered trade unions were prohibited from giving financial assistance to a candidate seeking election to a legislative body; now trade unions will neither be able to support such a candidate (e.g. through the union newspaper) or grant any assistance to a person seeking a position (e.g. party secretariatship) in a political party.[5]

Head offices

There were formerly no statutory limitations on where a trade union could have its head office. Now all trade unions must have their head offices in the Republic, excluding 'self governing homelands' (Section 11(4) (a)). The effect will be that trade unions operating in South Africa will not be able to have their head offices in KwaZulu (a 'self-governing homeland', though part of the Republic) or Transkei ('independent' and not part of the Republic), for example.

Strikes

The act has introduced a new offence. All trade unions or federations of trade unions are prohibited from granting financial or other assistance to a striker with the object of 'inducing' or 'enabling' him to take part in an illegal strike (Section 65(3A)). The effect of this is to make it a crime for a union or federation to provide strike pay for workers engaged in an illegal strike. The fine for supplying such assistance is R1 000. Participants in an illegal strike now run the risk of a fine of R1 000 or one year's imprisonment or both (Section 82(1)(b)). Previously the maximum fine was R200.[6]

Administrative controls

Unions have always been required to submit copies of their constitutions to the industrial registrar as part of the process of registration.

Now an unregistered union is (within six months of its formation or three months of the act taking effect) required to submit a copy of its constitution to the industrial registrar. It must also give the registrar the address of its head office and the names of its office bearers and officials (Section 4A). Failure to do this renders the union liable to a fine of R1 000. Should the unregistered trade union alter its constitution it must notify the registrar within thirty days (Section 9(b)). No stipulations are, however, contained in the act as to what the constitution of an unregistered union is required to contain.

Unregistered unions are now required to comply with a variety of administrative duties that have previously been imposed only on registered unions. All unions are now required to:
(a) maintain a register of members (including details of subscription payments),
(b) keep proper books of accounts which must be audited at least once a year and the auditor must make a report; and,
(c) prepare annual financial statements and balance sheets which must be submitted to the members (Section 8(5)).

Restrictions are placed on voting and election procedures:
(a) all voting by ballot must be in secret;
(b) an official of the union is not allowed to vote at an executive meeting. This does not apply to a president or chairman employed by the union in a part-time capacity (Section 8(6)(a) and (b)); and,
(c) the union secretary must submit the names and addresses of persons elected or appointed to a position as office bearers or officials to the registrar (Section 11(3)).

The union secretary is required to keep all documents for three years. This includes ballot papers, books of account, financial statements, registers of members, records of payments, minutes and correspondence (Section 11(1)). The secretary must submit to the industrial registrar annually:
(a) the number of paid-up members and members not in good standing,
(b) financial statements, the balance sheet and the auditor's report.

The secretary must respond within thirty days to any request by the registrar for details about the above (Section 11(2)). Where a trade union changes the address of its head office the secretary must notify the registrar of this within thirty days (Section 11(4)). Where a new branch is established the registrar must be given details as to the office bearers, officials and membership (Section 11(5)).

Controls over federations of trade unions[7]

The Industrial Conciliation Act provides for registration of federations 'consisting wholly or partly of registered trade unions' and which has as their object, or as one of their objects, the promotion of the interests of employees (Section 80(1)). A federation applying for registration is required to submit certain information to the registrar (Section 80(2)). Once registered the only duty previously placed on the federation was to notify the registrar of amendments to its constitution, elections and appointments, the names and addresses of its members, and the number of workers each member represents (Section 80(4)). The act places further controls on federations of trade unions, whether they are registered in terms of the act or not (Section 80(8)). The restrictions on political activity, assistance to strikers and the location of a head office now apply to all trade union federations in the same way as they apply to trade unions.[8] Federations will have to keep audited books of accounts and retain these and financial statements, registers of members, records of payment and correspondence for three years in the same way as trade unions. The secretary of a federation will be obliged to respond to requests for information by the industrial registrar in the same way as a union secretary. No restrictions, however, are placed on voting procedures in a federation and an unregistered federation is not required to inform the registrar of the names and addresses of its members and the number of persons each member represents.

Special powers of the registrar

Prior to this act the registrar was entitled to conduct an enquiry into the affairs of a registered trade union on certain grounds (Section Twelve). The grounds are any material irregularity in respect of an election, or any act by an official, office bearer or committee which is unconstitutional, unlawful, unreasonable to the members or has caused serious dissatisfaction among a substantial number of members. After the enquiry, the registrar can make a recommendation to the minister to remedy the situation, and the minister may, at his discretion, make this recommendation binding on the union. The act now gives the registrar the same powers to intervene in the affairs of a registered federation.[9]

Inspectors' powers
Section Sixty makes provision for the appointment of inspectors to monitor the application of the act. These inspectors are now given various powers of investigation to determine whether any trade union, federation, employers' organisation or industrial council is carrying out the provisions of its constitution and the act (Section 61). Previously these powers, which include powers of search and interrogation, did not apply to federations.

Repeal of the Black Labour Regulations Act

The act has repealed the Black Labour Relations Regulation Act 48 of 1953. This act provided for the system of liaison and works committees (a form of representation for Africans primarily at plant level), a mechanism for determining minimum wages and working conditions for blacks in particular industries or trades, and a complex procedure for settling disputes. Provisions to replace the first two features have now been included in the Labour Relations Act.

Works councils
The Black Labour Relations Regulation Act provided for the establishment of works and liaison committees at factory level for blacks only. The courts have held that these committees enjoyed only those limited powers given to them by statutes.[10] The act has now introduced a new forum for plant level negotiation (Section 34A). An employer and all or some of his workers may set up a works council. No mention of race is made in the section constituting these councils. Such a council may be set up for a section of a factory, a factory or where an employer has more than one factory in the same industry, two or more factories. At least half the members of the council must be elected representatives of the workers. The remaining members will be representatives of management. What functions these councils can perform are not specified in the act, and they can perform any function that the employers and workers agree upon. All liaison committees in existence in terms of the Black Labour Regulations Act will be regarded as works councils (Section 34B). (Works committees cannot

be regarded as works councils as they do not have management representatives on them.)[11]

Determination of wages and working conditions
The Black Labour Relation Act provided for a separate mechanism for setting minimum wages and working conditions for African workers. These standards were determined by the minister upon the recommendations of employers or employer organizations in their particular industry. No provision was made for reference to the workers affected, and the minimum wages and working conditions were promulgated in the government gazette as a Black Labour Order. These provisions have now been included in the Labour Relations Act (Section 51A). The effects of this is that a labour order could now be made in terms of this procedure to regulate wages and working conditions for workers of all races. Black Labour Orders will remain in effect until superseded by an Industrial Council Agreement (Section 51A(7)).

Dispute procedure
The Black Labour Relations Regulation Act had a special disputes procedure for black workers. This procedure, which provided for disputes to be referred to a variety of committees, labour officers and boards has given way to the conciliation procedures contained in the Labour Relations Act. This will do away with the anomalous situation that previously existed which required black workers to exhaust the disputes procedures under both the Black Labour Relations Regulation Act and Industrial Conciliation Act before staging a legal strike.

The removal of racial discrimination

The act has deleted all reference to race. In some cases, this was achieved simply by deleting the offending words, in others the process of extraction was more complex.

Definition of employee
The definition of 'employee' has been used as a device to exclude Africans from participating in the official collective bargaining

system instituted by the act. The Industrial Conciliation Amendment Act 94 of 1979 included African workers in the definition, but excluded migrant and 'foreign workers'. After substantial criticism, this definition was extended by the minister so as to include all workers except foreign workers.[12] Foreign workers were those from internationally recognized states such as Mozambique, Lesotho, Botswana, Malawi. The act has removed all these exclusions and extensions and defines an employee as any person in work and receiving remuneration (Section One). The effect is to open the official collecting bargaining system to all workers.

Registration

The Industrial Conciliation Act introduced the notion of racially separate unions in 1956. Section 4(6) of the act prohibited the registration of mixed unions without the authorization of the minister. This power enabled the minister to deal with those unions registered under the 1937 act which had mixed membership. Such unions were then allowed to register provided their constitution provided for an all white executive, racially separate branches and racially separate meetings (Section 7(3)). Section Six made provision for one racial group to split from a mixed union and form a racially separate union. To facilitate such splitting, the act provided for a division of assets between the 'racially separate' and the 'mixed' unions. These provisions have now been removed from the statute book with the following consequences:

(1) the prohibition of mixed unions has been repealed in its entirety as well as the similar prohibition existing under the procedures for the variation of registration (Section 4(b) — repealed),
(2) the specific constitutional requirements for mixed unions such as a white executive, separate branches and the like have been repealed. The effect will be to allow the mixed unions to arrange their constitutions racially as they see fit (Section 8(3) — repealed),
(3) the special provisions absolving white unions from the representative requirements under the registration procedures have been removed. Registration under Section Four of the act follows roughly the following course. The applicant union applies for registration for certain interests (e.g. industries or job categories) in certain areas. The registrar gazettes the application and invites objections to the registration by other registered unions (or unions

seeking registration at the same time). In the light of any such objection and further representations by the applicant union, the registrar can register the applicant. He may opt to limit its scope of registration, if need be by taking into account the extent to which the area and interests applied for are 'served by' the applicant union, and the representativeness of the objecting union. If the objecting union is sufficiently representative in any of the areas or interest applied for then the applicant union may not be registered in respect of such areas of interest. Previously special provisions of the act absolved racially exclusive unions from objections based on representativeness provided that they had fifty percent of the racial group as members working in the area applied for. This provision has now been repealed,[13]

(4) Section Six of the act provided for a division of assets of unions. It was enacted in 1956 to facilitate the racial separation of mixed unions registered under the 1937 Act. Where a racially exclusive union broke away from a mixed union, the new union could apply for a division of assets of the original union in proportion to the relative sizes of membership of the two unions. The concept of the division of assets has now been removed from the act so that a breakaway group will not be able to force the original union to divide its assets with them.[14]

Registration procedure

The act makes two amendments to the registration procedure, other than those related to the removal of racial terminology. Where an existing union objects to an application by a union for registration, the registrar must now assess the representativeness of the applicant only in respect of those members of the objecting union who are eligible for membership of the applicant union (Section 4(4)(c)). The effect of this is that although a union has over fifty percent of the employees in an industry it will not necessarily be representative in every section or category of worker in that industry. If the applicant union so limits its scope, whether racially or by occupation, it will be registered despite the fact that the objecting union is representative of the industry as a whole. This will allow racially exclusive unions, by defining their scope of interests racially, to be regarded as representative, despite the fact that the special provisions relating to the registration of such unions have been repealed.

The concept of provisional registration introduced in 1979 has been abolished. Section 4A gave the registrar wide powers to register trade unions provisionally and impose conditions on such registration. Should the registrar believe that such conditions have not been complied with, he was empowered to withdraw the registration. Unions provisionally registered at the time the act became law, are dealt with as if the section had not been repealed.

Stop order facilities

Prior to the 1981 act an employer could grant stop order facilities to any trade union, whether registered or unregistered. Section 78 (1C)(a) now makes it an offence for an employer to grant stop orders to an unregistered trade union without the consent of the minister. A registered union can compel an employer to grant stop orders by application to the minister. For an application for compulsory stop orders to succeed, the applicant union is required to be both representative and registered in respect of the industry or undertaking concerned. The minister retains his right to refuse an application for compulsory stop orders (Section 78(1A)(a)). A provision that allowed racially exclusive registered unions to be granted compulsory stop orders even though they were not representative of the industry or undertaking concerned has been repealed.[15]

Sexual discrimination

The explicit power given to industrial councils to discriminate on the grounds of sex in industrial council agreements has been repealed. This means that no new industrial council agreement which discriminates sexually in the setting of minimum wages and working conditions can be declared binding by the minister in terms of Section 48. Similarly, the minister cannot extend an agreement if the exemption might operate to allow sexual discrimination. This brings industrial council agreements into line with wage determinations which may no longer discriminate on grounds of sex.[16]

Notes

1 Notice 235 of 1981, G.G. 7521, 27 March 1981.
2 Labour Relations Amendment Bill (W.59 — 1981). According to the Explanatory Memorandum accompanying the bill a number of more controversial proposed amendments have been referred to the National Manpower Commission.
3 This article refers to the controls placed on trade unions. It should be noted that similar controls are placed on employers' organisations, whether registered or not.
4 This is the right of an inspector appointed in terms of the act to carry out an investigation to determine whether any trade union is observing the provision of its constitution and the act. The control has been dealt with under the heading 'Controls over Federations' as the way in which it effects trade unions has not been altered. The power of the industrial registrar to investigate the affairs of a registered union has also been dealt with under 'Controls over Federations'.
5 The controls in the act on political activity are considerably narrower than those proposed in the draft bill. The bill extended the definition of a political party to include the single person. The intention was to close the loophole in respect of 'independent' candidates, who registered trade unions were (and are still) able to support. More importantly, the draft bill introduced the concept of a 'political organization'. This was defined as any person or association with the purpose of promoting the 'political interests' of all or some of its members. What constituted 'political interest' was not defined in the bill. Had this section been enacted, it would certainly have affected relationships between trade unions and community organizations, and might well have affected unions affiliating with each other as a union could quite conceivably constitute a 'political organization'.
6 The restrictions in this section also apply to employers' organizations giving assistance to employers involved in illegal lock-outs. In the draft bill it was proposed that assistance to strikers by anybody should be made an offence. The bill contained an additional amendment dealing with strikes which has now been dropped. A registered trade union may not call or take part in a strike without first conducting a strike ballot to ensure that the majority of members in the undertaking, trade or industry involved support the strike. The bill proposed to place certain controls over the holding of such ballots.
7 Equivalent controls are placed on federations of employers' organizations.
8 These are dealt with above in 'Controls over Trade Unions'.
9 In the draft bill the powers of the registrar were, in addition, extended so as to include the power to recommend the deregistration of a registered union or federation. If the registrar recommended deregistration the minister, the bill proposed, had to invite the union to make representations. It would, however, remain within his discretion to give effect to such a recommendation. Upon deregistration the union would cease to be a

body corporate and once the union had been deregistered by the minister it would be subject to compulsory winding up. The effect of these proposed amendments was that the minister would have the power to deregister a union or federation for unlawful, unconstitutional or unreasonable acts and upon such deregistration the union would be wound up. The assets of the union or federation would be distributed to federations or unions registered in respect of the same interests.

10 See Piet Bosman Transport Works Committee v P.E. Bosman Transport (Pty) Ltd (1980) 1 ILJ 66; 1979 (1) S.A. 389 (T) in which the court held: '. . . a works committee . . . is a statutory body with the limited functions of establishing and maintaining dialogue with an employer of blacks . . . and negotiating with him on behalf of his black employees . . . the statute does not vest a committee . . . with the power of going to court' (at 69 A — C).

11 In the draft bill no provision was made for a legislative framework for bargaining at plant levels. Employers' organizations protested against the failure to replace the works and liaison committees with alternative 'official' system of plant level representation.

12 R2167 in G.G. 6679 of 28 September 1979.

13 The draft bill contained a provision which would allow a section of a registered trade union to break away from that union if it changed its membership qualification as a result of the repeal of the prohibition on mixed unions. The new union would be exempt from a number of the registration requirements. The effect would be to allow a section dissatisfied with the opening of membership to other races to set up and have registered a separate union despite the fact that the original union might be representative in all the areas and interests applied for. This would have precluded registration in the normal course of events.

14 The section remained in the draft bill but all references to white and coloured were removed. The effect of this would have been to allow a new union of undefined membership to divide off from the original union and take with it a proportion of the assets of the original unions, provided it could satisfy the membership requirements stipulated in the section.

15 In the draft bill the granting of stop order facilities to registered unions was made compulsory provided the application for a stop order was submitted in the prescribed form by the union and had been signed by both the employee and the secretary of the union.

16 The type of discrimination that has been prohibited is the setting of lower minimum wages for women doing identical work to men.

Part IV

Overview: The Registration Debate and Industrial Councils

Jon Lewis

The debate on whether or not and on what terms unions should register was to seriously divide the South African independent trade union movement. The findings of the Wiehahn Commission, published in 1979 advocated legal recognition for African trade unions. The legislation which followed and made possible for the first time the registration of unions representing African workers, had the explicit aim of controlling the resurgent black union movement.

In responding to the state's initiative the independent unregistered unions were faced with difficult tactical decisions, which had a bearing on questions of principle and wider strategic considerations. Initially all groupings — FOSATU, the Consultative Committee of Black Trade Unions, the African Food and Canning Workers' Union (A.F.C.W.U.), the Western Province General Workers' Union (W.P.G.W.U.) and even the TUCSA parallels — rejected the terms on which registration was offered. Faced with this united response to its reform package the state conceded the right of migrants to belong to registered unions. This was enough to satisfy the immediate objections of the Consultative Committee and the TUCSA unions which proceeded to register. Thereafter FOSATU parted ways from A.F.C.W.U. and W.P.G.W.U. (joined later by the community unions, principally

SAAWU) over the appropriate response to the whole registration package.

The FOSATU unions finally opted for registration on a nonracial basis (despite the legislation's opposition to mixed unions) with the threat of deregistering if their terms were not met. FOSATU was to argue that registering strengthened their hand against recalcitrant managements and was necessary to combat attempts by the TUCSA parallels to inflate their membership.[1]

The positions adopted and the increasingly bitter terms in which the debate was conducted are reflected in the pages of the *South African Labour Bulletin* over the period 1979 to 1982. For the *South African Labour Bulletin* it was a difficult period. The divisions in the wider labour movement were reproduced in the editorial board making it increasingly impossible to adopt a united editorial position. However these years were to establish the *South African Labour Bulletin* as a forum for debate, independent of any one faction — despite initial reluctance to publish the W.P.G.W.U's original memorandum without FOSATU presenting its side of the argument as well.[2]

The W.P.G.W.U.'s memorandum (Reading Twelve) was timed to coincide with the joint meeting with FOSATU and A.F.C.W.U. in November 1979 which was called to discuss registration and was also used to try to pressurise FOSATU into not registering. In retrospect the memorandum — and the G.W.U. would now agree with this criticism — exaggerated the controls implied in the registration package. The W.P.G.W.U.'s opposition to registration was born out of its own democratic trade union practice and its overriding concern to maintain worker control against attempts at cooption. Their's was a practical calculation about how best to safeguard trade union democracy and autonomy from state control. The full scale theoretical critique of their tactics contained in the article by Fine, De Clerq and Innes (Reading Thirteen) which appeared nearly two years later came as something of a shock since nobody had been willing to criticise them publicly before. The intervention by Fine et al provoked bitter exchanges which continued until the end of 1982. By this time however the terrain of the debate had shifted radically.

The Fine et al piece was interpreted as a direct statement from FOSATU although the authors deny any close collaboration. Nonetheless Innes and De Clerq were closely involved with FOSATU and certainly their role was to provide a defence of FOSATU at a time when that body was coming under increasing attack from the community unions and exile organisations. For the authors their task went beyond the registration question to a critique of traditional anti-apartheid 'boycottism'. Moreover they argue that their article implied a critique of FOSATU 'survivalism' and was an attempt to raise the central question of the relationship between unions and the state. This actually ran counter to FOSATU orthodoxy at the time which was to confront capital (by which was meant employers), leaving the state to the political organisations.

The intervention by Fine et al was seen as offensive in its tone by those still opposed to registration, and unleashed a series of replies couched in even more immoderate terms. G.W.U. regarded the charges of 'boycottism' as a caricature and restated its position on the original terrain of democratic trade union practice and the need to maintain worker control[3] (Fine et al had opened themselves to attack in this regard by seeming to argue that 'delicate' issues could only be discussed at leadership level because of repressive security measures). Other responses from Hirsch and Nicol, and Haysom moved further into the terrain opened up by Fine et al with a critique of the latter's theory of law and the state.[4] They also rejected the 'boycottist' tag and pointed to the wider debate over the boycott strategy already under way in response to the school boycotts. Beyond this the exchanges reflected growing political differences over the question of class alliances and the relationship between trade union and community issues in terms which prefigured the later debate over trade union affiliation to the U.D.F. This shift was grasped in particular by Haysom who argued that those who favoured registration had overestimated the advantages and those opposing registration had exaggerated the controls. The real question was what form of politics would the unions adopt in order to transcend their narrow survivalism?

The final word went to Fine et al[5] although by the end of 1982 the immediate issue of registration had in any case receded. Concessions on migrant members and provisional registration, FOSATU's successful defence of nonracialism despite registration and changes in the law which extended controls to unregistered unions contributed to diffusing the registration question. But the extension of the registration debate to encompass the whole area of 'unions and politics' had obscured differences in the anti-registration camp, and polarised the labour movement on a very different terrain. On the registration question there had in fact been three different positions (leaving aside

CUSA): FOSATU's tactical acceptance; the G.W.U.'s rejection of registration on the ground that it would hamper the democratic functioning of the union; and the more fundamentalist opposition of the community unions to what was seen as collaboration with the apartheid regime. It was to be some time before the differences in the anti-registration camp came to the fore.

In the meantime the G.W.U. was to play a mediating role in the unity talks from late 1981. However the talks also sharpened the divisions between G.W.U. and the community unions, a process which was intensified by demarcation battles with SAAWU particularly in the Durban docks. G.W.U.'s clear opposition to affiliation to the United Democratic Front (U.D.F.) marked a further stage in its break with the community unions. G.W.U.'s leading role in the two debates — over registration and U.D.F. affiliation — involving as it did a radical shift in alliances, was ironic but wholly consistent. Its reservations over U.D.F. affiliation were largely located on the self-same terrain of safeguarding democratic trade union practices and worker control.

Focus shifts to industrial councils

In retrospect although the registration debate did open up important questions about the relationship between trade unions and the state it also suffered from overkill. This may help explain the more muted response to the decision in 1983 of some FOSATU unions to take part in industrial councils — a decision which was much more fraught with dangers of cooption. There was also a real conciousness of the dangers of cooption and of the necessity for safeguarding worker control across a wider layer of union leadership. Significantly Fine et al had argued that at a certain point in time it might be tactically advantageous for the independent unions to participate in industrial councils, and that there would be no *a priori* objection to such a course (at the time FOSATU was opposed to joining industrial councils).

In fact in the early days of the registration debate all the protagonists shared a deep distrust of the industrial council system. By mid-1982 however widespread discussions were taking place, especially within FOSATU, over the possibility of entering the industrial councils for tactical reasons.[6] FOSATU was to decide that, provided plant bargaining and recognition rights were not sacrificed, affiliates could enter industrial councils if it appeared advantageous to the union. In 1983 MAWU and N.U.T.W. decided to join industrial councils. In an article published in 1983 in the *South African Labour Bulletin,* Eddie Webster analysed pressures behind MAWU's decision to join the National Industrial Council (N.I.C.) for the metal industry.[7] Two years later an assessment of this tactic must remain tentative. MAWU's minority position on the industrial council, its defeats in the strikes of 1982 and the advent of recession and mass retrenchments mean that no dramatic gains have been registered during that time.

On the other hand MAWU has gained some control over the industry's pension fund and has successfully defended its organisational principles: shop steward structures, plant based bargaining and worker control. Several agreements have been signed, particularly in Natal, which effectively breach the guidelines of the employers' federation in the metal industry (SEIFSA). In the Transvaal, and in alliance with the South African Boilermakers' Society (S.A.B.S.), MAWU has mounted a local challenge at Highveld Steel to the 1984 N.I.C. wage settlement which both unions refused to sign.

More recently the FOSATU affiliate, Paper Wood and Allied Workers' Union, has joined its industrial council to become the majority union there. This move was preceded by the establishment of a national shop stewards' council for the major company in the industry,[8] and has actually entrenched the right to negotiate at plant level, following a breakdown in negotiations at national level.

On the industrial council itself MAWU has not been out-manoeuvred by the conservative Council of Mining and Building Unions. Rather MAWU's joining the N.I.C. has split the C.M.B.U. wide open, with the S.A.B.S. now cooperating with the emerging unions. This major realignment of unions in the metal (and auto) industry is reflected in defections from TUCSA and in the re-establishment of the South African Coordinating Council of the International Metalworkers' Federation in March 1984.[9] Whether this new 'economistic' grouping of trade unions can contribute to the wider political goals of the emerging unions remains to be seen.

February 1985

Notes

1 FOSATU, 'Memorandum — the parallel union thrust', *S.A.L.B.* V, 6 and 7 (March, 1980), p. 16; in *S.A.L.B.* VII, 1 and 2 (September, 1981), pp. 32 — 35, the *Bulletin* editors produced a 'balanced' summary of the arguments for and against registration.

2 FOSATU's position was that these issues were too sensitive to debate publicly. See Halton Cheadle's letter in *S.A.L.B.* V, 6 and 7 (March, 1980), pp. 7 — 9. For the G.W.U.'s reply see *S.A.L.B.* VI, 7 (July, 1981), pp. 16 — 25.

3 G.W.U. 'Reply to Fine, De Clercq and Innes', *S.A.L.B.* VII, 3 (November, 1981), pp. 16 — 25.

4 F. Haysom, 'In search of concession: reply to Fine et al,' *S.A.L.B.* VII, 3 (November, 1981), pp. 26 — 41; A. Hirsch and M. Nicol, 'Trade unions and the state — a response', ibid., pp. 42 — 50.

5 D. Innes, 'Trade unions and the state: rebutting our critics', *S.A.L.B.* VIII, 1 (September, 1982), pp. 34 — 46; B. Fine, 'Trade unions and the state once more: a reply to our critics', ibid., pp. 47 — 55; D. Innes, 'Trade unions and the challenge to state power', *S.A.L.B.* VIII, 2 (November, 1982), pp. 60 — 71.

6 See J. Copelyn, 'Problems in collective bargaining', *S.A.L.B.* VIII, 1 (September, 1982), pp. 69 — 80.

7 E. Webster, 'Mawu and the Industrial Council', *S.A.L.B.* VIII, 5 (April, 1983), pp. 14 — 19.

8 P. Horne, 'PWAWU: Organising Mondi', *S.A.L.B.* X, 2 (October/November, 1984), pp. 37 — 43.

9 J. Lewis, 'International Metalworkers' Federation: South African Coordinating Council', *S.A.L.B.* IX, 6 (May, 1984), pp. 1 — 4; M. Golding, 'TUCSA: Another one bites the dust', *S.A.L.B.* X, 3 (December, 1984), pp. 3 — 6.

Reading 12. (1979)

Comments on the Question of Registration*

Western Province General Workers' Union

The Wiehahn Commission and the subsequent legislation has exposed certain important differences within the unregistered trade union movement in South Africa. The differences by now concern the question of registration.

Registration is, and always has been, a key question in the trade union movement. Whatever one's feeling about the entire concept of special registration for trade unions, it is difficult to deny that the fact that white and coloured workers have been permitted to form and join *registered* unions, and the African workers have not possessed this 'right', has constituted a major aspect of racial discrimination and is a factor of fundamental importance in understanding the oppression of African workers. But is the opposite equally true? Is it true that the extension of any registered status is a positive advance? Is it not true that the strength of the unregistered trade union movement has largely accounted for the decision to extend registration to trade unions of African workers? Surely it is correct to say that what is at issue is not 'registration or no registration,' but rather 'registration on what terms'. And surely we are in a position to demand terms which can constitute the basis

* First published in more extended form in *S.A.L.B.*, V, 4 (November, 1979), pp. 114 — 134.

for the development of a united, democratic trade union movement. That the state and the bosses will attempt to undermine such a development will not be surprising. But at least, we must not accept terms which guarantee the development of a weak, divided and bureaucratically controlled union movement.

It seems that the report of the Wiehahn Commission and the subsequent legislation can, for our purposes, be divided into three major categories. Firstly, those recommendations that seek to divide the unions by determining the eligibility of particular groups of workers for union membership. Secondly, those recommendations and provisions that are concerned with the control and supervision of those unions that seek registration under the terms offered. And, thirdly, we must examine the situation potentially facing those unions which decide not to register.

Division of the unions

On the face of it, the Wiehahn Commission Report itself adheres to the principle of freedom of association. Particularly, the Commission recommended that the racial make up of the unions be left to each individual union. This is by now history and we all know that initially the state refused to accept these recommendations. Particularly, the state refused to permit the registration of multi-racial unions, and it initially refused to permit contract workers to join registered unions. In the face of widespread opposition from the majority of the trade union movement, the state has backed down on the latter restriction and, by proclamation published at the end of September, contract workers have been included in the definition of 'employee' in the Industrial Conciliation Act. They are hence eligible for membership of registered unions. To date the ban on 'mixed' unions remains effective, but there is probably good reason to believe that this too might be amended in the near future.

Prior to the concession announced a few short weeks ago, it is probably true to say that none of the unregistered unions intended seeking registration. However, the ministerial proclamation has changed things considerably — the TUCSA parallels have got what they want and are gleefully seeking registration and simultaneously claiming victory for their policy of 'moderation'; the independent trade union movement is clearly divided, with some unions and groupings reportedly inclining towards registration, despite some strongly held reservations and misgivings; others, clearly inclining towards nonregistration, but who fear strongly for the future of the unregistered union movement should the state's overtures once again be rejected; and a small handful of unions who reaffirmed their decision not to seek registration.

It is crucial to recognise that what the state has done by its recent concession is to implement in all major aspects the report of the Wiehahn Commision. It is important to recognise that the trade union movement had been unable to respond coherently to this concession. The reason for this is that we *initially almost without exception concentrated our attacks on the state's deviation from the Wiehahn Commission and by implication called for the implementation of the commission.* We protested that the state had refused to implement what one trade union leader described as the 'major positive aspect' of the Wiehahn Commission. What has now happened is that the state has answered our protests and backtracked on its refusal to implement this 'major positive' recommendation by belatedly including contract workers within the scope of the definition of 'employees'. And the unions have been predictably caught unawares. We concentrated all our attacks on this single aspect of the new dispensation and in the face of the state's apparent generosity and rectification of its previous position, we are faced with registration under a system which is, by implication or omission, acceptable to us. It is our argument that it is still not too late to state clearly our objections to the Wiehahn Report itself and to the whole registration package. And, of course, the most effective statement of our opposition would be to refuse, *en bloc*, to register.

Registration and control

As progressive trade unionists we all stand on two non-negotiable principles, viz., the right of workers to join unions of their choice, and control by workers over every aspect of their unions' activities. *Our objections against the violation of workers' control of the unions have taken second place to the storm raised surrounding the prohibition of contract worker membership of the unions.* In other words, whereas we have stated emphatically that we will not register if contract workers may not join our unions, *we have not stated that we will not register if the state insists upon removing control of the unions from the hands of the workers.* And yet the one is no less serious than the other; *we* hold the principle of worker control no less sacred than we do the principle of freedom of association. We are not revealing anything unknown if we claim that the aim of the Wiehahn Commission and that of the state as a whole is *control of the unions.* This objective is enshrined in the report of the Wiehahn Commission and has been repeated on a number of occasions by the minister himself. But knowing the state's objectives, does not mean accepting them. And the only way of really refusing to accept the state's objectives is to refuse to accept registration under the conditions offered by the state. Let us just list some of the more blatant of the provisions.

The precise functioning of the industrial court is still a matter for speculation. The problem is, however, that it is always likely to remain a matter for speculation. What is absolutely clear is that the court is going to possess enormous *law-making* power. One need only refer to the introduction of the notion of an 'unfair labour practice' to realise precisely how extensive the powers of the court will in fact be. The act defines an 'unfair labour practice' as 'any labour practice which in the opinion of the industrial court is an unfair labour practice'.

Secondly, the criteria for registration are not specified — it is likely that they will remain unspecified, with both the initial application for registration and maintenance of registered status, being at the whim of a registrar who in many cases is not required to motivate his or her decision. The new clause on provisional registration in the act states baldly that '... the registrar may at any time (and without giving reasons therefore) withdraw the registration of a trade union or employees' organisation contemplated in this section if he is of opinion that such union or organisation has not complied with any of the conditions imposed in terms of subsection (1)...' It is necessary to add that the registrar is in no ways constrained in the application of the conditions he imposes on those unions granted provisional registration. And thus of course, as stated above, the criteria in terms of which provisional registration is granted, remain locked in the minds of the registrar ... or the industrial court. And then, of course, there are a variety of other controls suggested by the Wiehahn Commission — financial controls, possible vetoing of election and appointment of office bearers and officials, etc.

It is not necessary to recognise that the *unusual strength* of the unregistered unions (unusual, that is, in the context of South African unionism) rests precisely in the democratic functioning of the unions; it rests precisely on the fact that our unions are *controlled by the workers.* If we hand over to the state the right to control our unions then surely we are behaving in a manner which is not only unprincipled, but is ultimately self defeating, for we shall be removing the very basis of our strength — the fullest participation of the workers in the control of their unions.

Let us be clear — we do not expect that any concession granted by the state will be free of conditions and restrictions. And we acknowledge that it is our task to maximise the gains and minimise the effects of additional controls. But do the *potential* gains of registration under the terms offered outweigh the potential losses? It is on this basis that our decision ultimately rests.

Registration or nonregistration? carrots and sticks

The carrot

Clearly, the big carrot that is being dangled in front of the eyes of the unregistered unions is participation in the industrial council machinery. But already we know that membership of the industrial councils will not follow automatically from registration. The employers and the existing registered unions (many of whom are extremely antagonistic to the minimal concessions now granted by the state) will be responsible for deciding on our participation in 'their' industrial councils. What will we have to give in return for a seat on the industrial council? No less than our strength. We will, in a word, have to start behaving like 'responsible' unions or, in the words of the Wiehahn Commission, *'bona fide'* unions. The view of progressive unions is surely that a *'bona fide'* union is one that is controlled, *in every aspect,* by the members, by the workers. As we will show below, this is certainly at odds with Wiehahn's view of a *'bona fide'* union. It is therefore necessary to ask: *what point is there in sitting on an industrial council, if, in order to do so we are compelled to emasculate ourselves? Will we be able to make any gains on the industrial council if our structures and policy are altered so as to conform to the standards applied by the industrial councils?* We can all point to a large number of industrial councils which have brought minimal gains to the workers precisely because all the trade unions ever do is sit on industrial councils. It is our fear that we too will precisely have to give up our other activities in order to achieve the sort of 'respectability' which the industrial council will demand.

The other carrots that are being offered to us are the 'right' to stop orders, the 'right' to enter into legally binding agreements with the clear rider that, if we do not register, we will not possess these rights. We are also being offered the right to run a training program: however, given the controls the state envisages over the registration of training programs, it is unlikely that we shall be able to decide on the content of such training programs. And finally, we are possibly being offered the right to continued existence. Having said that, let us examine the potential consequences of a refusal to register.

The stick
There are a number of possible consequences arising from a continuing refusal on the part of the independent unions to register.

Firstly, there is already in the legislation a prohibition on unregistered unions negotiating stop order facilities with management. Moreover, the Wiehahn Commission has suggested that legally binding agreements between unregistered unions be prohibited. There is a clear attempt by the state to bleed the unregistered unions by removing from the sphere of our activities what is conveniently believed to be the flesh and bones of trade union work. But is this true? Is it correct to say that we cannot continue our trade union work in the face of these prohibitions? It is necessary to note that there are extraordinarily few effective agreements in force between management and the independent unions. We certainly do not underestimate the significance of these advances. But do they constitute the *sine qua non* of trade union activity? Is it not true to say that we are all operating in a stable fashion, with *de facto* acceptance by management, in a great many factories in which we have not entered into legally binding agreements. Is it not also true to say that in those factories where we are operating effectively *and* in those few factories in which there are legally binding agreements, our successful operations are absolutely dependent upon vigilant organisation and the maintenance at all times of considerable factory floor support. The point that we wish to make is simple: *no amount of legislation is ultimately capable of determining the relationship between the workers and the bosses. As progressive trade unions, we know that the relationship between the workers and the bosses is dependent ultimately upon the organised strength of the workers in each factory.*

But we do not deny that the prohibition on legally binding agreements and stop order facilities will hamper us in our work. However, what are we asked to do in order to be allowed to have the right to enter into such agreements? We are being asked to register. And as we pointed out: *by registration we will be precisely compelled to give up that factor which has accounted for our success to date, namely our organised strength in each factory.* As for the question of stop order facilities: is it not enough to say that no organisation was built up by a stop order. And, if we are having problems in gathering our subscriptions, is that not because over the years we have become lulled into complacency by easy access to overseas money? If, on the other hand, we are unable to collect subscriptions because of the apathy and lack of commitment of our members, then we cannot ask the state to raise subscriptions for us: we cannot sell our organisational principles for a union subscription.

Secondly, there can be no doubt that if we refuse to register, others will be prepared to register on our ground and we will enter into competition with these newly registered unions. We do not underestimate the importance of this factor. One has only to look at one of the major industries in the western Cape to see the functioning of a registered union which despite all the legal advantages of an industrial council, closed shop and stop order facilities, does quite clearly not enjoy the support of the workers. And yet it is extremely difficult to challenge the domination of this union from the outside. We do not underestimate the importance of this example. Yet we should also not be overly troubled by this and other examples. Firstly, these unions have a long history and many of them were, arguably, established in a period when there was not a strong progressive force to challenge them. Moreover, recent political developments in South Africa make it far less likely that the workers will, in these times, support unquestioningly the domination of a bosses union. Secondly, one has only to look at the experience of the Textile Workers' Industrial Union in Natal, and Smith and Nephew in particular, to realise that registered unions do not necessarily constitute an insurmountable obstacle to a well organised, albeit unregistered, union which enjoys the support of the workers. Thirdly, and most importantly, we cannot argue on the one hand that the terms of registration are unfavourable to the workers and that therefore we reject them; and yet argue on the other hand, that the workers will turn to these unions in force. It is tantamount to arguing that the workers are incapable themselves of seeing through the deceptions of the state, that the workers have no idea what is good for them. Undoubtedly some workers will voluntarily join the puppet unions; undoubtedly the bosses will not hesitate to force many workers to join these unions. It is even possible that, in time, the nominal membership of these unions may exceed that of the independent unions. But to admit that is a far cry from arguing that their real organisational strength will ever exceed that of ours.

Finally, the most severe consequence possibly arising out of a failure to accept the state's registration package is the outlawing of unregistered unions. The Wiehahn Commission certainly suggested that in its scheme there was no place for unregistered unions. The minister's initial response indicated that unregistered unions would not be outlawed but that they would be bled to death and challenged by the construction of an alternative trade union establishment enjoying all the advantages of official patronage. We do not believe that puppet unions will ever be an effective challenge even if a simultaneous attempt is made to prohibit stop order facilities and legally binding agreements.

Then, surely, the next alternative is outright prohibition, and recently there has been considerable talk of the possibility of 'compulsory registration'. *Why was 'compulsory registration' not introduced from the beginning? Precisely because the trade union movement in a united response refused to be party to the blatant attempt to destroy the unions.* Is it not true that the state has seen, because of the shallowness of our initial response, that in fact our opposition to Wiehahn was highly superficial? *And hence, by introducing what we all understand to be only superficial changes, the unregistered trade union movement has been thrown into disarray and confusion. A perfect time to introduce 'compulsory registration'.*

The union responses

Soon after the Wiehahn Commission Report was tabled, the controll-

ing committee of the W.P.G.W.U. foresaw the possibility of the introduction of compulsory registration, and, indeed, went as far as formulating a response to this eventuality. In a resolution adopted by the
controlling committee, after extensive discussion with the rank and
file, it was decided that the union would not seek registration. In fact,
the resolution specifically states that *if the state attempts to force us to
register under the conditions proposed by Wiehahn we would then
disband the union ourselves.* This undoubtedly expresses our rejection
and anger with the Wiehahn proposals. *But is it not a perfect invitation to the state? We are in effect asking the state to introduce
compulsory registration because we are saying that if this is done then
we will close ourselves down.* The error of this line was pointed out to
the union and we would certainly not expect other unions to adopt this
utterly mistaken position. But has the response of the other unions
been markedly different? We would argue that it has not been. It is
clear that the majority of the independent unions were saying: *'We do
not approve of seeking registration but if you force us to, then we will
register'.*

Surely the only correct response is for all of us to say: *We do not
approve of the registration conditions proposed by the state and, until
such time as the state agrees to accept our principles of freedom of
association and workers' control of the unions, we will continue to
operate as unregistered unions.*

*We must bear in mind that the new dispensation cannot succeed
without our active cooperation.* If we refuse to cooperate, the state will
be faced with two alternatives: either the state must outlaw and ban
the existing unions, or it must go ahead with its plans and register
those organisations that are prepared to accept the restrictive conditions. If it outlaws us then it will be outlawing *all* the trade unions
which enjoy the support of the advanced and organised workers of the
country and the support of our fellow workers all over the world. By
so doing, the new dispensation would be revealed for what it is:
another attempt to foist an utterly unacceptable system onto the black
people of this country, another form of urban bantu council for the
black people. *We believe that the state is unlikely to take this radical
step if, by so doing, its intentions are so clearly exposed.* If, on the
other hand, the majority of the progressive trade union movement
registers, the state will then, *with the implicit support of the unions
opting for registration,* be able to outlaw those that refuse to seek
registration.

Alternatively, the state will register the reactionary trade unions and attempt to challenge our dominance in the trade union movement by establishing a new national network of trade unions operating with the full support of the state. We do not deny that this will be a hard fight but we cannot shy away from the fight by accepting the state's conditions now.

The state's third possible alternative is to agree to *our* conditions and to permit registration on *our* terms. We do not believe that this will happen immediately. But surely this is what we are fighting for? If we accept the restrictive conditions now, we will not be able to fight for our principles at some later stage. We will be too weak, we will be too thoroughly controlled by the state to muster the reserves necessary to fight for our principles. *In a word, accepting the state's present conditions means that we ultimately lose the support of the workers.* As progressive trade unions, we cannot countenance this possibility.

Addendum to Original Memorandum

All the responses thus far — and indeed much of the discussion at the 3 November 1979 meeting attended by the FOSATU affiliated unions, the Food and Canning Workers' Unions, the African Food and Canning Workers' Union and the W.P.G.W.U. — has indicated a number of related areas of disagreement with our memorandum. Firstly, it has been argued that we exaggerate the controls inherent in the registration package. Many of the unions in fact argue that whereas a degree of protection and respectability is achieved by registration, the most troublesome controls can be simultaneously avoided! Secondly, it is argued that we underestimate the threat from the parallel unions. Thirdly, and far less importantly, it is argued that if our arguments against registration are to be applied consistently, then we must call for the deregistration of the few progressive currently registered unions. Finally, there is considerable divergence over the tactical question — over how best to meet the threats contained in the new labour dispensation.

The question of control

It has been argued that our memorandum has exaggerated the controls contained in the new labour dispensation. It is pointed out that currently the controls are — with the exception of the entire question of provisional registration — no more stringent than those which already apply to the currently registered unions. The highly exceptional examples of the progressive registered unions are then raised and it is argued that, provided we refuse provisional registration and accept only final registration, then we too could operate as effectively as the progressive registered unions. At one level the argument is persuasive — it is in any event objectively true that no additional controls have been imposed. To this we can only reply: Wiehahn is not yet finished. There are more reports to come and there is more legislation to come, and already the first Wiehahn report has strongly recommended the imposition of additional controls. Moreover, the minister has consistently, and blatantly, stressed that the entire objective of registering the black trade union movement is precisely in order to control it. Currently, the only additional controls are contained in provisional registration, but it is argued that we can possibly avoid provisional registration. Whilst we disagree with this assessment (and we disagree strongly with the tactics suggested by most of the other unions for avoiding provisional registration), we have to admit there is currently no legal requirement to apply for or accept provisional registration.

However, if additional controls are introduced, this will not be the case. *They will be mandatory instructions to labour department bureaucrats and there will be no question of applying for exemption from these controls.* If we do not object in the strongest possible terms now to the first clear evidence of additional controls, i.e., if we do not insist upon the removal of provisional registration from the law, but prefer to tamper with it selectively by means of exemption, how will we deal with controls over which similar discretionary powers of application are not given?

But there is more to this than the question of legally imposed controls. Because its has been argued that *if no additional controls are imposed then, on accepting registration, our organising practices and hence our real strength will remain unaffected.* We reject the argument because it fails to understand correctly the *political intentions* of the Wiehahn Report, particularly as they relate to the *industrial council system.* Secondly, it actually fails to understand precisely the real nature of the threat faced with respect to the parallel unions.

It appears to be generally agreed that the *real controls* in the entire industrial relations system are contained in participating in the industrial councils themselves. And — it is also generally agreed — that this is all the more so insofar as active participation in the industrial councils must inevitably result in a particular change in organising strategy. It forces us into a prescribed round of bargaining at the level of the total industry — i.e., at a level at which the bosses are 100% organised and yet at which the black unions are very weak. Even more importantly, the industrial council system presupposes that the state can establish a neutral body comprising boss and worker representatives who could be happily reconciled at all times. Our experience makes this view difficult to accept.

The fear of industrial council participation is apparently easily countered by those inclining towards registration. They argue that *there is no legal obligation to become involved in the industrial council machinery.* In other words, they argue, 'we can register to take advantage of the "protection" and/or "respectability" which this course provides' — i.e., 'protection' from state executive action, and 'respectability' in the eyes of management and hence the ability to conclude legally binding house agreements. The question of protection from state executive action has already been dealt with in our memorandum. The best protection against the state is a unified stand against registration under the present conditions. As for the 'respectability' we will supposedly gain by registering, will the bosses simultaneously allow us to refuse to become involved in the industrial council machinery, whilst continuing to permit us to negotiate individual house agreements in more favourable, better protected circumstances? Legally, there is in fact no obligation to become involved in the industrial council machinery; however, politically, it will be extremely difficult to avoid the industrial councils, Wiehahn's intentions are absolutely clear.

> In view of the overriding importance of the employer-employee relationship at the level of the enterprise, the commission believes that the establishment of works committees and works councils should be actively encouraged (3.119) .... It is, however, equally important that in promoting maximum consultation and negotiation at the enterprise level any possibility of undermining the industrial council system should be effectively precluded in the legislation (3.120).

At present, the response of the bosses is: 'You are not registered, we will not speak to you.' After registration the responses of the bosses will be: 'You are registered, we will see you at the industrial council.

We will discuss factory problems with our works council.' *Works councils for the workers, industrial councils for the unions. But in the end both for the bosses.*

Those unions which refuse a seat on the industrial council will be relegated to a grey area with no room for manoeuvre between the industrial councils and the works councils. They will find themselves in this unenviable situation because they will have effectively not accepted the whole registration package. The registration package is firstly *political* and only secondly *legal.* And the political imperatives, the clear intentions of Wiehahn, require that the entire registration package be accepted. The crucial part of the registration package is precisely participation in the industrial council system, and unions will only enjoy the 'advantages' of registration if they accept the whole package. We will still be unable to conclude legally binding house agreements. So having discovered that legally binding *house* agreements are beyond our registered grasp, why not accept legally binding *industrial* agreements. All that requires is a further step along the slippery road to 'respectability' — a seat on the industrial council.

Our point is simple. *Both before and after registration, any attempt to take the workers' struggle forward (be it by means of legally binding agreements or any other instrument) will depend on one factor and one factor only — the organised strength of the workers and not on the 'respectability' extended to us by registration.* In short: by staying outside of registration we will be compelled to fight exactly the same way as we have done in the past — with the worker's organised strength. As progressive trade unionists that is the way we know best, that is in fact the only way we can fight.

The threat of the parallel unions

It is not necessary to debunk at length the manner in which the parallels have organised and will continue to organise. In a word, the parallels are, at best, 'benefit' societies which in exchange for a subscription provide a variety of pension, medical, etc., benefits. Their membership is a *paper* membership. No progressive unions will disagree with this brief assessment.

In our memorandum we concentrated entirely on the ability of an unregistered union to counter the threat of a registered parallel union. We do not believe that it will be a simple task; but nor do we believe that it will be insurmountable. *As long as we retain our methodical, thorough attitude to workers' organisation; as long as we maintain our emphasis on a well informed, participating rank and file; as long as we can contrast our organisation with that of the paper parallels, then we will be able to retain the workers' support.*

If, however, we think that in order to gain access to management it is necessary to match member for member the parallel unions, then surely we must register. *But all that this means is that we will inevitably become involved in a race for paper members.* The inevitability of this, at least in the initial period following registration, has in fact been acknowledged by some progressive trade unionists. *This is a fatal path.* We know that there is no such thing as bad organisation initially, followed up by good organisation in the same factory by the same union. We know that if a union follows an incorrect organising path in the initial stages it is then impossible to reorganise that badly organised factory. We will have installed a particular organisational practice which we cannot attempt to alter the following week.

Tactical questions

At the joint meeting of 3 November 1979, the trade unions present released, after intensive discussion, a joint statement of principles which set out minimum conditions for registration. However, we cannot deny the fact that this joint statement does contain within it two very divergent strategies, two divergent views on how best to secure the acceptance of these principles. FOSATU have stated how they intend going about securing the stated principles and we must go about explaining our position.

In brief, FOSATU intends submitting an application for registration on the basis of these principles and they will only accept registration if the registration certificates are consistent with their principles; we on the other hand, do not intend applying for registration until these minimum conditions are enshrined in the law.

We should point out, firstly, that we do not believe that all the FOSATU unions will be registered under the conditions outlined in the joint statement. Only the weak, paper unions will escape these controls — it is after all unnecessary to control them. We do not believe that FOSATU unions fit this latter description and we therefore do not believe that the state will exempt them.

Secondly, whilst we do not doubt the sincerity with which the members of FOSATU hold to the stated principles, we do think that they are seeking to secure their acceptance in a misguided manner. The clearest statement of our opposition to this unacceptable system would be to refuse to have anything to do with it, until it is made more acceptable.

Finally, we must all agree that we will not have won acceptance of our principles, if they are accepted selectively. We can only quote the words of Isisebenzi, the official FOSATU newspaper.

> The Minister of Labour says that all problems will be solved by him. He will give what are called exemptions. But how can unions accept a system of exemptions to decide everything rather than a *system of law*.

We couldn't agree more. The acceptance of the workers' guiding principles must be for all workers — for workers in every union of their choice, for workers in the present, and for their children in the future. They must be guaranteed; they must not be given by a minister one day who, if we are 'naughty boys and girls', will take them away the next day.

Reading 13. (1981)

Trade Unions and the State: the Question of Legality*

Bob Fine, Francine de Clercq, Duncan Innes

Introduction: the debate

Ever since the Wiehahn Commission published its findings and the government introduced legislation enabling the registration of black unions, an important debate has emerged in South Africa and abroad concerning the response of black unions to the state's initiatives.

Although we welcome the debate, we are not happy with the predominant direction which it has taken so far. Most critics of the state's registration strategy have advocated that it should be boycotted by all black workers who value their independence from the state. This has been true of critics both inside South Africa and abroad, and it is the one common element that binds together radicals who otherwise hold very different or even antagonistic political perspectives.

The unfortunate features of the debate so far are that the reasons why FOSATU has led the drive to make critical use of the state's registration package have been scarcely articulated and, more generally, that the theoretical basis for an alternative strategy to boycott has barely been spelt out.

* First published in more extended from in *S.A.L.B.*, VII, 1 and 2 (September, 1981), pp. 39 — 68.

We begin this discussion with a brief statement of the positions which, broadly, characterise the two poles of the argument surrounding registration. This will provide a basis to examine the presuppositions in which these positions are rooted.

Among those black unions which have agreed to apply for registration there are important differences. Some, like those unions affiliated to TUCSA and to a lesser extent to CUSA, have not seriously challenged the advisability of registration. For these unions, registration has been welcomed as an unambigious victory for black workers, though they may have expressed some minor disagreements with aspects of the state's package. For others — and here we refer specifically to FOSATU unions — agreement to register is based on a far more complicated and contradictory analysis of the advantages and difficulties it brings to black workers.

FOSATU has set itself certain long term aims which it regards as crucial to the development of a strong trade union movement among black workers. These include: the elimination of legally enforced racial division in the labour movement; the radical limitation of state interference in labour relations; the establishment of workers' control in the unions, and an end to craft based divisions within the union movement.[1] FOSATU is adamant that 'our struggle has not been to achieve registration as an end in itself'.[2] However, while they reject registration as an *end,* FOSATU has not necessarily rejected registration as a *means* of achieving their long term aims: that is, they have adopted a tactical approach to the question, arguing that they would accept registration only if it served to help them win their long term aims. To this end, they agreed to apply for registration on condition that certain demands intended to promote their aims were met by the state.

FOSATU's position implies a different conception of the state from that advanced by TUCSA. By arguing that in amending the Industrial Conciliation (I.C.) Act, the state has at last come to its senses, TUCSA implicitly posits a conception of the state as more or less neutral in relation to the struggles between various contending social groups, comprising employers and groups of racially defined workers (white, coloured, Indian and African). FOSATU, on the other hand, through its continued protests against state interference, recognises its repressive character. However, this does not lead them to conclude that registration should be dismissed as *merely* an instrument of state repression. On the contrary, FOSATU argues that both the Wiehahn Commission and the amendment have been forced upon the state 'by years of struggle by workers and their representative organisations',[3] and therefore that these changes establish a new terrain of activity to which black workers and their unions must relate. The workers' movement, they continue, would be foolish to ignore that the state may be making real concessions under pressure, and therefore, FOSATU is willing to 'test'[4] the state's intentions by applying for registration under their own (FOSATU's) clearly defined terms. Implicit in all these arguments is a view of the state in which it appears not as a neutral arbiter between contending groups, nor *merely* as the repressive instrument of one class, but rather as a repressive force which is located in a nexus of contradictory social relations and whose character is determined by the changing relations between the classes involved. Unfortunately, since this theoretical position has not been explicitly developed by FOSATU, the organisation has found itself swayed at various times by different pressures, thus leading to a good deal of confusion within its own ranks about its overall position and tactics.

A rather different analysis of the state is implicit in the position adopted by those black unions opposed to registration. Here the basic argument is that both the Wiehahn Commission, which arose as a response to a crisis in the political and economic control of the black labour movement, and the legislation which followed are no more than a crude attempt by the state to intensify and rationalise control of the independent black trade union movement. The rhetoric of liberalization is a fiction behind which lies the harsh reality of the extended domination of the apartheid state. According to the G.W.U. which supports this view:

> Now suddenly it seems that formal recognition has become a real possibility. But only because the unions have been presented with a highly restrictive and limiting set of conditions for registration. Acceptance of these conditions raises the possibility ... of formal recognition being extended on a wide scale precisely because registration spells the death knell of workers' control of the unions .... It involves, in other words, a series of compromises on the question of workers' control, for this is what registration implies. Having compromised on the question of workers' control, the unions will have lost the most important element of their power. [5]

Clearly, in this analysis the state is seen as an uncompromising repressive force, capable of *adapting* its methods of repression towards the labour force, but never of *easing* repression. There is no room here for the kinds of manoeuvres which FOSATU seeks to adopt since any attempt to work, however critically, within the confines of the new legislation automatically implies a fatal subordination to the new forms of repression, to the power of the state.

The only way forward is to refuse the straightjacket of apartheid legality and to continue to build an independent union movement free of the restrictions of registration. As the G.W.U. states:

> Knowing the state's objectives does not mean accepting them. And the only way of really refusing to accept the state's objectives is to refuse to accept registration under the conditions offered by the state.[6]

This latter position is taken up to varying degrees by different unions. Within South Africa, SAAWU, the G.W.U., and the Food and Canning Unions have all argued the need to reject registration on the grounds that it will inevitably involve collaboration with the apartheid state, and therefore the weakening of the labour movement. In exile, SACTU has rejected the notion that peaceful reform of any kind can be meaningful under apartheid, and therefore dismisses registration as a fraud and mere window dressing for apartheid. But, whatever their reasons and different positions, all these varied groups have in common the fact that they regard the state's concessions as essentially fraudulent and therefore they all advocate a policy of boycott.

It is around this issue of the nature of these concessions — are they real as FOSATU argues or are they simply fraudulent? — that much of the debate turns. And underlying this question is that of the nature of the state which has offered these concessions and of its relation to the classes which constitute the social fabric of modern day South Africa. In attempting to answer these complex questions, we begin by examining historical experience in South Africa to see what lessons can be learned.

The legacy of history

Registration and the conditions of incorporation

In order to answer the key question of why the 1924 I.C. Act was able to undermine the majority of the white, coloured and Indian unions which registered under it, one has to look further than the provisions of the act itself. Law operates within the context of certain social, political and economic conditions, and to understand the implications of a particular law for society, one has to examine it within the context of these conditions.

The most important starting point is to situate the 1924 act within the productive and social relations which existed within the labour force at that time. Here the key elements would appear to be the existence of a well entrenched racial hierachy in the division of labour and the differential incorporation of the racial groups in the country's political structures. In addition to these objective conditions — all of which promote racial divisions within the labour force — are important subjective conditions which further entrenched these divisions. Of importance here is the tradition of craft unionism with its accompanying ethos of sectionalism and racial superiority which was imported from abroad and was prevalent among white workers. The point is that the I.C. Act of 1924 was inserted into a society whose objective and subjective conditions were already permeated with racial divisions.

It would be inadequate to argue that simply because the above conditions prevailed at the time, it was therefore *inevitable* that the act would have its intended effect of dividing and incorporating workers. However, in order for workers to be able to resist these tendencies the presence of a countervailing social force, capable of generating and sustaining a movement in the opposite direction, is necessary. In other words, the 'success' of the I.C. Act must be related to the relative strengths of the opposing classes. To resist incorporation, it was necessary that the mass of the labour force, African workers, should lead the movement as a whole. Yet in the mid-20s, the African section of the labour force, especially in industry, was relatively weak — and certainly far weaker than it is today. This is not to say that African workers did not fight important struggles against employers and the state during this period, but that they were not a strong enough force (numerically, organisationally, ideologically) to counter the intense pressure which the state was imposing on white workers.

Furthermore, it must be borne in mind that the 1924 I.C. Act was introduced after white workers had sustained a heavy defeat at the hands of the state. The crushing of the Rand Revolt brought with it a phase of demoralisation among these workers. Objectively divided, enmeshed in the grip of a narrow racist and sectional ideology, driven backwards and demoralised by the state, with no substantial countervailing force to sustain or rejuvenate them, is it any wonder that the majority of the white workers fell easily into the trap of incorporation which the state had laid for them through the terms of the I.C. Act?

To sum up, it was not the I.C. Act which led to the defeat of the registered union movement after 1924 (in terms both of its incorporation by the state and its rejection of nonracialism). What turned the I.C. Act into a defeat for the labour movement was the existence of definite historical conditions and a particular balance of class forces.

However to pose the question in this way runs the risk of missing an important aspect of the argument: that is, the I.C. Act itself cannot be treated as simply a functional appendage of the state which in some magical way would resolve all its problems. Rather, the act was an attempted solution to the contradictions faced by the state and therefore contained in turn, both advantages and dangers.

The contradictory nature of the I.C. Act

Some Marxist analyses of South African society crudely represent the law as being no more than an instrument of the dominant capitalist class; a weapon capable of unambiguously promoting the interests of this class. In positing this functionalist conception of the law, these theorists are perhaps reacting against an equally crude pluralist conception which treats the law in positivist fashion, as value free and therefore neutral in the struggle between social groups. In our view, both these approaches fail to grasp the essence of the nature of the law: that it both expresses and attempts to regulate a set of antagonistic social relations, thereby representing a form of domination through which the conflict between antagonistic classes is mediated. Law does not *constitute* social relations, but rather it acts upon forces already constituted. Consequently, we could reject the argument that it was the passage of the I.C. Act in 1924 which secured the incorporation of the registered unions, since the act itself could have no magical powers of this kind. Rather, we would see the passage of this act as an attempt by the state to resolve certain fundamental contradictions which faced employers at that time, but which simultaneously opened up a new set of contradictions which would have to be confronted.

There is no doubt that the I.C. Act of 1924 brought with it substantial advantages for the state and employers. Foremost among these were the denial of rights to African workers, the racial divisiions, which it encouraged within the labour force and the cooption of the white dominated labour aristocracy. Yet in noting this its seems to us just as important to bear in mind that the state paid a high price despite these advantages. In particular, the introduction of a statutory colour bar — a necessary device if white workers were to be enticed into collaboration with the state — imposed restrictions on the use employers could make of relatively cheap black workers in the more skilled positions. This in turn, led to the shortage of skilled labour becoming a serious economic problem. Further, by drawing non-African workers into collaboration with the state, they were prevented from fulfilling their role as a labour aristocracy able to exercise, on behalf of employers, a degree of ideological dominance over the African labour force.

Finally, the I.C. Act helped to create more favourable conditions for a convergence of the African workers' struggle and the nationalist struggle. Although an important advantage of the legislation was that it helped undermine the potential for solidarity among white and black workers, a corresponding disadvantage lay in the political danger to the state which emerged from the potential unity forged within the black population. This provided the basis for an alliance not only between black workers and other sections of the black population (based on their common expression as blacks), but also within the various sections of the black working class itself (based on their common subjection to discrimination under the I.C. Act). This further encouraged black workers to overcome such major divisions among themselves as between tribes, migrants and non-migrants, urban and rural divisions, etc. These and other implications of the act — implications which could not have been welcomed by the state — inevitably contributed to the politicisation of industrial conflict and placed political questions high on the agenda for those organisations which were to seek to represent the interests of black workers.

To ignore these points and to argue that history proves that trade union registration automatically implies incorporation by the state is not only erroneous but politically dangerous as well, in that it leads to a principle being made out of the tactic of boycott.

Exposing Wiehahn

Those advocating boycott have argued in essence that while the

Wiehahn strategy *appears as a concession of rights for black workers, it is in reality* merely a more rational subtle and intense form of state control. There are three related problems with this approach. Firstly, by placing exclusive focus on challenging the semblance of rights offered by Wiehahn, the boycotters accept uncritically the image, put forward by the commission itself, that its proposals represent a *rational* solution to the problems of labour control faced by the state. Secondly, by treating the liberal rhetoric of Wiehahn as *merely* an ideological fiction they fail to examine the ways in which registration might extend the rights of black workers and so augment the workers' field of action. Thirdly, by concentrating on exposing the repressive character of apartheid legality they neglect the equally vital, but less evident, task of revealing the *uses* which black workers can make of changes in the legal status of their unions.

Thus the boycotters, in their constant re-assertion that there is nothing liberal in the state's new measures, do little more than repeat what the representatives of the state themselves say — only in slightly more explicit form.

It is characteristic of the state to present its reforms both as a recognition of the rights of its citizens and as an optimum form of control over them. The temptation facing the state's critics is to reject the soft language of rights as no more than an illusory veil, while accepting the hard language of control as a true mirror of reality. But neither side of the coin is correct. On the one hand, it cannot be assumed that rights are *merely* a veil for power or a mystification which hides the brutal realities of class domination. The existence of rights constitutes a vital resource for the oppressed and an inhibition on the power of the oppressors. That is why the winning of rights from the state has been a vital part of all labour movements. Further, there is no reason to presuppose that even the most authoritarian regimes cannot be forced by working class movements to concede, at least for a period, crucial democratic rights. Even in Franco's Spain or, more recently, in Brazil, the opposition was able to squeeze a measure of liberalisation from the regimes and to make use of the rights afforded, however meagre and precarious. Thus, the notion that rights are nothing more than an illusion or that they are impossible to win under authoritarian governments is a false dogma that can only obscure the need — and sap the will — to fight for them.

The other side of this critique is also misplaced. It cannot be assumed — simply because the agents of the state say so — that the new labour policy does introduce a more rational or intense form of control over the unions. The state presents its Wiehahn strategy as a technical device for imposing more efficient control over black unions as a quantitative increase in the intensity of control. Our task is not to bow before this image of omnipotence, but to search beneath the surface for the contradictions inherent within the new regulations; not to accept the technical appearance of these reforms, but to grasp the shift in class relations they signify; not to assume that they represent a quantitative increase in control, but to assess the qualitative changes in the form of domination which they signify; and to find out, independently of the state's rhetoric, which side stands to benefit from these new arrangements.

We should add that for any capitalist state, control is not an end in itself, but is always subordinate to the demands of capital accumulation. There can be no certainty in advance that the imperatives of control will neatly correspond with the imperatives of accumulation.

For these reasons it is not sufficient for critics of Wiehahn to focus on the state's *intentions* alone. Protagonists of boycott have argued rightly that the state intends to use registration to divide, discipline, incorporate and isolate the black union movement. But our response to these innovations cannot be determined by the state's intentions; rather we must make our own assessment of the real effects of registration. For between the state's intentions and their realisation in practice falls a shadow: the struggle of workers. Whether the new forms of labour control will serve as a stimulus for its development (as the state fears) cannot be gauged by studying the state's intentions alone.

The vital task of black workers is to reach for means whereby they can take hold of the instruments which the state seeks to use against them and turn them around to their own advantage. This is not always possible. However, to exclude this course in principle merely ties the hands of the labour movement.

The exposure of the contradictions of state power is as vital as the exposure of its repressiveness. The tensions inherent in the Wiehahn strategy have a number of economic and political ramifications which make it a high risk policy for the state. On the economic level, difficulties arise out of the uneven nature of capitalist development. While the existence of organised African labour, if kept within certain bounds, might be compatible with the highly modernised sector of industry, this poses real problems for those businesses which still rely heavily on comparatively backward technology and large inputs of cheap, unskilled black labour. This kind of problem serves to remind us again that the imperatives of labour control must always be seen in the context of the imperatives of accumulation and do not automatically correspond with them.

The political difficulty which the Wiehahn strategy poses for the state is essentially this: if it is to incorporate successfully a section of African labour it must concede to them some extension, however meagre, of the restrictive rights which they currently possess. If the state offers nothing, then its policy of cooptation cannot hope to succeed. The risk from the perspective of the rulers is that whatever concessions or rights it offers will be used by black workers in ways that were never intended: to consolidate, broaden and strengthen the union movement. This is the weak underbelly of the government's strategy. Our argument is that by making a principle out of boycott the opportunity to exploit this weakness is lost.

The decisive issue with respect to registration is whether or not it represents, in relation to the existing situation of black workers, a real extension of their rights. If this is not the case, then boycott is clearly in order. However, if concessions are made (albeit for the purpose of cooptation), then it signifies — whatever the intentions of the state — an advance for black workers.

'Outside the law': the myth of no compromise

The boycotters achieve this metamorphosis of tactic into principle by rejecting in advance the possibility that black workers could force the state to make real concessions which they could usefully exploit. They argue that, to the extent that any real concessions are made by the state, it is only with the intention of incorporating a section of the black labour movement, and that the use of these concessions would necessarily compromise the unions involved. Thus, even when concessions are 'real' they are to be boycotted since, if unions took advantage of them, they would compromise their independence from the state. This approach treats advances made by workers as if they were traps that will automatically lead to their incorporation. The Wiehahn Commission's argument is that the persistence of African unions, 'outside the law' poses threats which can only be met by drawing them within the discipline of the law. This conception has been repeated uncritically by those of a boycott persuasion who simply reverse the value judgements, but retain the terms of the opposition. Outside the legal framework, they argue, African unions accord themselves 'freedom of action' forced back within the ambit of the law, they will be 'coopted' and 'rendered ineffectual'.

The idea that 'independent' unions have ever existed 'outside the ambit of the law' is nonsense, as the history of their legal suppression clearly shows. The commission may have had its own reasons for suggesting that 'independent' unions are not under the legal subjection of the state, but the fact that it is so deluded itself is no reason for its critics to do the same.

The issue before us is not to swallow blindly the mythological notion that any unions are free of legal constraints; rather it is to compare empirically the limited rights and severe controls facing black unions inside and outside the official negotiating machinery, and to decide policy on this basis. It is not enough to say that registration is tied to the imposition of constraints; the significant question is whether these constraints are more or less restrictive than those currently exercised.

Most boycotters would doubtless agree, when the question is put to them so baldly, the unregistered unions are subjected — and always have been — to the most intense legal controls by the state. However, they fall back onto a conception of inner freedom in the face of external adversity: they argue that unregistered unions have been able to maintain their internal integrity in the face of state repression, while participation in the official machinery of industrial conciliation is dependent on the unions' compromising themselves. It is this rhetoric of 'no compromise' with which we now take issue.

By its very nature all trade unionism is based on compromise, in that unions negotiate the rates and conditions of exchange between labour and capital without directly challenging the exchange itself and the dominance of capital implicit therein. Additionally in the South African context, there are specific compromises that are inevitable. The boycotters assert as fundamental principles that must not be compromised, workers' control of the unions (that is, internal democracy) and political independence from the state. We do not argue with these principles as goals to be attained: quite the reverse. But we do argue with the claim that these principles have already been put into practice by any of the unregistered unions. If democracy means anything, it must include full and open discussion on all pertinent issues, full accountability of the leadership, the open election and revocability of all officials, and so forth. But under the present repressive conditions, workers cannot possibly feel free to engage in full and open discussion of say, strikes or political associations which the state is likely to deem illegal. To the extent that discussions of this type do take place, they must do so in a manner that is discreet and so violate the norm of internal democracy. It is important to call things by their real name. The fact is that all unions are forced to compromise on fundamental principles. This is not a fault, but a strategic necessity in the context of a repressive state.

The alternative to boycotting

The alternative to boycotting the package is to try to exploit the contradictions which the state faces so as to counter the restrictions contained in registration, while, at the same time, taking full advantage of the extension of rights offered (broadly this has been the tactical response adopted by FOSATU). There is *considerable room* for unions to manoeuvre against the state's intentions precisely because of the contradictory position in which the state finds itself. In this regard it is worth mentioning that the tactics adopted by FOSATU unions so far have met with a good deal of success. For instance, confronted by the government's registration proposals, FOSATU decided to apply for registration *on its own terms* in an attempt to force the government to conceed FOSATU's right to a nonracial constitution and also its right to register unions with a racially mixed membership. However, the right to represent workers in a factory has been confined to workers defined in terms of race. FOSATU has challenged this latter decision and, at the time of writing, is continuing its campaign for unrestricted freedom of association, threatening deregistration *as a last resort* if their demands are not met. Of course, there is no *guarantee* that FOSATU will be victorious on these issues. Yet surely it is this kind of approach — critising every repressive aspect of the government's proposals, counterposing to them the unions' own demands, and ensuring no unnecessary sacrifice of the benefits to be derived from registration — which offers the most constructive way forward for the labour movement.

It must not be forgotten that the main reason for the state's embarking upon its Wiehahn reforms in the first place is that the previous position of refusing recognition to black unions was no longer tenable. The state has been pressurised from a number of sides (economic changes, mounting resistance from black workers and populist struggles, and from pressure groups abroad) into making concessions. The fact that the state chooses to turn this defensive manoeuvre into a positive advance for itself through its present registration package should not be allowed to obscure the fact that this new strategy is itself riddled with contradictions. It is these that must be analysed, exposed and manipulated — not boycotted. Just as the state is constantly seeking to divide and out manoeuvre the black union movement, so must that movement seek to turn the tables on the state by using every advantage offered it, all the time putting forward its own demands and rallying more and more workers to its side. Certainly, the state does not relish the prospect of officially recognising a strong trade union movement in the country, *but nor does it want a return to the status quo ante*. This is why it has conceded real rights to black workers. The prospects that have been opened up thereby pose a great challenge to the union movement. It would represent a major setback for that movement if this challenge was not met.

An example to consider is the introduction in 1977 of in-plant committees which were granted formal negotiating powers. As part of the struggle for the right of African workers to belong to legally recognised trade unions, some unions also began to make use of the machinery of the works committees with the view to consolidating the unions' position on the factory floor. They transformed these committees into democratic shop steward committees, seeking to ensure that the members were democratically elected by the rank and file, that full discussions were held prior to the meetings with management, that report back meetings were held and that close cooperation was maintained with both the union officials and the committee members in other factories and industries. The ideal was to *combine* different methods of struggle and not to *counterpose,* as the state intended, participation in these committees to the building of trade unions.

The same principle holds with registration and participation in the industrial council system. In the absence of unrestricted negotiating channels, the unions *may* wish to use the industrial council system in the same way that they used the works committee system. In doing so, however, the unions should fight to ensure, among other things that the fullest possible discussion takes place with the membership about the issues to be put forward at the industrial council meetings; that there be early report backs to the membership of discussions at these meetings; that the presence of shop floor representatives be made a condition for participation and that present restrictions such as veto rights be removed. By winning these and other demands, workers may succeed in injecting their own content into alien forms. However, even the winning of these rights should never result in the substitution of plant level by industrial council bargaining. The former must always be protected as a primary channel for the pressing of workers' demands. As presently constituted, the industrial councils threaten the power of black unions. To meet this threat, the unions could combine the struggle to transform the character of these official institutions with the struggle to extend alternative open channels of negotiation. What is important is that the unions use their rights of representation at industrial level to put forward a set of minimum demands which would apply to all workers of that particular industry, thus opening up the possibility for unions to gain access to the unorganised section of the African work-force.

Finally, it is important to recognise that for the first time in South African labour history some African workers have been granted official trade union rights. When the state poses an immediate and constant threat to black unions, the winning of basic rights of trade union representation provides some measure of protection from the worst excesses of state repression and executive action. State recognition, however limited, makes it less difficult for unions to recruit members, to gain access to the work-place, to win management recognition, to secure stop order facilities, etc. In addition, trade union recognition facilitates access to bargaining channels. At one level all the state is doing through the law is giving formal recognition to a *de facto* situation; at another level this extension of legality provides more favourable conditions for the real extension of workers' power.

The politics of legality

Within the different strands of opinion that together comprise the boycott position one belief predominates: namely, that unions must be political and that the only correct *political* response to registration is that of boycott. In one way or another, the various boycotters all share the view that in South Africa politics and economics are inseparable; that economic struggles (over narrow trade union issues of wages and conditions of work) and political struggles (over pass laws, influx controls, etc.) are so closely intertwined that any attempt to fight for the former without the latter would be doomed to failure and is as such regressive. While we do not disagree with the view that there is a close relation between economics and politics, we do challenge the boycotters' conception of the unity between them — and in particular their belief that boycott registration is an appropriate way of securing their unity in practice.

Behind this argument lies an old shibboleth for the opposition movement in South Africa: namely, that illegality (or non-legality) is more radical than legality and that the use of legal means of struggle is inherently reactionary. There is nothing inherently wrong in workers using legal openings afforded them to press for the extension of their legal rights. To deny this and to present illegality as an absolute rule of conduct is a chimera of the ultra-left. In our view, it is one that has seriously impeded the historical development of the struggle for black political rights in South Africa (witness the defeat of the black trade union movement which accompanied the turn to illegality in the early 1960s). The call to boycott legal registration expresses in a new form just such a perspective.

Underlying the boycott view is a serious misconception of the relationship between trade unions and politics. According to the boycotters, in order to extend narrow economic trade unionism into politics, the unions need only develop their own political activities (e.g. in campaigns against the pass law) and/or enter into alliances with political organisations. However, such extensions of the trade union movement into politics, while not necessarily wrong, are not the key elements in the process. Most important of all, is the struggle for recognition from the state, since it is this which establishes membership of trade unions as a political right for workers.

However insignificant the boycotters consider state recognition to be, the state does not reciprocate this neglect. It coordinates and focuses management's attacks on the black unions, it establishes the coercive framework within which all unions must operate; and it prepares and organises the police, army and prisons, not to mention the spies and scabs, whose goal is the destruction of independent unionism. In this context, the struggle by the unions to extend the sphere of workers' power through state recognition is crucial: in terms of winning space for the unions to organise; in terms of establishing general conditions conducive to the organisation of black workers where the establishment of unions is almost impossible; in terms of coordinating and centralising the workers' movement in the face of the coordinated and centralised policy of the state; and, finally, in terms of extending the narrow economic concerns of unions into larger political concerns of democracy and influence over the state.

So far we have discussed the boycotters as if they were a single entity; but behind their common agreement lie diverse and sometimes antagonistic political positions. There are two major tendencies within the boycott position between which it is important to differentiate (although these strands do not necessarily coincide with particular organised groupings).

One tendency reflects the view of those who will try to find any excuse to channel the workers' struggles to their own ends. They do not want the unions — that is, the workers' own organisations — to take up issues pertaining to the state, for they wish to reserve this task for hands other than those of the workers. According to them, the workers are only useful as a kind of battering ram for a movement they themselves seek to lead. In fact not only are they unhappy when the unions take the initiative with the state, but in general they are reluctant to see any show of independence by the unions as this threatens their own political leadership. The 'unity of economics and politics' is the subordination of unions to a movement headed by and serving the petty bourgeoisie.

The second tendency is found among those boycotters who are genuinely committed to the movement of black workers. They have fought hard precisely to free workers' organisations from dependence on both the state and the petty bourgeoisie and to build them up as an independent force in their own right. They advocate boycott not to prevent unions from taking the initiative, but with a view to preserving their independence from any force outside themselves. For them, the substance behind the principle of 'the unity of the economic and the political' is that trade union struggles in South Africa are in themselves political.

As against these boycott tendencies, the position represented by FOSATU has recognised the significance of state recognition. Like the latter group of boycotters, FOSATU has also struggled to create a black worker movement independent of both the petty bourgeoisie and the state. FOSATU, however, has had its shortcomings as well, in that its response has tended to identify independence from petty bourgeois politics with independence from politics in general. This has lead to the charge of economism being levelled against FOSATU. However, FOSATU appears to have undertaken the fight for recognition in a defensive way, vaguely apologetic for their decision, treating it for the most part as a technical exercise bringing with it technical advantages, and therefore failing to reveal its significance either to its own members or to other black workers.

What is crucial in our view is that all those who are concerned to promote the position of black workers recognise the struggle for state recognition of black unions as their primary political goal. There is agreement that the state's denial of trade union recognition to black workers over the past fifty odd years has been one of the most serious obstacles to their development. Now that the state, in the face of consistent and militant opposition, appears finally prepared to make its first concessions on these demands, it would seem to us the height of folly for the unions to turn their backs on these concessions.

Notes

1 See FOSATU Central Committee statement, *FOSATU Workers News,* November 1979.
2 *Ibid.*
3 *Ibid.*
4 *Ibid.*
5 Western Province General Workers' Union, 'Registration, Recognition and Organisation,' *South African Labour Bulletin,* V, 6 and 7 (March, 1980), pp. 73 — 74.
6 Western Province General Workers' Union, 'Comments on the Question of Registration,' *South African Labour Bulletin,* V, 4 (November, 1979), p. 120.

Part V

Overview: Trade Unions and Politics

*Doug Hindson**

Union involvement in political struggles outside the work-place raises numerous important questions. Under what conditions and in what ways should the unions take up workers' problems such as housing, transport and repressive administration? What forms of organisation are appropriate to tackling these problems? Should the unions themselves represent workers in conflicts with the authorities in the townships or should they encourage the formation of separate organisations to take up such issues, organisations whose membership is community rather than factory based? What should be the relationship between the unions and such community based organisations? What should be the relationship between the unions and the emerging national political organisations?

Underlying these questions is the central issue of the presence and leadership of different social classes within the trade unions, community and national organisations. The reason why this is important is that the class composition of both the membership and leadership of these organisations affects the class interests they pursue. Insofar as these organisations exert an influence over broader social and political processes their class content affects the path taken by social change in South Africa.

* My thanks to Johann Maree, Phil Bonner and Mark Swilling for their comments on an earlier draft of this introduction.

These questions have recently been taken up publicly by the independent union movement in South Africa, and are reflected in the following four papers. The first three contributions, which appeared in the *South African Labour Bulletin* between 1982 and 1983, reflect official union thinking on the issue of relations between unions and political organisations. The fourth paper, written in 1984 but only published in the *Bulletin* in 1985, examines the November 1984 stay-away in the Transvaal. This practical demonstration of successful cooperation between unions (the most powerful of which had previously eschewed such involvement) and community organisations may mark the beginning of a new phase of political unionism in South Africa.

For most of the 1970s the energies of the independent unions were expended mainly on the painstaking task of building up organisational strength on the shop-floor. They wished to avoid a repetition of the experience of the South African Congress of Trade Unions which, as a full participant in the campaigns of the Congress Alliance, had been destroyed in all but name by state repression in the 1960s.

The emphasis on building union strength meant that the major union struggles for most of the decade of the seventies were over elementary rights: to organise, to be recognised and to bargain with management over wages and working conditions. While recognising the connection between economic exploitation and political oppression, the unions held back from full engagement in political struggles outside the work-place arguing that to take up issues which they had little chance of winning at that stage, and thereby risk destruction of the unions, was politically senseless.

Important changes both in the society as a whole and within the union movement at the end of the decade brought the question of union involvement in political action to the forefront of union debates. The wave of protest which swept South Africa's townships from 1976 onwards, followed by the deracialisation of industrial relations and the introduction of labour market reforms for urban Africans, revealed that the struggles of oppressed South Africans could force the state to make certain concessions. But it became equally evident that protest without organisation to sustain it led, at best, to changes which failed to yield substantial or lasting gains for most of the working class.

In the immediate aftermath of the 1976 urban revolts it was widely realised that not only had the independent unions survived for half a decade, but that they constituted the only effective, if still narrowly based, organisations representing South Africa's most oppressed people, the black workers. For some this was a vindication of the policy of political caution; for others it was grounds for greater union involvement in direct political action.

The decade of the 1970s ended with a sharp economic upturn and a surge of worker militancy. This, combined with the state's legitimation of African trade unions, led to a rapid expansion of union membership. In the climate of boom and reform new more overtly political unions mushroomed into existence. In contrast to most existing independent unions, which organised factory by factory on industrial lines and emphasised shop-floor strength, the newcomers favoured general unionism and the mass township meeting. At such meetings the focus would be on problems afflicting all Africans as township residents and not merely or primarily the specific problems facing workers in their factories.

A further development was the emergence in the late 1970s of alternative foci of power to the unions, in the form of multi-class local and (from 1983) national organisations. Following the example of the Port Elizabeth Black Civic Association (PEBCO) in 1979, many of the township based community organisations began organising working class constituencies and succeeded in attracting workers in increasing numbers. A parallel development was the growth of organisation amongst school children and unemployed youth in the black townships. This trend coincided with a shift within most of these residentially based (or 'community') organisations from black conciousness ideology towards a nonracial, democratic ideology. The impact of community organisation amongst urban workers and their families was great enough for some independent unions, in the late 1970s and early 1980s, to feel the need to begin to debate openly their relationship to such organisations.

The issue of union-community cooperation was first raised in a practical way in the western Cape, in 1979, when the Food and Canning Workers' Union (F.C.W.U.) called for and received community support for its boycott of Fatti's and Moni's products. Difficulties were experienced, during this and a number of subsequent commodity boycotts, in the relationship between unions and some of the community based organisations which offered support. Not only did coordination of a campaign often prove problematic, but in some instances disputes arose over the conduct of a boycott: when and where it should be started and called off. The leadership and direction of the unions was sometimes questioned by those who had originally set out only to offer support (see Liz McGregor, 'The Fatti's and Moni's Strike', *S.A.L.B.* V, 6 and 7 (March, 1980). As greater experience was acquired community support for commodity boycotts in some instances strengthened union-community relations, as in the case of the Colgate boycott in 1981, the Rowntrees boycott in 1982 and, most spectacularly, the threatened Simba Chips boycott which immediately preceded the 1984 November stayaway.

With the formation of embryonic organisation around township issues in the late 1970s the demands were made increasingly in the opposite direction: unions were asked by community militants to support campaigns over issues such as rent increases, housing and residential controls, and the boycott of local political elections. When union leaders failed to attend meetings to initiate action on such issues this led to resentment and criticism. However, these calls were often made at short notice: union leaders were sometimes asked to sit on platforms in meetings their unions had not helped organise, with agendas which had not been discussed by their membership. These experiences led to mounting tensions between a number of industrial unions and some of the emerging community organisations in the late 1970s, and to resistance on the part of some unions to participation in community action led by other organisations. However, with the growth of working class participation in community organisations and township based campaigns over rents, bus fares and repressive administration, union leaders found themselves under increasing pressures from within their own organisations to take up the problems of workers in the townships.

These tensions within and between organisations led to discussions about the differences between union and community organisations and how to establish improved relationships between them. Some of these issues were raised in an important article published in the *S.A.L.B.* in July 1982 (VII, 8), entitled 'Search for a Workable Relationship', in which the Food and Canning Workers' Union (F.C.W.U.) set out an approach to union-community cooperation and, by implication, to union involvement in issues beyond the factory.

> Our viewpoint is that a union should not split the struggle of workers in the factory from struggles outside the work-place, on community and political issues. We do not believe that the problems of the workers in

the factories are separate from the problems in the areas where they live. Nor can we ever say that it is no concern of workers that they have no say in the government of the country (p.55).

The F.C.W.U. went on to argue that this did not mean that unions could take up all issues raised in the communities on their own. Such struggles required a different form of organisation:

> ... we do believe that separate forms of organisation are needed for these struggles. A trade union is not a community or political organisation. A union which tries to be a community or political organisation at the same time cannot survive. It can also not afford to neglect the problems and organisation of the workers for wider issues ... (p.55).

The reasons why it was necessary to form different organisations to take up such issues were not only to do with the dangers for unions of state attacks, but also the class composition of the townships and the leadership of community organisations. The membership of the unions, it was argued, comprised only workers, although this class was itself divided in important ways: for example by state racial policies, differences in skill and in terms of the distinctions between migrants and settled urban workers. These divisions were however within a class exploited in common by bosses.

In contrast the constituencies of the community organisations included both workers and the middle classes, groups with sharply opposed interests over the issue of economic exploitation, albeit, in the case of Africans, a shared opposition to racial oppression. Furthermore, leadership within community organisations, it was argued, was dominated by people with educational or language skills not available to ordinary workers, which made it difficult for the latter even to express their particular needs within such organisations, let alone to aspire to control or leadership. While it was acknowledged that the unions themselves had a sprinking of highly educated people with middle class origins in key official positions, it was argued that union practices developed over the decade, such as regular branch and national meetings, had insured that the leadership and officials were directly controlled by workers. Furthermore, official positions in the unions had increasingly been filled by workers who had come up from the shop-floor.

Many of the independent unions doubted whether the community organisations that sprang up in the late 1970s had in fact organised ordinary people within the townships, working class or otherwise. It was widely feared that most organisations claiming to represent their communities in fact comprised small groups of activists with little organisationally grounded support from the mass of residents in their areas. Union-community relationships, they argued, should not be restricted to relationships between leaders, but should rather be forged through the full involvement of the ordinary membership of both types of organisations (*S.A.L.B* VII, 8, pp.56 — 57). Events were to prove that some union leaders had underestimated the extent to which their members were becoming involved in the community based action and the degree of frustration at the lack of union assistance in fighting township issues. Rank and file criticism of union complacency was eventually to induce these leaders to accept joint action with community organisations, notably in the Transvaal in 1984.

Until very recently, unions affiliated to the Federation of South African Trade Unions (FOSATU) were amongst those which were most resistent to involvement with community organisations. FOSATU's official position, set out in Joe Foster's keynote address to congress in 1982 (Reading Fourteen) differs in important respects from that expressed in the F.C.W.U's 'Search for a Workable Relationship'.

Foster's address expresses a concern that involvement with community organisations over nonfactory struggles could entail the loss of working class leadership and direction of such struggles, and expose the unions to state attacks for actions initiated and directed by leaders not subject to worker accountability. Why, it was asked, should workers, who had painstakingly built up their organisations over years of struggle, give over leadership to newly formed community organisations which had no substantial organised base and thus relatively little to lose from confrontations with the state?

An approach which would ensure that the working class maintained the leading role in political struggles without exposing it to opportunistic leadership was to construct a working class movement. The task of such a movement would be to defend workers' specific interests within the existing dispensation, and ensure working class interest would not be subordinated to those of other classes in the event of a multi-class political party coming to power. FOSATU's 1982 congress did however resolve to support progressive organisations in particular community campaigns, but gave no practical guidelines as to how to do this.

FOSATU's policy was influenced by the experience of anti-union state repression following the Durban strikes in 1973 - 74 and the

Soweto uprising in 1976. The leadership in the unions and groupings which were later to form FOSATU had developed a policy of caution towards union involvement in broader political struggles. However the formation and rapid extension of new general unions, the emergence of community based organisations which overtly associated themselves with a broader struggle for 'national' liberation, and a groundswell of interest in broader political involvement within FOSATU's emerging worker leadership forced a reconsideration of official policy. Foster's address represents FOSATU leadership's attempt to come to terms specifically with mounting criticism at its lack of involvement in community issues, and its distancing itself from the African National Congress and the strategic issues of 'national', as against class, liberation. While the address provided a theoretical answer to the criticism that FOSATU was not willing to engage in political struggle, this isolationist approach side-stepped the issue of how in practice the unions were to relate to emerging community organisations within that struggle.

As it turned out, no workers' political organisation was formed by FOSATU, although officially sanctioned political involvement increased, for example on the east Rand over squatter removals, and in Port Elizabeth and Uitenhague in opposition to the tricameral parliamentary elections. FOSATU's official policy was rapidly over-taken by the course of events. By 1983 political questions in South Africa had been redefined by the inauguration of two important multi-class national organisations, the black conciousness National Forum Committee (N.F.C.) and nonracial United Democratic Front (U.D.F.).

The immediate question raised by the formation of the N.F.C. and U.D.F. was whether or not the unions should affiliate to them, and on what basis. These questions were taken up in an interview the General Workers' Union (G.W.U., previously the Western Province General Workers' Union) gave to the *S.A.L.B* in 1983, reprinted here as Reading Fifteen.

The view adopted by the G.W.U. was that the U.D.F., and any other organisation which aimed to combat political oppression in South Africa, should be supported by the union, but that it was not desirable at that stage for the G.W.U. to affiliate to any particular political organisation. This position was endorsed by most of the larger, better organised and more established independent unions at the time, but not by the newly formed regionally based general unions.

One important reason advanced by the G.W.U. was that the members of this union held diverse political opinions despite the fact that all were workers. Affiliation to a single political organisation might meet with the support of some members but could not, as matters stood in the union at that time, accommodate all. Such a move might even lead to conflict and division within the union. Equally, official union identification with particular political organisations might foster divisions between unions. Union unity initiatives, which were making good progress in 1983, might be seriously retarded, if not entirely frustrated. The validity of this argument was forcefully brought home in the ensuing months as, one after another, unions experienced splits in which the issue of political affiliation was central — as a catalyst if not a cause.

Sisa Njikelana's contribution (Reading Sixteen) was written in response to the G.W.U. interview, and puts the case for affiliation to the U.D.F. While this paper was not published under his union's name, Njikelana's views express a position shared by many of the new regional-general unions which, like the South African Allied Workers' Union (SAAWU), decided that it was in the interests of their membership to affiliate to the U.D.F.

It was mainly from the regional-general unions that the criticism of union avoidance of political issues had for some time been strongly voiced. These unions argued that the workers' struggle in the factory and in the township was indivisible and that unions had an obligation to take up community issues. It was 'economistic' and 'reformist' for unions to restrict themselves to factory issues. This position was connected with a view about the class and racial nature of the society. It was held that racial oppression in South Africa was indispensible to the maintenance of the system of economic exploitation; that the principal antagonism in the society was between the oppressed black masses and the privileged white elite. Hence priority should be given to the struggle for national liberation. The release from class exploitation would follow.

These views were influenced by the manner in which the new general unions organised. The large open township meeting as an organisational tactic promotes issues and interests common to all classes of township dwellers, and not specifically the interests of workers. In the period preceding the formation of the U.D.F., many of the new general unions became increasingly involved in actions over rents, transport and local elections. Their approach to the issue of the 'indivisibility' of work-place and community struggles was to attempt to build indivisible organisations straddling both spheres. Inevitably this resulted in the neglect of shop-floor organisation, leaving these unions exposed to the full force of recession and state attacks from mid-1982 onwards. The rapid decline of regional-general unionism from 1983 onwards, through shrinkage of membership, splits and infighting, dramatically vindicated the warning given two years earlier that a union which tried to be a community or political organisation at the same time would not survive as a union.

Thus when in late 1984 the Congress of South African Students in the Transvaal called upon workers for assistance in their year-long struggle against the bantu education authorities, their appeal had to be directed at the industrial unions. The regional-general unions, as fellow affiliates of the U.D.F., would be expected to support the students' call, but given their weak organisational base, they could not be relied upon to mobilise workers on a significant scale. Only the independent industrial unions in the Transvaal, and especially affiliates of FOSATU, had the organisational depth and regional spread needed by student and civic organisations to mount a mass demonstration in the black working class townships of metropolitan Transvaal.

Reading Seventeen provides an account and assessment of the November stayaway, examining it against the background of crisis and conflict in the townships in the preceding months. The article argues that FOSATU's entry into joint action with student and civic organisations in the stayaway was made possible by the overlapping membership of these organisations and a growing congruence of objectives amongst their members over basic problems facing workers and their families in the townships: rising rents, transport costs, bantu education and an inefficient, corrupt and repressive local government system.

It argues that the Transvaal region of FOSATU was prodded into joint action with student and civic organisations by mounting criticism from within FOSATU's rank and file of the organisation's lack of political involvement; criticism which reached crisis proportions with the split in the Metal and Allied Workers' Union, FOSATU's largest affiliate, on the east Rand in mid-1984. This led to a growing appreciation amongst FOSATU's leaders of the fact that its own members were becoming increasingly involved in townships campaigns, and that to stand aside was to risk losing them to organisations more willing to take up their grievances outside the work-place. The decision to endorse some form of combined union-community action in the

Transvaal came after intense debates within FOSATU's leadership over problems in the townships, especially the issues of rents, and police and army presence in the Vaal Triangle.

What distinguished the action taken by the Transvaal unions in support of the students and residents in the townships was that the union and community organisations came together as independent organisations and forged a plan of joint action with specific objectives, to take place over an agreed period of time. The risks to the unions could thus be weighed up and minimised. This differed sharply from the political unionism typical in the recent past of the regional-general unions which saw themselves both as unions and community organisations, and made no clear distinction between the needs of their members as workers and the needs of the wider community. The action differed, too, from that of some industrial unions which advocated political abstention and also from the go-it-alone approach adopted by FOSATU only two years earlier.

The particular form of action taken in November 1984 — staying away from work — should be distinguished from the more general issue of cooperation between unions and community based civic, youth and other organisations. The costs of the stayaway were high for FOSATU — 5000 to 6000 workers at the Sasol plants in Secunda were dismissed and some union officials were detained.* Such action will be resorted to in future only after careful assessment. Nevertheless, as a model for union-community cooperation the November stayaway may herald a new and positive phase of political unionism, and, indeed, of nonracial democratic struggle in South Africa.

April 1985

*After a tough struggle the union however managed to compel Sasol to re-employ seventy percent of the dismissed workers.

Reading 14. (1982)

The Workers' Struggle — Where Does FOSATU Stand?*

The following is the full text of the keynote address, given by the FOSATU General Secretary, Joe Foster at the FOSATU congress in April 1982

Introduction

Three years ago — almost to the day — we met in this very same place to form FOSATU. Today we have set as our theme — the workers' struggle — in a serious attempt to further clarify where we as worker representatives see FOSATU to stand in this great struggle.

That we are discussing this theme today and resolutions that relate to it is a justification of our original decision to form FOSATU and shows how seriously we take the new challenges that face us three years after that decision. Clearly any such discussion raises many very important issues and the purpose of this paper is to try and bring together these issues in ways that will help guide our discussions.

*First published in S.A.L.B., VII, 8 (July, 1982), pp. 67 — 86.

It is the task of this congress to give a clear policy direction to our actions between now and the next congress — we believe that the issues raised in this paper are crucial to a political understanding of our policies and what we hope to achieve by them. We also believe that it is the task of congress to add and modify the views expressed through open and serious debate.

FOSATU — an assessment

In the three years that FOSATU has existed there is little doubt that we have achieved a lot in terms of growth and gains made for our members. However, I believe that our greatest achievement is the fact that at this congress we are determined to respond to new challenges and set new directions if this is necessary. We could have made this congress a great occasion open to parade our successes and hide our failures, however, we have chosen otherwise.

We have chosen to keep it closed and to once again self critically examine our position. I believe that this shows our determination to take the great militancy of our members and use this to build a just and fair society controlled by workers.

We have no intention of becoming self satisfied trade unionists incapable of giving political direction to the workers' struggle.

Yet we would only be dreaming of change if we do not strengthen and build our unions into large and effective organisations.

At our inaugural congress we stressed certain policies and set ourselves the task of establishing a tight federation of nonracial, national, industrial unions, based on shop-floor strength. We set ourselves the task of sharing resources between affiliates and of building up an educational programme. We further stressed our independence in regard to party political organisations and from international trade union organisations.

Now it is not my task to assess every success and failure of FOSATU. There are reports tabled that will allow delegates to draw their own conclusions. However, it is important to make certain assessments in order to go further and identify why we need to clarify our position and set new and clearer directions.

I believe that we have to ask ourselves two crucial questions:

● Have we established an effective organisation based on shop-floor strength and national nonracial industrial unions?
● Has our organisational activity developed worker leadership that can give guidance and direction to all workers?

In answer to both questions it would be wrong to expect a positive answer after only three years. However, we should be able to assess if we are going in the right direction.

Clearly in regard to the first question we made progress — it could even be said to be considerable progress — with NAAWU, N.U.T.W. and MAWU beginning to be a significant presence in major industries. However, there is a long way to go in these cases and more so in those of other affiliates.

It is, however, the second question that poses more problems. As the unions grow and are faced with new challenges it becomes crucial that the leadership knows what direction it is going in. What are the organisational strategies that are necessary as the unions become larger and more effective? What dangers to worker militancy lie in recognition and stability?

As these unions grow then the question is what role do they play in the wider political arena. There has been a great upsurge in political activity over the last few years and many different political groups are looking to the union movement to state its position. We must be sure our organisation and our leadership can confidently state its position and continue to organise in the way that will strengthen and not weaken that position.

The purpose of this paper is to set out the issues we should debate if we are to meet the challenges.

Working class movement

As a trade union federation we are clearly concerned with workers and their aspirations. If we were to think in terms of our members only, we would have a very limited political role. If, however, we are thinking more widely of the working class then we have to examine very much more carefully what our political role is. In particular we need to look at this role in the South African context.

If we look at the advanced industrial countries then we see what can be called working class movements. There are a number of different organisations — trade unions, cooperatives, political parties and newspapers — that all see themselves as linked to the working class and furthering its interests. These working class movements are, therefore, powerful social forces in those societies.

In the capitalist economies these working class movements have power and organisation, yet politically the working class is still subject to policies and practices that are clearly against their interests as the activities of Thatcher and Reagan show. This is increasingly leading to intense political and organisational activity to give the working class and the union movement a clearer direction so as to gather together the working class movement into a force that will more definitely put workers in control of their own destiny.

In the socialist countries similar battles are being fought. Whilst social, political and economic relations in these countries have been greatly altered and there have been great achievements to the benefit of workers, there is still the need for workers themselves to control their own destiny. Solidarity was not struggling to restore capitalism in Poland, its struggle was to establish more democratic workers' control over *their* socialist society.

Now my purpose in briefly looking at the working class movement in the advanced industrial countries was twofold.

Firstly, so that we can be clear that worker activities such as strikes and protests do not in themselves mean that a working class movement or working class politics exist. These latter are more than that — they are large scale organisations with a clear social and political identity as the working class.

Secondly, I wished to show that the pure size of working class organisation is itself no guarantee that workers will control their own destiny. In fact, as the struggle of Solidarity shows, even the fact that a country is said to be socialist does not guarantee that workers control their own destiny.

In short it could be said that workers must build a powerful and effective movement if they are to succeed in advancing their interests against some very hostile forces, but they must also ensure that this movement is able to take a clear political direction.

The experience of the great working class movements in the advanced industrial countries is a very important guide and lesson to us. However, it cannot provide all our answers. Firstly, in South Africa we cannot talk of a working class movement as we have defined it above. Secondly, whilst there is undoubtedly a large and growing working class its power is only a potential power since as yet it has no definite social identity of itself as working class.

The questions we should therefore address ourselves to, are:

● Why has no working class movement emerged?
● What are the prospects for such a movement emerging?
● What role can FOSATU play in such a process?

Political history and workers

It is not possible in a paper such as this to deal fully with all the developments in South Africa's history that have led to the non-existence of a workers' movement in South Africa.

South Africa's history has been characterised by great repression and the major political and ideological *instrument* for this repression has been *racism*. Yet the major effect of this repression has been to establish very rapidly a large capitalist economy.

Racism, and the violence and injustice associated with it, are very stark and clear forms of repression. Alongside this only about five to ten percent of the population has ever had the franchise. Clearly, therefore, there is a very identifiable oppressive force and the major political task of the oppressed peoples has always been to attack that oppressive and racist regime.

So what had developed in South Africa is a very powerful tradition of popular or populist politics. The role of the great political movements such as the A.N.C. and the Congress Alliance has been to mobilise the masses against the repressive minority regime. In such a situation mass mobilisation is essential so as to challenge the legitimacy of the state both internally and internationally.

Where virtually all the population is voteless and oppressed by a racial minority then a great alliance of all classes is both necessary and a clear political strategy. Furthermore, building such an alliance was a great task.

The A.N.C. had to overcome racial division so as to rise above the divisive racism of the oppressors. They had to deal with opportunistic tribal leadership, to organise thousands upon thousands of people and they had to do all this in the face of harsh repression by the state. In achieving this there is little wonder that the A.N.C. rose to be one of the great liberation movements in Africa.

In this context it is also easier to see and understand why the trade union movement acted in a particular way. The racial divisions in the working class, linked as they were to other objective factors, made it possible for capital to quite quickly suppress any serious challenge to their supremacy. It was possible to create the conditions that led to a politically tame union movement and thereby forced more militant and progressive unions to bear the brunt of state action, which in turn affected the politics of these unions.

Furthermore, at all times there were occasions when workers resisted by strike action, protest and organisation. Yet this by itself cannot constitute a working class movement. Whilst the unions were often prominent they were always small and weakly organised both nationally and in the factories. They could not provide an organisational base for a working class movement as we have defined it above.

Progressive and militant unions were continually the subject of state harassment, but, never managed to seriously challenge capital nationally or on a sustained basis. As a result, the effective political role of progressive unions and of worker activity was to provide a crucial part of any popular struggle and that was to give it its 'worker voice'. No mass popular movement can be effective or be seen to be effective if it does not have some worker involvement or representation. By the 1950s with the growth of South Africa's industry and the size of the working class, the need to include workers became essential and as a result SACTU became an important element of the Congress Alliance.

In these circumstances the progressive trade unions became part of the popular struggle against oppression. They did not and probably could not have provided the base for working class organisation. There is of course no doubt that their activities have been very, very important in creating the conditions that led to the emergence in the last ten to fifteen years of the present progressive trade unions. However, these unions are operating in a different environment.

Workers and their struggle became very much part of the wider popular struggle. An important effect of this development was that capital could hide behind the curtains of apartheid and racism. The political energies of the oppressed masses and of international critics were focused on the apartheid regime and its abhorrent racism. The government and Afrikanerdom became the focus of attack. In fact the position was such that learned liberal academics saw in capital the great hope for change despite the fact that capital and its lackeys were undoubtedly the major beneficiaries of apartheid.

Capital did its very best to keep in the political background and as a result this helped prevent the creation of capital's logical political opposite which is a working class political movement. However, of crucial significance was that capital was growing rapidly and changing its very nature into a more monopolistic, technologically advanced and concentrated form. Its links internationally were also growing as was its importance for international capital.

We find, therefore, that behind the scenes of the great battle between the apartheid regime and its popular opponents, the capitalist economy has flourished and capital emerges now as a powerful and different force. Capital:

- is highly concentrated in truly gigantic corporations;
- has access to international information on how to deal with working class challenges;
- has access to the state's security information;
- is able to rapidly share and assess information;
- is able to use the objective circumstances in its favour such as unemployment and influx control to weaken worker organisations;
- is now an important part of international capital and cannot, therefore, be lightly discarded by international capital;
- is able to hide behind politics and as a result can hide its sophisticated attacks on labour because no one is paying any attention.

Yet as the upsurge of popular political activity emerged again in the 1970s some of its new forms such as black conciousness also place little emphasis on capital. So there is a growing gap between popular politics and the power of capital and as a result the potential power of workers. It is in this context we should look at the likelihood of a working class politics emerging.

Need for a working class movement

The growing size of the economy and the dramatic changes taking place have to take into account the speed and manner in which the economy has developed. In discussing the working class movements in the advanced industrial economies, we have to bear in mind that in most cases they took about 100 years or more to fully develop. Industry started first by building larger and larger factories, and bringing people together in these factories.

The new capitalists had to struggle politically with the older ruling classes over labour, taxation policy, tariff protection, political rights and political power.

Then mechanisation became more important and there was a definite change in production processes. As this happened the skilled workers who had usually given leadership to the craft unions found themselves in a very difficult position. As a result leadership problems in the organisation of trade unions and the political environment, developed in a complex and relatively slow way.

In South Africa this has been condensed into sixty to seventy years and from the outset large scale capitalist enterprise dominated. The birth of capitalism here was brutal and quick. The industrial proleteriat was ripped from its land in the space of a few decades. At present capitalist production massively dominates all other production. There are no great landlords on their agricultural estates and there is no significant peasantry or collective agriculture. Virtually everyone depends for all or part of their income on industry or capitalist agriculture.

The working class have experienced a birth of fire in South Africa and they constitute the major objective political force opposed to the state and capital. There is no significant petty bourgeoisie or landed class with an economic base in our society.

In the economy capital and labour are the major forces, yet politically the struggle is being fought elsewhere.

The existence of this industrial proletariat and the rapid transformation of capital are very powerful reasons why a working class movement could rapidly develop in South Africa. There are a number of factors that will assist in the organisation of workers:

- the great concentration of capital has also meant a greater concentration of workers. These workers generally have a higher level of basic education and skills than before and their links with the past are all but broken so that more and more a worker identity is emerging;
- this is reinforced by the sophisticated strategies that are designed to 'deracialise' industry and some other areas of society. The effect of

this is to divide off certain privileged members of black society leaving workers at the bottom of the privilege pile;

● the concentration of workers in industry has also concentrated them in the great urban townships;

● the particular structure of the South African economy with its high degree of state involvement, price controls and heavy dependence on international markets has made it a very sensitive economy. As a consequence attempts to 'buy off' the major part of the working class will fail. It is more likely that as some readjustments of privilege are attempted it will have to be workers that suffer through inflation and lack of basic commodities;

● the above factors and South Africa's international economic importance are likely to force capital into the political open and as a consequence develop a worker response;

● although capital can at present hide behind apartheid it is also the case that if workers organise widely enough they can get great support from the international labour movement. Also international public opinion has to be very carefully watched by capital because both international and South African capital are dependent on their links with the rest of the world.

These then are some of the important factors that are favourable to the development of a working class movement in South Africa. However, this does not mean that this will automatically happen. To understand this, we need to look at the present political environment more carefully both to see the present political tendencies and to establish why some active leadership role should be played by the unions and FOSATU in particular.

Workers need their own organisation to counter the growing power of capital and to further protect their own interests in the wider society. However, it is only workers who can build this organisation and in doing this they have to be clear on what they are doing.

As the numbers and importance of workers grow then all political movements have to try and win the loyalty of workers because they are such an important part of society. However, in relation to the particular requirements of worker organisation, mass parties and popular political organisations have definite limitations which have to be clearly understood by us.

We should distinguish between the international position and internal political activity. Internationally, it is clear that the A.N.C. is the major force with sufficient presence and stature to be a serious challenge to the South African state and to secure the international condemnation of the present regime. To carry out this struggle is a difficult task because South Africa has many friends who are anxious to ensure that they can continue to benefit from her wealth. The fact that the A.N.C. is also widely accepted internally also strengthens its credibility internationally. However, this international presence of the A.N.C. which is essential to a popular challenge to the present regime places certain strategic limitations on the A.N.C., namely:

● to reinforce its international position it has to claim credit for all forms of internal resistance, no matter what the political nature of such resistance. There is, therefore, a tendency to encourage undirected opportunistic political activity;

● it has to locate itself between the major international interests. To the major western powers it has to appear as anti-racist but not as anti-capitalist. For the socialist east it has to be at least neutral in the super power struggle and certainly it could not appear to offer a serious socialist alternative to that of those countries as the response to Solidarity illustrates. These factors must seriously affect its relationship to workers;

● accordingly, the A.N.C. retains its tradition of the 1950s and 1960s when, because there was no serious alternative political path, it rose to be a great populist liberation movement. To retain its very important international position it has to retain its political position as a popular mass movement. This clearly has implications for its important military activities.

Internally we also have to examine carefully what is happening politically. As a result of the state's complete inability to effect reform and the collapse of their bantustan policy, they are again resorting to open repression. Since 1976 in particular this has given new life to popular resistance and once again the drive for unity against a repressive state has reaffirmed the political tradition of populism in South Africa. Various political and economic interests gather together in the popular front in the tradition of the A.N.C. and the Congress Alliance.

In the present context all political activity, provided it is anti-state, is of equal status. In the overall resistance to this regime, this is not necessarily incorrect. In fact without such unity and widespread resistance it would not be possible by means of popular mass movements to seriously challenge the legitimacy of the present regime.

However, the really essential question is how worker organisation relates to this wider political struggle. I have argued above that the objective political and economic conditions facing workers are now markedly different to that of twenty years ago.

Yet there does not seem to be clarity on this within the present union movement. There are good reasons for this lack of clarity.

As a result of repression most worker leadership is relatively inexperienced and this is made worse by the fact that their unions are organisationally weak and unstable. The union struggles fought against capital have mostly been against isolated companies so that the wider struggles against capital at an industry or national level have not been experienced. This also means that workers and their leadership have not experienced the strength of large scale worker organisation nor the amount of effort required to build and democratise such large scale organisation. Again state repression and the wider political activity reinforce previous experiences where the major function of workers was to reinforce and contribute to a popular struggle.

Politically, therefore, most unions and their leadership lack confidence as a worker leadership, they see their role as part of a wider struggle but are unclear on what is required for the worker struggle. Generally, the question of building an effective worker organisation is not dealt with and political energy is spent in establishing unity across a wide front.

However, such a position is clearly a great strategic error that will weaken if not destroy worker organisation both now and in the future. All the great and successful popular movements have had as their aim the overthrow of oppressive — most often colonial — regimes. But these movements cannot and have not in themselves been able to deal with the particular and fundamental problems of workers. Their task is to remove regimes that are regarded as illegitimate and unacceptable by the majority.

It is, therefore, essential that workers must strive to build their own powerful and effective organisation even whilst they are part of the wider popular struggle. This organisation is necessary to protect and further worker interests and to ensure that the popular movement is not hijacked by elements who will in the end have no option but to turn against their worker supporters.

Broad and complicated matters have been covered and it is difficult to summarise them even further. However, I shall attempt to do so in order for us to try and examine the role that FOSATU can play in this struggle.

1. Worker resistance such as strike action helps build worker organisation but by itself it does not mean that there is a working class movement.
2. There has not been and is not a working class movement in South Africa.
3. The dominant political tradition in South Africa is that of the popular struggle against an oppressive, racist minority regime.
4. This tradition is reasserting itself in the present upsurge of political activity.
5. However, the nature of economic development in South Africa has brutally and rapidly created a large industrial proletariat.
6. The size and development of this working class is only matched by its mirror image which is the dramatic growth and transformation of industrial capital.
7. Before it is too late workers must strive to form their own powerful and effective organisation within the wider popular struggle.

FOSATU's objective

From what has been said we believe that FOSATU must set itself the task of giving leadership and direction to the building of a working class movement. Our efforts so far have equipped us to do this. Our organisation is nationally based, located in the major industries and the militancy of our members has generally developed a politically aware and self critical leadership.

FOSATU as a trade union federation will clearly not constitute the working class movement nor would this place FOSATU in opposition to the wider political struggle or its major liberation movement.

FOSATU's task will be to build the effective organisational base for workers to play a major political role as workers. Our task will be to create an identity, confidence and political presence for worker organisation. The conditions are favourable for this task and its necessity is absolute.

We need have no fear of critics — our task will contribute to the wider liberation struggle and will also ensure that the worker majority is able to protect and further its interests. Ours is a fundamental political task and those who ask of workers their political support without allowing them the right to build their own organisation must answer for *their* real motives.

As was said above, capital has transformed itself and has a greater capacity to tolerate worker organisation because it is now more powerful and better able to deal with a worker challenge. Also because of its absolutely central position it will have the full support of the state in its actions and in the bitter struggles that are to come.

This requires a very much greater effort to establish worker organisation and requires thorough organisational work and ceaseless mobilization of our members. The growth and transformation of capital has created the very preconditions for large scale worker organisation.

Our concrete tasks and challenges

If we see the above as our general direction then we must deal with concrete tasks and challenges.

Organisation

What is crucial in organisation is the quality of that organisation — the quality that gives it its overall political direction and capability. As is clear from the experience of the advanced industrial countries that we looked at earlier, organisational size alone is not enough, yet without size there can be no effective counter to capital.

Broadly one can distinguish three factors that affect the quality of worker organisation — the structure of organisational strength and decision making; the location of organisational strength and the political qualities of its leadership structures.

Structure

The structure of an organisation should be such that it correctly locates worker strength and makes best use of that strength.

FOSATU's experience in this has been very important. Our

organisation is built up from the factory floor. As a result, the base of the organisation is located where workers have most power and authority and that is where production takes place. This also has the effect of democratising our structures since worker representatives always participate from a position of strength and authority in the organisation. By stressing factory bargaining we involve our shop stewards in central activities and through this they gain experience as worker leadership. It should be said that they do battle every day.

These factory based structures are the key to transforming pure quantity of members into a flexible and effective quality. Capital's hostility to factory organisation forces members and shop stewards to struggle continuosly or else to have their organisation crushed.

At the union level FOSATU has attempted to build broad industrial unions on a national basis. We, in effect, have one affiliate per industry. We have chosen industrial unions because of the organisational advantages we gain in our struggle against capital. However, FOSATU's role is to link these industrial unions into a tight federation that is based on common policy and a sharing of resources. Our aim is to keep a unity of purpose among affiliates at all levels of their organisation.

Our task in the three years to come must be to consolidate and develop factory organisation, a national presence for our unions and to reassert unity of purpose among affiliates.

The structures we are developing are an essential basis for effective and democratic organisation and are the basis for greater worker participation in and control over production.

Location

The question of location is closely related to structure. Without correct structures then the location of one's organisational strength is not as important.

We must accept that it will take many years to organise all workers and at present that should not be our aim. Our present aim must be to locate our organisation strategically. We need to look at the location of our organisational strength in relation to the industry, geographic area and the points at which we can most effectively carry our collective bargaining.

Our major affiliates should be located in the major industries. Within these industries we must become a substantial presence by carefully building our organisation in major factories, companies and areas.

Geographically we must clearly aim to be a national presence both as FOSATU and as the affiliates. Our organisation should be able to dominate major industrial areas. By doing this we create the major means whereby worker organisation can play a significant if not dominant role in the communities that surround these industrial areas.

Successful collective bargaining requires that the organisation is capable of mobilising its members behind demands. Thus far our unions have only really been able to mobilise at the plant level. However, the experience of NAAWU which is exceptional in FOSATU has shown what can be gained by them if we are to serve our members. We must be able to mobilise across factories and in local areas across industries. We must see industry bargaining or regional bargaining not as something to be feared but as the logical extension of our present structures and practices.

Worker leadership
Here we must be immediately clear that we are not talking about leadership in the sense that it is usually discussed — which is in terms of individuals and 'great men'. This view of leadership is not what is important for a worker organisation. What we are interested in is the elected representatives of workers and the officials they appoint to work within the organisation.

We are interested in how the leadership is elected or appointed: who it is answerable to and how this accountability is achieved: how experienced leadership is, how it gains this experience and how it develops the means of training and educating leadership so that it remains self critical and politically active.

The challenges facing worker leadership are undoubtedly different to other leadership groups. For worker leadership in a capitalist society, their everyday struggle is related to their job and therefore their wage and therefore their very ability to survive. The most appropriate comparison is with that of the guerilla fighter who has to develop the strength to resist daily, the knowledge of his terrain that will give him every tactical advantage and the support of those for whom he is struggling. Probably of most importance, because both the worker leaders and the güerilla are fighting a powerful enemy, is the development of a sense of when to advance and when to retreat.

These skills are not easily learnt and not easily replaced. So worker leadership cannot be wasted by opportunistic and overly adventuristic actions.

We are also concerned with worker leadership in a wider arena than only that of the union struggle. Giving leadership to the working class requires an organisational base. Without this base, then the poverty and the lack of education, information and time that workers are struggling against will be the very factors which will force workers to surrender leadership of the community to other strata in society.

Our aim is to use the strength of factory based organisation to allow workers to play an effective role in the community. Worker leadership will have:

● gained invaluable political experience from their factory struggles;
● organisation and resources behind them;
● organisational structures and location that will give them localised strength;
● the ability to speak with a clear and democratically established worker mandate.

The points made here should be our guide for action and we have a long way to go in building a larger leadership structure that has the political qualities of clarity, determination, discipline and the ability to be self critical.

Working class identity
The task of organisation outlined above and, more important, the quality of the organisation will absorb most of our energies in the next three years, and is, therefore, our major priority. Yet to give leadership in the building of a working class movement we must start to build a greater identity for worker organisation.

In a very important way the building of effective trade unions does create a worker identity. However, there is the danger that the unions become preoccupied with their members and ignore workers generally. By establishing a clear political direction we can avoid this.

One answer that is often proposed is to be involved in community activities. That FOSATU should be involved in community activities is correct since our members form the major part of those communities. However, as we have argued above we must do so from an organisational base if we are truly to be an effective worker presence.

Without this base, it is more likely that we will destroy a clear worker identity since workers will be entirely swamped by the powerful tradition of popular politics that we examined earlier.

It is also the case that there has emerged into our political debate an empty and misleading political category called 'the community'. All communities are composed of different interest groups and for a worker organisation to ally itself with every community group or action would be suicide for worker organisation. Under the surface of unity, community politics is partisan and divided. FOSATU cannot possibly ally itself to all the political groups that are contesting this arena. Neither can it ally itself with particular groups. Both paths will destroy the unity of its own worker organisation.

This simple political fact is the reason for one of our founding resolutions. It has nothing to do with not wanting to be involved in politics. Our whole existence is political and we welcome that. Our concern is with the very essence of politics and that is the relation between the major classes in South Africa, being capital and labour.

We need to state this more clearly and understand it ourselves more clearly. There is also no doubt that we must take our own newspaper very much more seriously as it can be a major instrument in building a worker identity.

At the level of organisation we have a sound base on which to work. Probably our main problem has been that we did not clearly state why we had chosen certain structures and what could be achieved by them.

As our political clarity and confidence grows, so we must state our position more clearly in our meetings, among our members and through our own newspaper.

Unity in the labour movement

Our first step must be to address ourselves to unity in the labour movement. If we are to create a working class movement then trade union unity has to be dealt with very early on in our struggle. Because we take working class politics seriously we must take trade union unity seriously.

At present there is a very great momentum to unity in the labour movement and we have to carefully consider and analyse what is happening.

The first point to understand it that all the unions involved in the talks are relatively weak in relation to their potential — some appallingly so. Many are too easily fooled by their own propaganda and the great interest shown by everyone in believing that they are now a strong force.

Furthermore, with a few exceptions (mostly in FOSATU), these unions are not yet a national or an industrial presence. Their strengths lie in isolated factories and very few have any real geographic concentration. As a result, both the leadership of these unions and their membership have no clear conception of the organised power of capital nor for that matter of its weakness. There is no real experience of the difficulties of large scale worker organisation nor of the difficulties in building democratic worker structures. The bulk of the present leadership has no clear conception of the needs of worker struggle or of a worker dominated society. There is all too often a contradiction between the political position and organisational practice. Radical political positions are adopted but the organisational practice makes little headway into the power of capital nor is it effectively democratic. A number of factors result from this — often capital is attacked in the 'abstract' by making it all powerful and accordingly seeing an attack on the state as the only answer, or political energies are spent in widespread campaigns. Actual worker organisation and advance is left weak and based on sporadic upsurges rather than on organisational strength.

As a consequence of these factors it is not possible for people to draw any distinction between worker struggle and popular struggle let alone understand the relation between the two in South Africa. The unity talks are therefore conceived of as being within the wider popular struggle and as another area where anti-state unity can be achieved. A formal unity rather than a working unity against capital is therefore seen as the prime object.

There are broadly speaking three forms of unity to the union movement at present and we should look at each fairly carefully.

'**Ad hoc unity**': this is what has occurred at present where unity is issue-located and there are attempts to take a common stand. At present this unity is significant in that it creates unity out of apparent disunity. However, its significance will rapidly decline. Such ad hoc unity can only achieve anything on specific issues and it is inevitably forced to take more and more concerted and concrete actions unless it merely wants to be the source of endless press statements. Such further actions require a more permanent organisational link.

'United front unity': here the organisations remain autonomous but they set up a permanent platform of contact. Some people seem to see the solidarity committees as such a platform. However, although this provides a more definite organisational link, considerable new problems are posed. Again the movement is towards more and more significant gestures of protest and the question now posed is how are decisions to be taken and on what mandate. Does each organisation have an equal vote or is voting by size? If decisions are on a consensus basis — then on what mandate? Should each organisation get a formal mandate on each issue and if they don't, how representative of rank and file membership is each decision? Is there not a greater than usual danger of decisions being taken by a few officials who have easy access to the meetings?

A permanent organisational link requires a process for making decisions that is democratic and equitable. Furthermore, if solidarity actions are to be successful they require organisational coordination — this in turn requires the power to sanction. How can this be done if participants are entirely autonomous?

A further step in this type of unity can be a 'loose federation' such as TUCSA, where the unions are now all in the same federal organisation and the symbolism of unity is far greater. However, such a federal body — not being based on any clear principles — is unlikely to generate working unity as it would contend with numerous problems of jurisdiction between unions and it is unlikely that organisational rationalisation could take place without firm policies and particular structures.

In fact 'united front unity', with or without a loose federation, can destroy the hope of greater unity by creating unresolved differences and no acceptable way of resolving these.

'Disciplined unity': this requires common political purpose, binding policy on affiliates and close working links based on specific organisational structures.

If such a federation is based on industrial unions then FOSATU is the closest to being an example of such 'disciplined unity' — in the present circumstances.

If the federation were not based on an industrial structure but on a regional one, then it is more difficult to set out its working structures since there is no clear experience of how this would work. However, there is no doubt that some allowance would have to be made for industrial considerations and the industrial organisation of capital. In FOSATU we have argued that industrial unions in a 'tight federation' allow for maximum flexibility and efficacy.

It is clear from this that unity means little unless these factors are taken into account. To talk lightly of unity is to keep it within the framework of ad hoc or 'united front unity'. The effectiveness of such unity would rapidly disappear. So if that is what is meant by unity we have to imply certain possible motives of its proponents:

- inexperience and lack of thought on the matter;
- political expediency whereby this unity is for specific limited ends of embarrassing certain organisations;
- a preoccupation with popular politics and a lack of commitment to the building of a working class political position.

However, if we in FOSATU are to take our objective seriously and that objective is the building of a working class movement then we have to take unity very seriously. Clearly by unity we should strive for 'disciplined unity' since it is only such unity that can possibly meet our objective.

We must ourselves work out a programme for unity and on the basis of that programme we should not hesitate to attack those who are impeding the development of a working class movement.

Conclusion

The issues that have been covered in this paper are important and complicated — they are the basis for an understanding of the true nature of the workers' struggle in South Africa and the political role our organisation must play in that struggle.

We believe that in FOSATU we have a firm base on which to build organisationally. Our task in the three years to come is to firmly commit ourselves to a working class political position. With this greater political understanding we must:

- consolidate our organisational stuctures;
- give guidance and leadership in the building of a large working class movement in South Africa;
- seek out comrades and allies who will join us in this struggle;
- and in this way make our fundamental contribution to the libera-

tion of the oppressed people of South Africa.

In doing this we must all be clear that we shall never be so petty as to insist on our organisation's name as the only one in the trade union movement which can carry out this task. It is what the organisation does that is important — not what it is called. Yet equally, we shall never be so politically foolish as to abandon the worker struggle.

Reading 15. (1983)

General Workers' Union on the United Democratic Front*

The South African Labour Bulletin interviewed the general secretary of the General Workers' Union (G.W.U.) on his attitude to the United Democratic Front (U.D.F.). The following preamble from the G.W.U. explains the context in which the union felt it necessary to clarify these views publicly. The preamble is followed by the interview.

Preamble

Amidst the controversy surrounding the position of many unions with regard to the U.D.F., the G.W.U. feels that it is important that our position and views on this issue are clear. In addition, we believe that debate of this nature is healthy within and between progressive organisations.

This controversy has involved much criticism. We do not see criticism as necessarily negative. Some criticism may be based on a detailed understanding of and disagreement with our reasons for not affiliating to the U.D.F. This merely reflects the fact that, quite predictably, different outlooks on political issues do exist within

* First published in a more extended from in *S.A.L.B.* IX, 2 (November, 1983), pp. 47 — 62.

the democratic movement. Some criticism has, however, been based on a distortion of our position. Perhaps this is due in part to the fact that there has not been enough detailed publication of our reasons for not affiliating to the U.D.F.

We take issue with claims and resulting criticisms that we do not support the U.D.F. or that we are 'not interested in politics'. The interview with our general secretary answers these allegations in detail. We stress again what we have repeatedly and publicly stated, that we support any organisation opposing the new constitution and other laws which deny democracy to the majority of South Africans. Our support obviously extends to the U.D.F. We have stated our willingness to participate jointly in campaigns and we give our general support in a variety of ways.

Neither do we say 'we will never join the U.D.F.', a view attributed to us in some reports. We do have real difficulties, however, in affiliating as a single workers' organisation to the U.D.F. One possible scenario for the future, mentioned in the interview, is that of a national union federation affiliating to a national political body. It must be emphasised once again however, that we are an organisation which acts on mandates from our membership. As such this kind of unity would have to be one called for by the rank and file members. As stated in the interview, a national union federation may provide workers with the necessary support to participate in a multi-class organisation. Participation of workers on the ground rather than through an alliance merely 'at the top' would still be imperative.

We put our views forward in the hope of clarifying the present misunderstanding and encouraging discussion.

Interview

Why has the General Workers' Union decided not to affiliate to the United Democratic Front?

The first point, which we've stated repeatedly, is that we are committed to supporting any organisation which opposes the constitutional proposals and the Koornhof Bills, and the U.D.F. would obviously be primary amongst those organisations. We are also committed to the ideal of joint campaigns with the U.D.F. in opposing the bills and the constitution. But we don't see our way clear to affiliating to the U.D.F. Our difficulties there relate to two broad issues. The first concerns the structures of many of the other organisations that are affiliated to the U.D.F., relative to the structure of a trade union. These structures are very distinct and critically different. Our second major area of difficulty relates to the essentially single class nature, working class nature, of trade unions, relative to the multi-class nature of the U.D.F. and of many of the organisations affiliated to the U.D.F.

What are the essential differences in structure between the General Workers' Union and other trade unions on the one hand, and many of the organisations affiliated to the U.D.F. on the other hand, and why do you think those differences present obstacles to affiliation?

The answer to that question is long and complicated. It's relatively simple, difficult as that has proved to be in practice, for one union to affiliate to another union, because trade unions to all intents and purposes have identical structures. They all have factory structures, so that one union can fairly easily lock into another union at all levels of both organisations. This is simply not the case with a great many of the organisations united under the banner of the U.D.F. To take two concrete examples from the western Cape: the Ecumenical Action Group called TEAM, and the Detainees' Parents Support Committee. The former is a grouping of progressive priests, and the latter is a grouping of individuals dedicated to opposing detention, and providing support for those in detention. Let me be clear from the outset that both of these are laudable and necessary ventures, but neither bear any similarity whatsoever to the structure of a union. The same can be said in varying degrees of a great number of other organisations affiliated to the U.D.F., all the youth and student bodies, for example.

The critical feature that all these organisations have in common, as far as we can see, is that they are primarily organisations of activists. To say they are organisations of activists is not intended as a slight in any way, and we believe that there is a great need for this type of organisation in South Africa. But we still insist that they bear no similarity in their structure or organisational practice to a trade union. This problem has been recognised by the U.D.F. in the western Cape where some organisations, referred to as mass based organisations, have been given a certain number of delegates. Other organisations, those that we would primarily refer to as activist organisations, have been given a smaller number of delegates. While this recognises that differences do exist, we believe that it is an inadequate recognition. The difference between an activist organisation and a mass based organisation is not one of size, and therefore of the number of delegates to a central body, but rather of the entire structure and functioning of the organisation.

As we see it, an activist organisation is essentially a grouping of like-minded individuals, who are brought together by a common political goal. Their activity consists in propagating their ideas amongst a constituency which they themselves define. Activists grouped together in this way, in an organisation of this sort, have a great deal of freedom to manoeuvre in the extremely flexible parameters within which they operate. They don't represent members in a strong sense. They propagate ideas amongst a certain constituency, or in a certain area, and as such play a very important political role.

Unions, on the other hand, are not organisations of activists, and union leaders are not activists in the same sense at all, because they are representatives in the strongest sense. Union leaders don't claim to represent the views of the working class. They represent the views of their members. Church or student activists, can claim to represent the broader social aspirations of church congregations or student bodies, and it doesn't really matter whether they are actually mandated by the broad mass of students or church-goers, or whether they are not. By propagating their ideas or their line they attempt to make students or church-goers aware of their broader interests and their social role. A union leader, on the other hand, can't go to a factory and claim to speak for the working class. He has to be mandated by workers in a factory, and he has to be reasonably sure that the particular workers who have mandated him back up his mandate. In a union situation there is no alternative to working in that way.

The critical upshot of this is that a union representative has to go through a long and very arduous process of receiving mandates and constantly ensuring that the mandates are backed. Union leaders don't derive their position from discussing ideas amongst a small group of comrades, and then propagating these ideas widely. They derive their position from the members whom they've organised, and who send them forward with a specific mandate. Unquestionably, union leaders can influence the rank and file, but ultimately they are very tightly bound to the specific decisions of members.

This is, as far as we see, what a mass based organisation means. It's got nothing to do with the size of the organisation, its got to do with the difference between organisational politics and activist politics. The structure of a union derives from the relationship between the shop steward committee and the members in a particular factory. It is undoubtedly at that level where the mandated relationship is the strongest, but it works in that way all the way up to the top of the organisation, all the way up to the national conference, and we cannot change our hats to suit different occasions and still retain our character as representative organisations. We have to go through the process of getting these mandates, we have to know that our members are willing to back the mandates and what they are willing to do. If we don't do that our participation is either meaningless or, even worse than that, our participation could be construed by our members as being in violation of the most basic trade union principle, namely the principle of representivity.

Those considerations simply don't apply to a large number of the organisations affiliated to the U.D.F. Most of the organisations affiliated to the U.D.F. have, as their legitimate political task, to appeal to the masses 'out there'. We have as our task the representation of the workers inside our organisation, and the painstaking process of drawing more and more members into the formal and disciplined structure of a trade union.

This is a major reason why we've found it difficult to envisage fitting into the structure of the U.D.F. We've experienced huge difficulty in explaining to our members how we would fit into the U.D.F. as a union, yet conversely we have found it very easy to explain to our members how we would fit into a trade union federation. The difficulties that we have don't arise from the issues which the U.D.F. has been set up to tackle. These have been discussed in the union, and they are very broadly appreciated. But affiliation has aroused very little interest.

There's one additional point that I want to emphasise. We've stated repeatedly that we'll encourage our members to join the U.D.F. Well, given the federation structure of the U.D.F., that's impossible, but we'll encourage our members to join organisations that are affiliated to the U.D.F. Should one of our members rise to become even a leader of the U.D.F., we would not view that as inconsistent with union policy in the slightest. In fact it would probably be a source of great pride to the union, just as it's a source of great pride to us whenever any of our members become leaders in their progressive community organisations. But we do not see our way clear to representing our members as a union in the U.D.F.

You referred earlier to problems in the relationship between the union as a single class organisation, and other organisations affiliated to the U.D.F. which are multi-class organisations. Could you elaborate on that?

It's not even primarily a question that the union is a single class organisation, but that the union is a working class organisation, and a working class organisation only. A union by definition is open to workers only. This is not to say that there are never divisions in a trade union — there obviously are. There is a group of people in a trade union who are not workers, namely all the full time officials, and their interests have always to be subordinated to the interests of the members. There are also divisions within a union on the basis of the skill categorisation of workers in a factory.

In South Africa there are also the inevitable racial differences, and potential divisions between Africans with Section Ten rights and contract workers. It's these divisions which the constitution and the Koornhof Bills have been set up to widen. They are divisions that we always have to work at overcoming. But notwithstanding these divisions, all our members are working class. They are all factory members, and they are all members of the broader society. This means that they identify, quite correctly, as their source of oppression, the bosses and the state. That has a bearing on the question of our affiliation to the U.D.F. For one thing, unions will inevitably be organisations that incorporate a great diversity of political views and affiliations. We'll have within our ranks members with militant political views, and we'll have in our ranks members with fairly conservative political views. We'll also have within our ranks a great many members who have few political views at all, people who have joined the organisation purely to fight their bosses. With a certain degree of tension now and again, those diverse views can all be contained within an organisation, because they are all held by workers.

To a certain extent this could also be said of any other mass based organisation. It could be said of student organisations where these are mass based; it could be said of women's organisations where these are mass based; it could be said even of community organisations. It is conceivable that a woman joins a women's organisation to fight women's issues. Such an organisation should be able to contain within it a fair diversity of general political views as well. But there are two key differences. The first is that student and community organisations, and, although not necessarily correctly, women's organisations, tend to identify the state as their source of oppression. This means that they are inevitably more clearly politically defined, and their membership is more clearly a politically based membership. They don't have the bosses to intercede in the struggle in the same way that workers in a trade union do. Secondly, the fact of the matter is that in South Africa, most non-trade union progressive organisations, tend to identify themselves quite strongly with one or another political tendency.

This of course involves particular problems in Cape Town. I don't know if these problems are the same everywhere else. But here the community organisations are divided quite clearly into two groups. There was a possibility that affiliation could jeopardise the unity of, if not directly our union in Cape Town, certainly some other unions in Cape Town. This is also especially sensitive when we've identified as a priority the formation of a trade union federation, with the even greater diversity of views that are contained therein.

I'm aware that opens us up to what has become a currently fashionable charge, namely that we are economistic. Although it's not always clear from those levelling the accusation, I take this to mean that we concentrate our activities exclusively on wages and working conditions, that we're not concerned with political struggle, that the only basis of our unity is the struggle in the factory. It's as such, a unity that makes little positive contribution to the national democratic struggle.

There are two answers to this: the first is that a union must inevitably carry within it the tendency towards economism. A factory based organisation by definition sets itself certain limits, and the General Workers' Union has never made any claim to mystically transcend these limits. The second answer to the question is that the accusation reflects a very narrow, formalistic notion of what politics is, and that's what really brings us to a point pertinent to the question of the class composition of the union.

It has to be acknowledged that workers are a very special group in society. They are the class, unfashionable though that term might be, that produces the wealth of the country. As such they are the most exploited and oppressed members of society. This special place of the workers in society is currently recognised in a very peculiar and inverse way by other groups in society. The way in which it's recognised in South Africa is in frantic attempts by other groups to eliminate the differences between themselves and the working class. Positions range from the laughable assertion made some years ago to the effect that all blacks are workers, to more serious assertions made by community leaders and very often trade union leaders today, that the community is the workers and the workers are the community, or student activists who assert they are the workers of tomorrow, or women's organisations who assert they are the wives and daughters of the workers. All these assertions have a kernal of truth, but to be a worker of tomorrow is not to be a worker of today.

More pertinently it doesn't go any way towards transforming a student organisation into a workers' organisation. To say that workers constitute the majority of any black community in South Africa is obviously true, but it doesn't mean that workers constitute the majority of members in community organisations. In fact, it's lamentable, but nonetheless true, that community organisations have had relatively little insertion into the ranks of contract workers, for example. In those rare cases where the majority of a particular community organisation is in fact working class people, it's possible that these working class members will have little influence at the top of the organisation in the decision making structures of the organisation.

I want to be clear about one thing: when we say that workers are the most oppressed and exploited members of society, that means, at the general level that workers do not have access to the means of production, and that to be workers, they have to be deprived of the possibility of turning themselves into bosses. This, even at that general level, is not necessarily true of students. But what it means at a level more specific to our problems with affiliation to the U.D.F., to a multi-class organisation, is that workers as a class are necessarily denied access to skills and education, other than those that are directly required by the bosses in production. They are denied the skills of articulation and language, of literacy, numeracy, in fact of the whole culture which a smoothly functioning organisation seems to require. This is not to mention the fact that workers also have very little time at their disposal, or at any rate the time at the disposal of workers is very rigidly controlled.

It is in fact control that is a key defining element of what it means to be a member of the working class. Every minute of a workers time is controlled. He's told when and how and where he'll work; he's told when and where and how he'll sleep; he has no control over whether he is employed one day and unemployed the next day. All workers have, in a sense, is their unity. This is why workers tend naturally to take and implement decisions *en masse,* and conversely why other groupings in society are so comfortable with taking decisions individually or in small groups, even, which is very characteristic of student organisations, to break up large gatherings into small groups to facilitate decision making and discussion.

The point of this digression isn't to say that workers should never work together with organisations of non-workers, or organisations in which non-workers are also members. We would expect this of our members. But we wouldn't be surprised, and nobody else should be surprised, if, when our members do so, they insist on carrying into these organisations the culture and the demands of the working class, and the culture and demands of a working class organisation. Because, and this is where I want to answer the charge of economism, unquestionably the democratic union movement in South Africa has won substantial economic gains, and to be sure we've spent a major part of our time and energy in making these economic gains. But in the democratic unions, the workers have in addition won a new pride and dignity, a self confidence in their ability to take and implement decisions. This is really the key aspect of unions' political work. The acquisition by our members of an awareness of their own power, an awareness of their ability to participate in their own way in the most complex and difficult decisions. We don't claim for one minute that this should or does represent the totality of our political work. Nor do we make the claim that we are absolutely certain that the level of organisation of workers in South Africa has reached a stage where they simply won't settle for any less than the right to participate fully in any political or community organisations that they form, or that they join. This is especially so if they join these organisations in their capacities as union members. They won't be satisfied with formal symbols of power, nor will they be satisfied with power where the ability to exercise that power resides with the more skilled and educated union bureaucrats, where they become in a sense silent but nevertheless muscular participants in the whole process.

We don't here want to get into a detailed critique of the U.D.F. as such. But the U.D.F. has to ask itself whether its style and tone, whether the language spoken, whether the pace at which it has developed, whether its programme, facilitate the fullest participation by working class people. Our members simply do not feel that way. They've never, for example, appreciated the need for the sophisticated structures which the U.D.F. has introduced. This is not because they are backward or stupid, but because they are advanced leaders of their own organisation, an organisation which has been in existence for ten years. We've never in the ten years of our existence found the need to set up subcommittees, let alone a highly sophisticated and complex structure. The workers have not felt that they've had the time to participate in the endless debate surrounding the setting up of the U.D.F. This is not because they are uninterested in politics, but because they do arduous full time jobs and they believe, unlike activists generally, that meetings are only necessary when the meetings have a very clear and defined objective, and when there's the possibility of that objective being fulfilled at the meeting.

We encouraged, for example, our members to attend the launching of the U.D.F. A fair number attended, but the vast majority of those who attended didn't understand the meeting, because it was in English. The workers don't understand what programme of action is envisaged by the U.D.F., and this is obviously very critical. Given the above, there is a feeling on the part of the workers that they will not be able to participate fully in the decisions that lead to a programme of action, and this is anathema to an organised worker. They are not going to be drawn into an organisation in which they feel that they will have to take action blindly, without having participated in the decision making. These are really the key aspects of the class composition of the organisations: firstly, that we draw our membership from a very wide and diverse range of political views, unlike most of the organisations participating in the U.D.F. and secondly, that our members are working class people, and as a working class they come from a culture that is very distinct from that of other more privileged classes in society.

There has been a lot of talk about the importance of working class leadership in national political organisation. Are you saying that working class leadership does not amount to the presence of individual members of the working class within national politically oriented organisations, but rather that the working class should have a leading status, within national political organisations?

I think that I mean both. It is essential that working class individuals occupy leading positions in national political organisations inside the country. It's important because I believe the second to be true as well, that workers must have special status in multi-class organisations. Workers must have the opportunity to lead the pace, style, tone and language — in fact the whole discourse — of the organisation. The reason why it's important, and the reason why I think that it's important to examine the questions raised with respect to the U.D.F., is that democracy in this country is inconceivable without the fullest participation of workers in the national democratic struggle. This is not merely because the working class is the largest and most muscular group in society. Simply put, they are the only social grouping with a class interest in democracy. Other social classes or social groupings might have an interest in relative or partial democratisation of society. But the working class which has every aspect of it's life — it's economic life and it's political life, very rigidly controlled, is the one class in society that has an interest in a thorough going democ-ratisation of the economy and the polity. Working class organisation in South Africa has developed to the stage where workers insist on the right to participate fully in the structures of any organisation of which they are members.

You talked earlier about the fact that the General Workers' Union supports the development of other progressive organisations in the community, and that it encourages participation of General Workers' Union members in those organisations. In what concrete ways has the General Workers' Union supported the development of these organisations, and how does it aim to do so in future?

The primary way, in which we attempt to facilitate the development of broader community organisations is by taking up broader issues in our union. This we've always done, and we continue to do. The issue of the Koornhof Bills and the constitution has been very substantially discussed in the union right from the beginning, before many of the organisations that have been specifically set up to oppose the bills were even conceived of. This is really the primary way in which we support other organisations.

We would also support them, and we've said this repeatedly, by encouraging our members to join these organisations. We've fairly consistently been asked to give our members to other organisations. Well, our answer to that is that our members are not locked in concentration camps, our members are in the community, in the townships. They must be organised, and we would certainly encourage them to join those organisations.

What is the union's current relationship with the United Democratic Front, and what possible future developments do you see?

We definitely see a role for ourselves as a union relative to the U.D.F. We've said repeatedly that we are prepared to support U.D.F. campaigns. We hope to be informed of U.D.F. activities, of U.D.F. meetings, to enable us to encourage our members to go to these meetings. Both of a local or regional nature. We hope that we will receive U.D.F. newsletters and information sheets and that we will be able to hand these out to our members. For example, in the very near future in Cape Town the U.D.F. is holding a meeting to discuss what is going on in the Ciskei. We see what is going on in the Ciskei as critically important to us, obviously. We also see it as a critically important exposé of the constitutional proposals, and therefore legitimately within the U.D.F.'s ambit. We would certainly support them in that campaign.

As to the future, that's a little bit hypothetical at the moment, I can't ever envisage the General Workers' Union affiliating to the U.D.F. Although obviously I can't speak for any other union, I can envisage a situation where a formal relationship develops between a national/political/community centre like the U.D.F., and a national trade union centre. I should say on that score that there is a precedent for this in South Africa, for a relationship between a national explicitly politically based centre and a national trade union centre.

It's often been said by the unions that their priority is the formation of a federation, and that is the case. The reason why it's a priority, or the reason why that priority influences our decision with respect to the U.D.F., is not that we are spending so much time in forming a federation that we don't have time to devote any resources to affiliating to the U.D.F. Rather we see that as part of a national trade union centre, the workers would have the necessary support, the necessary base, from which to participate in a multi-class organisation. That is a possible development. Obviously it would be a highly complex development, and one that would require a broad agreement in the trade union movement. But certainly it's a possibility, it has been done before, I don't see why it shouldn't be done again.

Reading 16. (1984)

The Unions and the Front: A Response to the General Workers' Union*

Sisa Njikelana (in a personal capacity)

Given that the state is preparing to introduce the new constitution in an attempt to coopt sections of the oppressed majority and halt the advance being made in the struggle for a democratic trade union movement and to reject any attempts to isolate workers from the national democratic struggle.

With the above in mind, it is necessary that a contribution be made in response to the views expressed by the general secretary of the General Workers' Union, David Lewis, in regard to working class participation and the nature of this participation in the U.D.F. Special emphasis is placed on the role that should be played by the trade unions in the broad democratic front.

Class alliances

Certain points need to be made with regard to the issue of class alliance which seems to underlie much of this debate. This debate has sometimes been reduced to the level of individual contributions without the dynamic participation of the class forces themselves, especially the working class.

* First published in *S.A.L.B.* IX, 7 (June, 1984), pp. 76 — 83.

From our experience in struggle we know that an individual or group's political actions, in terms of what class position they adopt, do not mechanically correspond at every instance to the ultimate interests of their class. Rather, they assume positions which at any given moment, to some degree, depend on political, ideological and historical factors. It is therefore important to note that continuing national oppression and its resultant limitations, insecurity and deprivation, are continually felt by every class and group within the black community.

While the state is attempting, through various concessions, to coopt groups and individuals within the black community, we must be careful in our endeavours to unite our people for liberation, not to allow positions to be adopted which might push them unwittingly into the state's camp.

We also have to recognise that there are those whose experience or awareness of national oppression and economic exploitation will prevent them from going all the way in accepting cooption and/or collaboration with the state. These people must constantly be encouraged to play their part in the struggle for national liberation. With this firmly in mind it becomes all the more important that the black working class, as the most determined and consistent force in the struggle for national liberation, must lead the way forward.

Why a broad democratic front?

A front is an alliance of a broad spectrum of autonomous organisations of differing class origins who come together having identified a common political grievance. It is a forum, a rallying point, providing a structural form which guarantees the broadest possible unity in action of different social groups. It is a mechanism that ensures the maximum concentration of energies and resources of organisations previously acting independently.

The representatives of affiliate organisations of a broad front democratically decide the direction of the front. For instance, if a union or any other organisation feels it cannot take part in a particular campaign, it would make its opposition or inability known. This threatened abstention, hence the weakening of the campaign, requires a compromise to be forged in order that the broadest unity be secured in taking up the specific political issue at stake. If no compromise is reached the front faces a dilemma and the campaign may fail.

Trade unions: a particular organisational form

Much has been made of the 'critical' difference between a trade union as an organisational form and other forms of organisation. Trade unions, it is said, 'to all intents and purposes have identical structures'. This may be the case but to follow this by asserting, 'this is, as far as we see it, what a mass based organisation means', raises a number of questions.

It must be noted that the organisational form within which any mass based organisation operates is related to the specific conditions in which such an organisation develops. Likewise, the form of democracy adopted by such organisations is determined by those conditions within which the organisation operates. Any organisation which upholds the principles of democracy has to ensure that maximum participation of its members in decision making takes place. The concentration of workers within a single factory, concern or industry creates the conditions under which unionists organise. All factories have a limited and fixed number of workers (normally) and the workers are concentrated within that environment for the period of each working day. As such this environment allows the establishment of formal structures, an established membership and regular contact among members of the organisation through the form of shop stewards. This particular form of mass based organisation, made possible by the conditions within which it operates cannot be simply transposed onto all other historical and environmental conditions.

A mass base

Although it may be desirable that community, women's, student and other organisations establish formal and working structures, this is not always possible. It would be unreal to insist that a student organisation establish formal branch structures from classroom to classroom and school to school in a historical situation where student organisations are banned from the schools. For a community organisation to have a committee in each street may be the ideal, but under certain conditions this is extremely difficult to accomplish. To say as a result that a community organisation does not have a mass base is to be totally out of touch with the realities of the environment in which those organisers are working. Whatever the conditions, activists must never-theless continue to build organisations if they are serious about advancing the struggle for fundamental change.

The mass base of organisations which are unable to issue member-ship cards, collect dues, have dues deducted, pay full time organisers and operate through formal structures, can only be assessed according to the support their programmes enjoy. Therefore it is primarily in the struggles waged by these organisations that the extent or lack of a mass base can be assessed. Even formally structured organisations such as Buthelezi's Inkatha movement cannot be judged as mass based merely on the ground of their annual membership figures. It is the organisa-tion's ability to act and respond in struggle that exposes the degree of support, or the mass base, that it can call upon. In considering the question of organisational forms and their validity or lack thereof, it is important to note Gramsci's warning not to fetishise any particular form of organisation, but to adapt to the terrain offered by reality.

Working class organisation

Union organisation has historically been a tremendous step forward for the working class. The emergence of the union organisation has created and solidified workers' unity and, by spreading organisational experience, has advanced the cause of working class organisation. The experience gained through economic struggles serves to raise workers' consciousness, develop organisational ability and teach the value of unity and united action.

It is here that the question of the relationship between trade unions and the working class needs to be considered. It seems that there is a tendency to conflate the definition of the working class as a class with that of trade union membership, and hence to see trade unions as the only true form of working class organisation. This tendency emphasises the distinction between the trade unions, which are characterised as single class organisations and other organisations, which are characterised as multi-class organisations and hence not working class organisations.

Although it is recognised by Lewis that unions do have other elements within them which 'influence the mandate that is given', it is asserted that they will always 'represent the views of their members'. Again it is affirmed that 'unions will inevitably be organisations that incorporate a great diversity of political views, ...members with militant political views, and ... members with fairly conservative political views'. And yet it is asserted that 'workers', and by inference the trade unions themselves, 'must have a special status in multi-class organisations'.

This implied claim by a certain trade union leadership to 'special status' within multi-class organisation needs to be carefully examined.

Other forms of working class organisation

It is questionable whether trade unions, with their accepted ambiguities, will represent the interests of the working class any better or more thoroughly than community organisations based within the residential areas of the same workers who are members of the trade unions.

To conflate the working class with union membership, is to confine the membership of the working class to union membership only, to the exclusion of dependants (husbands, wives, elderly parents and children) of those union members. Non-unionised workers and the unemployed constitute a vast portion of the working class. The community, women's, student, youth and other organisations based within working class communities, are also in a position to express the views of the working class and are also legitimate organisations of the working class.

It is true that these other mass organisations will include other elements who often participate in the leadership as activists. But this level of activists, of often petty bourgeois (and sometimes even bourgeois) origins and backgrounds, exist both in the mass organisations and in the trade union movement.

The distinction between trade union struggles and struggles engaged in by other mass based organisations has tended to be exaggerated in an attempt to show that the economic struggles waged by the unions are far more real and working class in nature than other mass based struggles. How real is this distinction within the context of the historical conditions imposed by the apartheid system? Are workers' struggles for higher wages that unrelated to rent boycotts or bus boycotts? Even those community and other struggles which are not so clearly economically based, such as those waged in the schools for a free and better education system, are issues which directly affect the working class. These issues link the community based and often more political struggles directly to the economic struggles being waged by the unions. Then the broad democratic front which takes up these wider struggles, undoubtedly represents the interests of the working class to the extent that the working class must combine economic struggles with political struggle. It must be recognised that the economic struggle cannot be successful or even conducted on a large scale if workers have not won elementary political rights such as the freedom to organise without the threat of bannings, detentions and the violent breaking of strikes. Although some of these struggles have been won over the last few years these areas still remain contested terrain.

Trade unions and the broad democratic front

What is the role of trade unions in relation to the U.D.F. and its affiliate organisations?

The starting point of any programme aimed at securing fundamental changes in society must be an understanding of who the main enemy is and, on the side of the struggle for such fundamental social change, who the principal social grouping and its allies are. Looking to other revolutionary experiences such as those in Vietnam and Nicaragua, teaches us that the progressive forces, unlike the 'left' sectarians, drew the broad strata of the population into the revolutionary struggle; and had to struggle for leadership of the democratic organisations of the peasants, small shop owners, professionals, artisans, students and other petty bourgeois strata. In these experiences the working class did not become the leading force of the broad democratic front spontaneously, nor by demanding that 'workers must have the opportunity to lead the pace, style, tone and language — in fact the whole discourse — of the organisation'.

The mere presence of the union, or of individual members of the unions who are 'encouraged' to take part in the broad democratic front, is not going to guarantee that the front expresses the view of the working class or has working class leadership. Unions, by the very nature of their organisational forms and activity are not, and cannot be, political parties of the working class. As such they cannot demand to lead the broad democratic front, for as is argued above the working class is not reducible to trade unions and trade unions do not necessarily even express the views of the working class — do we want to say that Lucy Mvubelo's National Union of Clothing Workers expresses the views of the working class?

The only way the working class can lead the broad democratic front, as learnt in the experiences of other struggles, is through active participation within the organisations and structures of the broad democratic front.

The responsibility of the union leadership in this situation, if it has the interests of the working class at heart, demands of them that they lead the union's membership into the broad democratic front and into active participation with all its structures (regardless of their imperfections), to struggle for and ensure maximum working class participation; and finally working class (not just union) leadership of the broad democratic front.

Reading 17. (1985)

The November 1984 Stayaway*
*Labour Monitoring Group***

The successful two day stayaway of black workers in the Transvaal
on 5 - 6 November is not simply the re-emergence of past forms of
opposition. It marks a new phase in the history of protest against
apartheid: the beginnings of united action among organised labour,
students and community groups — with unions taking a leading
role.

In comparison with past stayaways this was one of the largest.
Precise calculations are extremely difficult. Adopting the figure of
an average sixty percent stayaway in the Pretoria-Witwatersrand-
Vaal (P.W.V.) area (this being the consensus figure of employers
and the media) then anything up to 800 000, and certainly not less
than 300 000, participated.[1] The numbers involved are considerably
more when one includes the approximately 400 000 students who
stayed away from school.

The significance of this stayaway in comparison with the student

*First published in a more extended form in *S.A.L.B.* IX, 6 (May, 1985),
pp. 74 — 100.

**Bill Freund, Stephen Gelb, Jon Lewis, Mark Swilling, Graeme Simpson,
Eddie Webster, John Davies. The L.M.G. was formed specifically to
monitor the November stayaway, and this report was originally completed
in November 1984. Publication was delayed pending the outcome of
charges laid against the stayaway committee.

led stayaways of 1976 was the active involvement and leading role of organised labour. Most unions over the last ten years have been pre-occupied with building organisation on the shop-floor and have eschewed overt involvement in issues beyond the factory. It is a measure of the extent of the crisis in the townships that these unions responded so rapidly to the student call for support.

Origins of the November 1984 stayaway

Three localised stayaways had already taken place in the Transvaal since September. During this period the beginnings of a working relationship between community and student organisations and the trade unions had been formed in the Vaal and east Rand townships. The elements of this relationship first came together during the Simba Quix boycott campaign launched from Tembisa in August.[2]

On 3 September a successful one day stayaway was mounted in the Vaal to protest against proposed rent increases of R5.90. The Vaal township authorities charge the highest rents in the country. The lowest rents in Sebokeng, R50 per month, are higher than the highest rents in Soweto which are R48. More than fifty percent of the households were in arrears on their rents by April — again the highest number in the country. Protest meetings were held in all the Vaal townships during August. Although these meetings were addressed by leading members of the United Democratic Front (U.D.F.), Azanian People's Organisation (AZAPO), Federation of South African Women, Soweto Civic Association, and Congress of South African Students (COSAS), the main organisational forces were the Vaal Civic Association and local shop stewards. At the final meetings in the Vaal townships on Sunday 2 September, it was decided that residents should refuse to pay their rents. In Sharpeville, the meeting decided to call a stayaway for the following day. The Monday ended in violence, with 31 deaths, as demonstrators clashed with the police on the streets.[3] It is estimated that at least sixty percent of the workers in Sharpeville stayed away. The police reacted in a particularly violent manner which set the tone for the next two months as unrest spread throughout the Vaal and the east Rand townships. 'Heavy handed police action', in the words of the Progressive Federal Party (P.F.P.)

leader, Van Zyl Slabbert, also led to escalating violence on the east Rand.[4]

Two weeks later the Release Mandela Committee (R.M.C.) called a stayaway in Soweto to express solidarity with the Vaal residents, and to protest against police action in the townships. This stayaway generated considerable confusion as the pamphlets originally distributed by the R.M.C. did not stipulate how long the stayaway should last. Only later did the R.M.C. and U.D.F. make it clear that the stayaway was to last only one day. Estimates of the numbers who stayed away range from 35% to 65%. Three youths died during clashes with the police, this being the first major clash between Soweto residents and the police since the 1976 — 77 crisis.

The third stayaway took place over a month later in Kwa Thema, Springs and lasted one day. Unlike the Soweto stayaway, however, it was extremely well organised, had a clear purpose, and ended successfully. The Kwa Thema stayaway is analysed at greater length below.

The November stayaway was the culmination of three different but inextricably linked processes: in the townships, the factories, and the education system.

The crisis in township government

The present township crisis is caused by a popular reaction to the bankruptcy of the government's urban policy. After the November 1976 student led township revolt that left the ineffectual urban bantu councils in ruins, the state established the community councils with slightly wider decision making powers. As part of its constitutional reform package the Botha government sought to give greater autonomy to African local authorities as a prelude to drawing them into a regionalised 'multi-racial' second tier level of government. This was the aim of the Black Local Authorities Act (Act 102 of 1982) which came into operation in August 1983. The elections for the new town councils were held in November with only a 15 — 25% poll.[5] Less than a year later, they were to become the target of mass resistance that has reached levels unprecedented in South Africa's history.

The Black Local Authorities Act was more the product of a constitutional conjuring act than of a real understanding of the material needs of the townships. Firstly, the town councils were given limited autonomy but no viable fiscal base. The stated objective is that they should be self financing and the government has drastically reduced its contributions to town council budgets. The townships, however, are little more than dormitory towns that have no taxable industrial enterprises. Furthermore, the predominantly working class residents, many of whom are unemployed, do not earn enough to provide a viable tax base. Consequently most of the councils are in debt. The Soweto council, for example is budgeting for a R30 million deficit in 1985, which it hopes to reduce by R10 million by increasing rents and service charges, in some cases by 100%. The proposed Vaal rent increases were in response to similar fiscal difficulties.

Secondly, whereas the state insisted that the town councils were adequate, democratically elected, representative structures, they were not linked up to central state representation, and hence were no substitute for full political rights. This lack of legitimacy was reflected in the low polls at the elections, the criticism of the system from councillors themselves, and eventually in the direct attacks on their property and personnel that was to be a central feature of the the recent unrest. A large number of councillors have now resigned, some in protest over the unviability of these institutions, and others because the state could not guarantee protection of life and property. As one councillor expressed it:

> I am virtually in hibernation in the board offices since my home was burnt down. If I just resign I will have two enemies — the board on the one side and the people on the other. I am pleading that I be accepted back into the community.[6]

Many of the councils were rendered inoperative and it was to address this crisis of legitimacy that a special cabinet subcommittee was established.

The financial and political crisis of the town councils helps explain the present wave of resistance. It has also given rise to new oppositional organisations — the civic associations — that constitute an alternative source of legitimacy to the discredited creations of state policy. It is significant that employers' organisations are calling on the state to negotiate with these bodies over the real problems in the townships — instead of simply detaining their leaders. However, given that all the main civic associations and community organisations in the Transvaal are affiliated to the U.D.F., no resolution of the township crisis is possible which does not address the fundamentals of the apartheid state. Nor has the extensive use of military force, which has only raised the level of violence, proved successful in undermining the resilience and new found power of the civic organisations. It was this failure to negotiate, together with the limitations of state repression, that resulted in the stayaway which was in effect a bid to decisively alter the balance of forces in the townships.

Trade union organisation and worker militancy

Recent years have witnessed a phenomenal increase in trade union membership amongst black workers. It was this growth in trade union organisation which made possible the successful November stayaway. What is particularly striking is the continuing growth since 1980, despite the fact of recession and heavy retrenchments.[7] Nor has recession and the threat of unemployment dampened the militancy of these newly organised workers — as shown by the stayaway itself. If one looks purely at work related stoppages, the number of strikes which took place in the first ten months of 1984, is fourteen percent higher than for the same period the previous year: 309 as compared with 270 strikes in 1983.[8] However the number of workers involved has doubled from 53 998 to 119 029.

Beyond the basic struggle for recognition and decent wages, the emerging unions have challenged management on a number of issues such as arbitrary dismissals, retrenchments, and health and safety.[9] In this way the frontiers of management control have been rolled back. There have been a number of responses to this. The state has sought to depoliticise at least one potential area of conflict — health and safety — thus its Machinery and Occupational Safety Act.[10] Employers have sought to reassert areas of 'management prerogative' as part of a continuing ideological battle to sell the free enterprise system to black workers[11] and at a practical level, in their conduct of shop-floor relations.[12]

With growing politicisation in the townships particularly since the formation of the United Democratic Front (U.D.F.) and the National Forum Committee (N.F.C.) in 1983, unions have been under pressure to take up political positions. There have been a number of different responses: the development of political/community unions, the growth of black consciousness unions,[13] whilst the Council of Unions of South Africa (CUSA) has dealt with the issue by affiliating briefly to both U.D.F. and N.F.C.

Ironically, the very process of reform by the state has obliged unions to adopt a direct political stance. Thus FOSATU's active support for the boycott of the elections earlier in 1984 was the result of pressure from its Indian and coloured members. The point must also be emphasised that those trade unions which had followed a 'survivalist' policy of concentrating on factory issues were under intense pressure to abandon this approach.

With growing polarisation in the townships, unions have been under pressure to give a political direction to their members. The split inside MAWU in mid-1984 brought these tensions to the fore, albeit in a confused way.[14] Unable to resist this pressure, intensified in the Transvaal with the entry of the defence force into the townships, these unions were catapulted into a central role in the stayaway.

COSAS and the crisis in education
The Congress of South African Students (COSAS) was established in 1979 to represent the interests of black school students on a national basis. Its principal aims include alerting students and the wider community to the repressive nature of schooling in South Africa, and to participate in drawing up an educational charter for a future nonracial democratic education system. Although rooted in the educational sphere, COSAS views the struggle in the schools as part of a much larger struggle against oppression and exploitation, and is an active affiliate of the U.D.F. Furthermore, COSAS has promoted the establishment of youth organisations to serve the interests of young workers and unemployed.

Since the Soweto uprising of 1976, black educational institutions have become sites of struggle as increasingly politicised students challenge the state's authority and contest discriminatory education. By October this year, some 200 000 students, primarily in the P.W.V. region, were boycotting classes and many of them had been out for most of the year. That was demonstrated again recently by student opposition to the coloured and Indian elections, and by the role students have played in the turbulent protests which erupted in the Vaal.

Throughout the year, COSAS took the fight to the Department of Education and Training via a series of concrete demands which include the establishment of democratically elected Student Representative Councils (S.R.C.s), abolition of the upper age limit of twenty years for school attendence, abolition of corporal punishment, and an end to sexual abuse of female students by male teachers.

The initiative towards what became the November stayaway came from students. There was a slowing down in the momentum of student protest by the beginning of October due to three main reasons: firstly, the failure of the state to respond adequately to students' demands; secondly, students as a whole and particularly COSAS activists were subject to detention — 556 in all in 1984 — and in some cases have been killed,[15] leading to a weakening of organisation; thirdly, end of year examinations were approaching and school principals and particularly the town councillors were attempting to mount a campaign to entice students back to school. Large numbers of boycotting students would not return to school unless the terrain of struggle could be shifted and the support of broader social forces enlisted.

Consequently, a call was made by the students for parent solidarity, and meetings were arranged in a number of townships with a view to establishing local parent-student committees. At the same time, an approach for assistance was made to other organisations within the U.D.F. and a meeting was arranged for 10 October. At this meeting it was argued that the student struggle would be advanced only if the trade union movement as a whole was willing to act in solidarity. Accordingly, COSAS at a later date invited the trade unions to join them and community organisations in the stayaway.

In the meantime a highly significant meeting attended by 4 000 people was taking place in KwaThema on 14 October. This led to the establishment of a KwaThema parent-student committee consisting of ten students and ten parents. Many of the parents were active trade unionists, and included MAWU and the United Metal, Mining and Allied Workers' of South Africa (UMMAWSA) shop stewards, as well as Chris Dlamini, president of FOSATU. This committee was mandated to send telexes to the Minister of Cooperation and Development and Education, G. Viljoen, as well as to the Minister of Law and Order, L. le Grange, listing the following student demands: scrapping of age limit regulations; election of democratic S.R.C.s; withdrawal of white teachers (usually members of the defence force); removal of security forces from the townships; release of all detained students; the resignation of all community councillors; and calling on students to boycott school until an appropriate response was received from the Department of Education and Training. If these demands were refused by the ministers concerned, then parents would take action in solidarity with students.[16]

No response was forthcoming and at a lengthy follow-up meeting the next Saturday, which was punctuated by shouts of 'Azikwelwa' ('we shall not ride' — the traditional boycott slogan), it was decided to call a local stayaway for Monday, 22 October, and if this failed to produce the necessary response, a further stayaway would occur on the 29th.

The stayaway on the 22nd was highly successful due to strong organisation and clear purpose. Press reports indicate that over eighty percent of workers stayed home. The stayaway involved violent clashes between youths, who set up barricades in the streets, and the police. The setting up of barricades, however, was a tactic that was not approved by the student-parent committee. It was the success of this stayaway which, according to Chris Dlamini, guaranteed support for the later call for a Transvaal regional stayaway in November.

The stayaway committee

The momentum built up in the KwaThema stayaway prepared the way for a larger regional action. On 27 October, a broadly based and very important meeting took place in Johannesburg in response to the original COSAS appeal for worker support. The meeting was attended by 37 organisations, including representatives of youth congresses, community organisations, and the R.M.C. COSAS called on unions to show solidarity with the specific student demands articulated earlier.

All organisations came prepared to take concrete action. In the case of FOSATU representatives, the process by which they reached this decision is illuminating. As mentioned above, FOSATU officials were already involved in the KwaThema campaign, and there is no question that there was a groundswell of shop-floor support for the students' demands — due in part to student solidarity with unions during the Simba Quix boycott. Chris Dlamini, at a public meeting in Johannesburg on 7 November, explained how the dividing lines between student and worker struggles were increasingly becoming blurred; how S.R.C.s were similar to shop stewards' councils; how age restrictions on students would force them onto the labour market during a period of high unemployment. Furthermore, workers are parents and they have to finance their children's education from their own pockets, Dlamini argued.

In terms of its deliberations, the central committee of FOSATU met on 19 — 21 October. Following reports from Transvaal locals on the crisis in the townships, all Transvaal representatives on the committee, irrespective of political affiliation, felt some action was necessary. A subcommittee, made up of Transvaal members of the central committee, was established and given wide powers to both monitor the situation and to take appropriate action where necessary. Chris Dlamini was chairman of the committee, and Bangi Solo the information officer. Both were detained after the stayaway. Meetings were held with students and student-parent committees. Thus FOSATU representatives arrived at the 27 October meeting with concrete proposals and empowered to take action. As far as can be ascertained, a debate over the length of the stayaway resulted in a compromise on two days. It was also agreed that the stayaway be broadened to encompass the demands of trade unions and community organisations. The representatives of the 37 organisations present formed a general committee (the Transvaal Regional Stayaway Committee as it was to be dubbed by the press), and a four member coordinating group was elected to handle practical preparations. This core coordinating committee consisted of Moses Mayekiso (of FOSATU and MAWU), Themba Nontlane (of Municipal and General Workers' Union of South Africa — MGUWSA), Oupa Monareng (of Soweto Youth Congress — SOYCO, and the Release Mandela Committee — R.M.C.), and Thami Mali (of R.M.C.) — i.e. two union organisers and one unemployed worker from SOYCO, and one ex-detainee out on bail. U.D.F. was not formally represented because it did not initiate the stayaway itself, and some organisations involved were not U.D.F. affiliates. Also since U.D.F. affiliates were present there was no need for the U.D.F. to be formally represented. It was also felt that it was not possible for the U.D.F. to assume leadership because the struggle was seen as specific to the working class African townships of the Transvaal.

Two days after the meeting of the 27th, FOSATU convened a meeting of all the Transvaal unions to coordinate action for the stayaway. This was followed by a series of meetings of unions, locals, and shop stewards to report back to members on the proposed demonstration. The decisions taken by the subcommittee were ratified by the full central committee when it met after the stayaway on 10 November. This meeting reiterated the central demands of the stayaway: the clear removal of age limits; democratically constituted S.R.C.s; withdrawal of the army from the townships and an end to police harassment; and a suspension of rent and bus fare increases.[17]

The initial pamphlet calling for a stayaway for 5 and 6 November issued the following demands: democratically elected S.R.C.s; the abolition of corporal punishment; an end to sexual harassment in schools; the withdrawal of security forces from the townships; the release of all detainees; no increase in rents, bus fares, or service charges; reinstatement of workers dismissed by Simba Quix. The last demand, a work-place demand, shows the continuity with previous campaigns. In the event, the Simba workers achieved their goal before the stayaway began.

The object of the stayaway was to articulate student, worker, and civic grievances, and to put pressure on the state to redress these. The entire community faced severe problems during the current recession. Also it was felt that the education issue could not be divorced from workers' problems — they could not be comfortable at work when their children were dying in the streets and whilst jobless parents were unable to afford an education for their children. On the question of reaching non-unionised workers on the shop-floor, each organisation was given specific tasks in this regard. In particular, hostel dwellers who in the past have been ignored, were a main target. In contrast to 1976 many hostel dwellers, particularly on the east Rand, were now unionised. In addition, 400 000 pamphlets were printed for distribution. However, there was little activity on the west Rand and in rural areas. Finally, COSAS specifically addressed its student constituency to ensure the stayaway in the schools whilst the unions undertook to ensure the stayaway from work.

Monitoring the stayaway

The stayaway from work

In our attempts to monitor the stayaway we sought to investigate the relationship of trade union organisation to the size of the stayaway. Thus our sample of factories consisted exclusively of establishments organised by trade unions. Using the SALDRU (Southern Africa Labour and Development Reseach Unit) Directory of Trade Unions as our data base, we phoned every firm in the P.W.V. area which had a recognition agreement with an independent union. We spoke to 71 of these, with only six refusing to talk to us. Our findings were:

1. Unionised factories gave overwhelming support to the stayaway. Seventy percent of our sample had a stayaway rate of over eighty percent (Table I).

2. These unionised factories were concentrated on the east Rand and the Vaal — the areas where the stayaway rates (as also indicated by management bodies) were highest. All surveyed establishments in the Vaal and far east Rand had over eighty percent participation, with sixty percent of the near east Rand and 91% of Kempton Park/Isando also showing over eighty percent participation (Table I). The poor showing in Pretoria reflects the limitations of our sample group. We know from other sources that the stayaway in Atteridgeville was almost total. However commuters from the neighbouring 'homeland' came to work in Pretoria as normal. A similar situation occurred in Brits with location dwellers supporting the stayaway and commuters working normally.

3. There was no weakening of the stayaway on day two as had been anticipated by some observers: 56% of establishments maintained the same level of stayaway for two days, twenty percent weakened, and 24% actually intensified on day two (Table II). In the past extended stayaways have failed, such as the call for a five day stayaway in November 1976 which simply petered out.

Table I: Stayaway participation rates by area

% Part-icipation	Vaal	Near east Rand	Far east Rand	Kemp-ton Park Isando	Pretoria	Jo'burg	West Rand	P.W.V. Total
90-100	70% (7)	48% (13)	100% (11)	82% (10)	-	20% (1)	-	59% (42)
80-89	30% (3)	12% (3)	-	9% (1)	-	20% (1)	-	11% (8)
70-79	-	7% (2)	-	-	-	-	-	3% (2)
60-69	-	7% (2)	-	9% (1)	-	20% (1)	-	6% (4)
50-59	-	7% (2)	-	-	25% (1)	-	-	4% (3)
Below 50	-	19% (5)	-	-	75% (3)	40% (2)	100% (2)	17% (12)
Tot. no. estab-lishments	14% (10)	38% (27)	15% (11)	17% (12)	6% (4)	7% (5)	3% (2)	100% (71)

Table II: *Stayaway participation rates on day one and day two*

Stayaway intensified on day two	17 (24%)
Stayaway weakened on day two	14 (20%)*
Number remaining the same	40 (56%)
Total	71 (100%)

*Of the twenty percent that weakened, half of these began weakly on day one with less than sixty percent staying away.

Table III: *Stayaway participation rates by sector*

% Participation	Metal	Chemical	Food	Auto., Build. & Trans.	Retail	All sectors
90 — 100	50% (12)	67% (8)	70% (14)	43% (3)	63% (5)	59% (42)
80 — 89	4% (1)	17% (2)	—	29% (2)	37% (3)	11% (8)
70 — 79	4% (1)	8% (1)	—	—	—	3% (2)
60 — 69	4% (1)	8% (1)	5% (1)	14% (1)	—	6% (4)
50 — 59	8% (2)	—	—	14% (1)	—	4% (3)
Below 50	26% (7)	—	25% (5)	—	—	17% (12)
Total no. establishments	34% (24)	17% (12)	28% (20)	10% (7)	11% (8)	100% (71)

4. All sectors where unions were present were equally affected. Mining was an exception where lack of participation was probably due to their isolation from the townships and the aftermath of their own recent strike (Table III).

5. There seems to have been no significant difference in the participation of migrants and township dwellers. In nine of the 71 establishments surveyed migrants were a significant proportion of the work-force. In five of these there was over ninety percent participation in the stayaway (Table IV). Secondary evidence later confirmed these findings.

6. None of the employers interviewed envisaged disciplinary action. The most common response was to deduct wages for the two days' absence. Some employers treated it as paid leave; others, more sympathetic, accepted employees accounts of 'intimidation' and paid

wages in full. There is evidence of dismissals in small and unorganised factories.

7. Many employers commented that coloured and Asian staff worked normally.

Table IV: Stayaway participation rates for migrants

% Participation	Proportion of migrants in the work-force*		
	1/4 to 1/2	1/2 to 3/4	3/4 to all
90-100	1	2	2
50-89	-	-	-
Below 50	1	2	1

*In only nine of the 71 establishments surveyed were migrants a significant proportion of the work-force.

The stayaway from school

According to press reports some 400 000 students observed the stayaway. In the Transvaal some 300 schools were completely closed. The Minister of Law and Order put the number of boycotting students at 396 000.

In terms of regions the overwhelming majority of schools in the Vaal Triangle, east Rand and Atteridgeville were deserted. The Department of Education and Training claimed that in Soweto attendence ranged from thirty percent to ninety percent. However, our investigation indicates a much lower attendence level — although most matric students did write their exams on 6 and 7 November.

In addition, students at the University of the North observed the boycott.

Responses to the stayaway

The state and the stayaway

State response to the stayaway needs to be assessed from several perspectives. During the stayaway itself response was relatively restrained: no serious effort was made to actually force strikers back to work. It was only after the conclusion of the stayaway that the state moved sharply towards a counter-attack that began with the Sasol dismissals and brought on a wave of detentions apparently linked to a conspiracy view of events. The state's delayed response makes sense when the broader context of the stayaway is considered.

Economic grievances and student unrest came together during the winter of 1984 in Transvaal and Orange Free State townships in a mounting wave of attacks on state authority and symbols of South African capitalism (e.g. with the destruction of banks and building societies).

The stayaway was marked by township revolts in which at least 23 people died,[18] with Tembisa being the most seriously affected community. The South African Police were so stretched that the South African Defence Force was put at its disposal. Already by October, the Minister of Law and Order, Le Grange, was justifying the use of the army in this way in a speech to the Transvaal Annual Conference of the National Party at Alberton. The state is clearly anxious about the possibility that township youths may try to develop no-go areas where police and army can appear only in force. Thus however menacing the withdrawal of labour may have seemed at the time to officials, the security forces were too thinly spread to make possible a physical suppression of the stayaway. Direct interference was largely limited to pamphlets mainly aimed at Soweto which called upon workers to unite against the strike. No sign was found of an effective attempt, on the lines of 1976, to create an anti-strike force among migrant workers; the hostility of Inkatha to the stayaway had a negligible effect.

During the five years before the stayaway, a broad disparity developed in South Africa between the terrain of activity tolerated for work-place and trade union organisation among Africans, and that for African politics which remains harshly constrained. Such a disparity is inherently unstable in the long term. The stayaway appears to represent the culmination of a movement away from acceptance of the fissure between community and work-place, and a return, particularly on the part of CUSA and FOSATU, to a more political trade unionism as defined by the state.

The first sign of a counter-blow by the state came in the form of mass dismissals of some 5 000 to 6 000 production workers at the Sasol Two and Three plants in Secunda, virtually the entire African work-force. Although management insisted that it took this action as a private sector employer, Sasol is a parastatal of great strategic significance and, one might speculate, requiring state consultation and assistance to bridge over the dismissal of such a huge labour force. The contrast to the 'no work no pay' stance of most large private sector employers was very marked. Police with dogs, armoured vehicles and hippo's were quick to move in and patrol the streets of the Secunda township, eMbalenhle, to assure the compliant removal of workers from hostels to the various bantustans. This was followed by a series of arrests and detentions, about thirty, in connection with the stayaway, including trade unionists and student leaders.

Capital and the stayaway

The first response of employer organisations was to play down the stayaway and so defuse its effects:

> Not to over-react, not to vent a white backlash which in turn causes a black backlash and so fuels an ever-increasing cycle of action and reaction, must be the watchword.[19]

Most employers were taken by surprise by the extent of the stayaway, and were unsympathetic to what they saw as a political strike unrelated to the work-place. As Leon Bartel, President of the Afrikaanse Handelsinstituut (A.H.I.) expressed it:

> The responsible employer should seek to divorce politics from labour relations. The stayaway is clearly a political matter and the employers should make it clear that political demonstrations will not be countenanced.[20]

Any future stayaways are always likely to be met by a harsher management response. Already some employers were calling for a trimming down of the work-force, and could well use stayaways as a pretext for retrenchments. 'Enlightened' employers, however, would baulk at any direct attack on trade unions, and are keen to maintain the fragile relations established with unions in the post-Wiehahn period.

This was clearly demonstrated when the three major employer associations, Association of Chambers of Commerce (ASSOCOM), A.H.I., and the Federated Chamber of Industries (F.C.I.) sent a joint telex to the Minister of Law and Order after the detention of CUSA leader, Piroshaw Camay, warning that the wave of detentions were exacerbating a very delicate labour situation. Minister le Grange responded aggressively, questioning their support among employers.

Employers feared that the state's initial reaction would curtail even the current limited reform programme — and the working relationship established with the state since 1979 to implement the reforms. Beyond this, capital's response to the stayaway and the general crisis includes a call for further and accelerated structural reform — particularly over influx control — in order to head off any challenge to the social system itself. The subsequent conference convened by the United States/South Africa Leadership Exchange Programme, which brought together representatives of capital and potentially sympathetic black leaders called for: cooperative schemes in the work-place; consultation and community involvement; recognition from government of socially responsible investment as tax deductible; a programme of job creation and the development of skills; investment of pension funds in black urban areas; improved communication between the races.[21]

Beyond immediate reforms the Financial Mail and Finance Week, the two key financial journals, responded to the stayaway by suggesting a dialogue with the African National Congress (A.N.C.). Both drew on Tony Bloom's timely speech to the Wits Business School:

> It is difficult to establish just how great the support for the A.N.C. is among blacks in South Africa, but I venture to suggest that it is very substantial. There is an inherent inevitability about talking to the A.N.C. It is not a question of if, but rather when.[22]

Capital's reform proposals still stop short of one-person-one-vote — as Ackerman made clear.[23] However in the long-term, sections of capital may even be pushed to contemplate nonracial democracy, if the free enterprise system itself is threatened by the continuing crisis.

Conclusions and future implications

1. The stayaways crystallised the central contradiction of state policy — the 'liberalisation' of the industrial relations system without meaningful political and social change. Hitherto the major trade unions have focused on factory floor issues avoiding involvement in more overtly political issues. The state's failure to adequately respond to the educational demands of the students and the growing crisis in the townships have propelled the trade unions beyond the factory floor. In spite of the recession workers were willing to risk their jobs by taking part in the stayaway — even when faced by management

threats, as at Sasol. The state's response — the detentions and the sackings at Sasol — forced the trade union to take further action, such as the call for a 'Black Christmas' — leading to further politicisation. According to a recent FOSATU statement: 'the long-term implications of the stayaway could include more involvement of the unions in political affairs'. The government's failure to resolve the crisis in education and in the townships now threatens to undermine its own reform initiatives, particularly as regards the industrial relations structures created in the post-Wiehahn period.

2. The stayaway brought together the major opposition forces to apartheid in the Transvaal; groups which had not previously worked together. They share certain distinctive features: they are mass based organisations drawing predominantly from the working class: unions, student organisations — overwhelmingly from the children of workers, and youth organisations representing young workers and unemployed. In the end the stayaway was successful because it rested upon democratic grassroots support and organisation. It was because of the trade unions' deep roots in working class communities that they responded so rapidly to the requests of the students, and it was their highly organised and democratic structures which made it possible to mobilise at such short notice for the stayaway. One important implication of these new forms of trade union organisation is that any policy of repression, of attempting to 'behead' these organisations by detaining leaders, is much less likely to be successful.

3. This new alignment has involved a further polarisation of extra-parliamentary oppositional politics. Buthelezi's vocal opposition to the stayaway call distances him even further from the mainstream of opposition in South Africa. His interference in the Sasol dispute and his advice to workers to go back on management's terms will not endear him to the trade unions.[24] The high level of involvement of contract workers in the stayaway suggests a critical weakening of Inkatha influence amongst organised workers on the Rand. Forced to choose between loyalty to Inkatha and to their unions many supported the stayaway. Indeed it appears that migrants were systematically mobilised in support of the stayaway by student and community organisations, and the trade unions. The hostel dwellers were to play no small part in advocating the stayaway. Nevertheless Inkatha's conservative influence remains strong particularly in Natal — which underlines the regionally specific nature of the stayaway. This also has important implications for those unions attempting to build up nation

wide organisation. There is already evidence of an attempt on the part of Buthelezi to re-establish his presence on the Reef in alliance with other conservative township groups — such as the Sofasonke Party.[25]
4. Where strong trade union organisation and community student organisation coincided the stayaway was most successful. It may be that the relatively weaker response in Soweto reflects the fact that there is less correspondence between working class and community organisation and the class profile of the area is more varied. Similarly the non-participation of commuters in Brits and Pretoria indicates the absence of community organisation amongst commuters. Bearing in mind current decentralisation strategies this indicates a critical area for organisation in the future.

Where the stayaway was most intense — the Vaal, east Rand and Atteridgeville — school attendance was also negligible and student organisation was strong. As Dlamini put it, workers readily identified the demands of the students for democratic S.R.C.s with their own struggles for independent representation in the factories.
5. In previous stayaways a central tactic of the authorities has been to try and undermine the action by forcing workers out of their homes and back to work. That this did not happen on this occasion probably reflects two important developments: the scale and geographical spread of the action and the heightened forms of physical resistance adopted in the townships — barricades, attacks on state institutions, attacks on councillors and others who are viewed as collaborators. The security forces were thus thinly spread and had to concentrate their resources on sealing off the most affected areas in order to contain the situation. It should also be borne in mind that the earlier house to house search associated with Operation Palmiet was singularly unsuccessful in capturing 'subversives' and certainly does not seem to have intimidated people from taking further stayaway action.
6. Sasol's hardline approach revealed the vulnerability of workers to reprisals after a stayaway.* Even so, organised workers were in many cases able to secure undertakings in advance from employers that there would be no dismissals. It is perhaps necessary to stress the limitations

---

* As a result of strategic organisation and hard bargaining the Chemical Workers' Industrial Union (C.W.I.U.), an affiliate of FOSATU, compelled Sasol to re-employ seventy percent of the dismissed workers and grant the unions additional rights. The agreement was signed in March 1985. For more details see *S.A.L.B.* X, 5 (March/April, 1985), pp. 3 — 7.

of stayaways; workers do not have the large resources to sustain a long general strike. Moreover an action which is township based can be easily sealed off by the security forces. By staying at home the workers surrender the initiative and are cut off from fellow workers in other townships.

7. One feature of the stayaway was the absence from the scene of the black consciousness organisations. Whilst they did not oppose the stayaway, they offered no organisational support. A spokesperson from Azapo criticised aspects of the stayaway: 'its lack of political content — it was ridiculous for students to approach workers; it would be more correct the other way around. Its positive aspect was to force the unions into political activity.' It was also felt by Azapo that little consideration was given to the possibility of reprisals by the state. Also of concern to this critic was what appeared to be an 'Africanisation' of the protest. While this may be one view, in fact this point implicitly underlines the working class nature of the stayaway — since the composition of the working class in the Transvaal is overwhelmingly African. This was also reflected in the dominance of the African affiliates of the U.D.F. during the stayaway.

8. The decision to resort to stayaways reflects the absence of political rights for blacks — the vote, freedom of speech and association. So long as blacks are refused access to political power, the stayaway will re-emerge as a weapon. However given the recession, the degree of organisation and the limitations of the tactic, the major unions have stated clearly that there will be no more stayaways in the immediate future.

Stayaways remain essentially non-violent demonstrations of power — and not an organised challenge to the state. (The large number of deaths during the stayaway — 23 in all — were not a result of the tactic itself, but were part of the ongoing township unrest which has claimed 161 lives since January and resulted in over 1 000 detentions).[26] In the past the state has responded to such demonstrations of power in a repressive manner with the result that legitimate protest has been forced underground or into exile. A similar response in the present situation would further deepen the internal crisis — and has already led to international condemnation. The demonstrations outside the South African Embassy and Consulates in the U.S.A. have achieved considerable publicity. More important was the response of the international trade union movement and particularly the International Metalworkers' Federation — which earlier in 1984 pledged support to the struggle of black workers for trade union and political rights.[27]

The stayaway represents a new alignment of forces against apartheid. The question is, if it endures, what form will it take: a return to the tactics of the 1950s or the extension of working class politics?

Notes

1 The conservative figure of 300 000 is obtained by multiplying the total number of blacks employed in private industry in the P.W.V. area (374 313) by sixty percent and then making allowance for retail and services. The figure of 800 000 is obtained by multiplying by sixty percent the total number of blacks in paid employment in the P.W.V. area (1 485 000) minus the number of mineworkers (+/−150 000).

2 *S.A.L.B.* X, 2 (October/November, 1984), pp. 3 — 6.

3 *Sunday Tribune,* 9 September 1984.

4 *Rand Daily Mail,* 3 September 1984.

5 J. Grest and H. Hughes, 'The state strategy and popular response at the local level,' in *South African Review Two,* (Ravan Press, 1984).

6 *Star,* 21 November 1984.

7 See for instance, Ari Sitas, 'MAWU: Rapid Growth in Natal,' *S.A.L.B.* VIII, 8 and IX, 1 (September/October, 1983), pp. 1 — 2.

8 *Star,* 16 November 1984.

9 E. Webster, 'A new frontier of control? Changing forms of job protection in South African industrial relations', Second Carnegie Commission, paper 111, (Cape Town, 1984).

10 J. Myers and M. Steinberg, 'Health and Safety Organisation: A Perspective on the Machinery and Occupational Safety Act,' *S.A.L.B.,* VIII, 8 and IX, 1 (September/October, 1983), pp. 79 — 90.

11 See Paul Johnson in *Financial Mail,* 23 November 1984.

12 See *S.A.L.B.,* X, 2 (October/November, 1984), pp. 3 — 6, for an unsuccessful example of this at Simba Quix.

13 M. Golding, 'Black Consciousness and Trade Unions,' *S.A.L.B.,* X, 2 (October/November, 1984), pp. 29 — 36.

14 M. Swilling, 'Workers Divided: A critical assessment of the Split in MAWU on the East Rand,' *S.A.L.B.* X, 1 (August/September, 1984), pp. 99 — 123.

15 E.g. Benjamin Khumalo, Soweto Branch Secretary of COSAS; see *SASPU Focus III,* 2 (November, 1984). All figures on deaths and detentions supplied by the South African Institute of Race Relations (S.A.I.R.R.).

16 *Sowetan,* 19 October 1984.

17 Details from official FOSATU press statements, and statements from Alec Erwin, Acting General Secretary of FOSATU at the time.

18 Figures supplied by S.A.I.R.R.

19 *Finance Week,* 15 — 21 November 1984.

20 Ibid.

21 *Star,* 21 November 1984.

22 *Finance Week,* 15 — 21 November 1984; *Financial Mail,* 15 — 19 November 1984.

23 *Rand Daily Mail,* 23 November 1984.

24 *Rand Daily Mail,* 27 November 1984.

25 *Rand Daily Mail,* 26 November 1984.
26 Figures supplied by S.A.I.R.R.
27 Jon Lewis, 'International Metalworkers' Federation: South African Coordinating Council', *S.A.L.B.* IX, 6 (May, 1984), pp. 1 — 4.

South African Labour Bulletin
Volumes One to Ten
(April 1974 – August 1984)*
Judith Shier

Author**

A. T. QABULA: Working class poet. IX, 8 (July, 1984), pp. 21 - 26.

ADAPT or die: a documentary on the emerging trade unions, produced by Christopher Isham for A.B.C. TV. VIII, 7 (August, 1983), pp. 73 - 75.

ADLER, T.
Letter to the editor. VI, 8 (July, 1981), pp. 4 - 7.
The prevention of occupational diseases and industrial accidents in South African industry. IV, 9 and 10 (March, 1979), pp. 55 - 65.

AFRICAN Food and Canning Workers' Union in Queenstown. VIII, 3 (December, 1982), pp. 9 - 11.

AFRICAN Food and Canning Workers' Union in Queenstown revisited. IX, 6 (May, 1984), pp. 17 -21.

AFRICAN TRADE UNION CONGRESS
Memorandum for consideration and adoption by Interim Government of Zimbabwe, December, 1976. III, 6 (May, 1977), pp. 105 - 116.

AN AFRICAN union negotiates with the industrial council. I, 5 (August, 1974), pp. 15 - 17.

AGGETT inquest — police exonerated. VIII, 4 (February, 1983), pp. 3 - 6.

ALTMAN, J.R.
Leadership problems of registered trade unions in South Africa. III, 2 (September, 1976), pp. 35 - 41.

ALUSAF shop steward speaks. VIII, 2 (November, 1982), pp. 82 - 86.

AN ANTI-LABOUR BILL — Zimbabwe, VIII, 5 (April, 1983), pp. 1 - 6.

ARMSTRONG, Amanda
Micro-technology and the control of women in the office. IX, 3 (December, 1983), pp. 53 - 73.

ARRESTS and detentions. IX, 5 (March, 1984), pp. 1 - 3.

B & S struggles: interview with workers' committee from B & S Engineering and Steelbright. VIII, 6 (June, 1983), pp. 69 - 72.

BADSHA, Omar
A review of (by Richard Hyman.) *Disputes procedure in action: a study of the engineering industry disputes procedure in Coventry.* I, 5 (August, 1974), pp. 48 - 51.

BANTUSTAN attack on trade unions. IX, 5 (March, 1984), pp. 90 - 91.

BARDILL, John
Review of *Development and*

*Estelle Randall compiled the index of volume ten.
**Where an article is not attributed to an author it has been listed according to title.

II, 4 (1975), pp. 51 - 59.

COOPER, Carole

Details of strikes during 1978. V, 1 (May, 1979), pp. 57 - 66.

The mineworkers' strike. V, 3 (October, 1979), pp. 4 - 29.

The PUTCO strikes: a question of control. VI, 6 (March, 1981), pp. 3 - 23.

COOPER, Carole and ENSOR,Linda

The 1979 TUCSA conference moving in for the kill. V, 6 and 7 (March, 1980), pp. 116 - 121.

COOPER, Carole, *see also ENSOR, Linda and COOPER, Carole*

COOPER, D.

Industrial council medical aid and medical benefit schemes in South Africa. IV, 9 and 10 (March, 1979), pp. 85 - 110.

COPELYN, John

And what of Leyland? I, 3 (June, 1974), pp. 12 - 16.

Problems in collective bargaining. VIII, 1 (September, 1982), pp. 69 - 80.

A review of William Brown: *piece-work bargaining.* I, 5 (August, 1974), pp. 52 - 53.

CORNELL, Jud

Conference on working conditions and women's health. IX, 3 (December, 1983), pp. 20 - 23.

Workplace health services and employment in manufacturing industry in greater Cape Town. IX, 7 (June, 1984), pp. 42 - 58.

CORNELL, Jud and KOOY, Alide

Wiehahn part five and the White Paper. VII, 3 (November, 1981), pp. 51 - 74.

COUNCIL OF UNIONS OF SOUTH AFRICA a look at its past. VIII, 5 (April, 1983), pp. 72 - 74.

COUNCIL OF UNIONS OF SOUTH AFRICAN on political organisations. IX, 2 (November, 1983), pp. 86 - 67.

COUNCIL OF UNIONS OF SOUTH AFRICA press statement and policy document. VIII, 3 (December 1982), pp. 68 - 72.

COURT rejects workers' evidence. VIII, 3 (December, 1982), pp. 16 - 17.

A CRITICAL look at MWASA. VIII, 4 (February, 1983), pp. 77 - 79.

CRITIQUE of 'Problems of African trade unions'. I, 5 (August, 1974), pp. 10 - 14.

CRONWRIGHT, Rodney

The changing techniques of milk distribution industry over the past thirty years and the consequent labour implications, a case study. Crons Dairy, Fish Hoek. IV, 7 (November, 1978), pp. 41 - 54.

DANIEL, John

The political economy of colonial and post-colonial Swaziland. VII, 6 and 7 (April, 1982), pp. 90 - 113.

DAPHNE, Jeremy

Maternity rights: CCAWUSA shows the way. X, 5 (March/April, 1985), pp. 15 - 16.

DAVIES, R.J.

Leadership and unity in Rhodesian black trade unions. I, 9 (March, 1975), pp. 12 - 28.

Notes on the theory of the informal sector with reference to Zimbabwe. III, 6 (May, 1977), pp. 54 - 71.

A review of Gavin Maasdorp and A.S.B. Humphrey: *From shanty town to township, an economic study of African poverty and rehousing in a South Africa city.* II, 5 (1975), pp. 56 - 66.

DAVIES, Rob

The class character of South Africa's industrial conciliation legislation. II, 6 (January, 1976), pp. 6 - 20.

Evidence against the Schlebusch report: (a letter to the editor). I, 7 (November/December, 1974), pp. 62 - 63.

DE CLERCQ, Francine

The organised labour movement and state registration: unity or fragmentation? V, 6 and 7 (March, 1980), pp. 18 - 43.

see also FINE, Bob and De CLERCQ, Francine

DE KADT, Raphael

Mocambique and the South African

December, 1974), pp. 50 - 51.
A look at the open trade unions. I, 3 (June, 1974), pp. 46 - 52.
The problems of African trade unions. I, 2 (May, 1974), pp. 39 -48.
The problems of established trade unions. I, 3 (June, 1974), pp. 17 -21.
Recent strikes in Durban. I, 4 (July, 1974), pp. 49 - 56.
Recent strikes in Durban. I, 5 (August, 1974), pp. 41 - 44.
Review of Anthony Hocking: *Oppenheimer and son.* I, 7 (November/December, 1974).
Review of Hugh Tinker: *A new system of slavery: the export of Indian labour overseas, 1830 -1920.* I, 6 (September/October, 1974), pp. 58 - 61.
Reynolds': scene of struggle. I, 3 (June, 1974), pp. 36 - 39.
Rumblings of discontent. I, 7 (November/December, 1974), pp. 43 - 49.
The strike at Sterling Winthrop. I, 6 (September/October, 1974), pp. 50 - 53.
TUCSA's relationship with African trade unions: an attempt at control, 1954 - 1962. III, 4 (January/February, 1977), pp. 26 - 46.

ENSOR, Linda and COOPER, Carole
Summary of the recommendations of the Riekert Commission. V, 4 (November, 1979), pp. 7 - 36.
ENSOR, Linda *see also COOPER, Carole and ENSOR, Linda*
ERWIN, Alec
An essay on structural unemployment in South Africa. IV, 4 (July, 1978), pp. 51 - 69.
Is economic growth beneficial to workers? I, 2 (May, 1974), pp. 7 - 9.
Review of Francis Wilson: *Labour in the South African Gold Mines.* I, 7 (November/December, 1974), pp. 64 - 72.
Review of G.G. Maasdorp: *Economic development for the homelands.* I, 4 (July, 1974), pp. 57 - 85
A review of M. Buraway: *The colour of class on the copper mines: from African advancement to Zambianization.* I, 2 (May, 1974), pp. 52 - 58.
Suggested strategies for rural development. I, 4 (July, 1974), pp. 31 - 41.
Wage increases and inflation. I, 3 (June, 1974), pp. 9 - 11.

EVANS, Gavin
The Leyland strike. VIII, 2 (November, 1982), pp. 13 - 44.
The emergence and decline of a community organisation: an assessment of PEBCO. VI, 2 and 3 (September, 1980), pp. 46 - 52.
EVIDENCE submitted to the Wiehahn Commission by the S.A.L.B. on the settlement of disputes. V, 1 (May, 1979), pp. 83 - 93.
EXTRACTS from the report of the Inter-Departmental Committee of Inquiry into Riots on the Mines in the Republic of South Africa. IV, 5 (September, 1978), pp. 49 - 65.

FAVIS, Merle
The Ford Workers' Committee: a shop flawed victory? VI, 2 and 3 (September, 1980), pp. 38 - 45.
FEDERATION OF SOUTH AFRICAN TRADE UNIONS
The parallel union thrust: memorandum issued on 8 November, 1979. V, 6 and 7 (March, 1980), pp. 76 - 98.
Principles of collective bargaining. VIII, (September, 1982), pp. 81 - 84.
Report November 1980 - November 1981. VII, 4 and 5 (February, 1982), pp. 104 - 116.
Resolution of the proposed Amendment to the Industrial Conciliation Act No 28 of 1956 passed by the Central Committee at its meeting April, 1981. VII, 1 and 2 (September, 1981), pp. 16 -17.
Central Committee: Statement on the Amended Industrial Conciliation

JACOBS, Mike
'We are One' - Fishtrip Phillips in India. X, 4 (January/February, 1985), pp. 12 - 13.

JAFFEE, Georgina.
The struggle of the B & S workers. IX, 5 (March, 1984), pp. 94 - 95.

JOSHI, Ravindra
Forbo Krommenie strike case. IV, 8 (January/February, 1979), pp. 87 - 89.

KADALIE, Clements
Economic and political programme for 1928. I, 6 (September/October, 1974), pp. 22 - 26.
What of the I.C.U.? I, 6 (September/October, 1974), pp. 35 - 37.

KALLAWAY, Peter
Labour in the Kimberly diamond fields. I, 7 (November/December, 1974), pp. 52 - 61.

KAPLAN, David and MORRIS, Mike
Manufacturing capital and the question of African trade union recognition 1960 - 1964. VII, 1 and 2 (September, 1981), pp. 86 -107.

KAPLAN, David
see also *MORRIS, Mike* and *KAPLAN, David*

KAPLAN, Russell
Interview with Sarah Chitja, deputy general secretary of the National Union of Clothing Workers. III, 4 (January/February, 1977), pp. 54 - 59.

KATLEHONG removals. VIII, 6 (June, 1983), pp. 18 - 22.

KATZ, A.
A review of M.W. Murphee and others: *Education race and employment in Rhodesia.* II, 7 (February, 1976), pp. 78 - 80.

KATZ, Elaine N.
Silicosis of the Witwatersrand gold mines: incidence and prevalence; compensation; 1902 - 1978. IV, 9 and 10 (March, 1979), pp. 66 - 84.

KEENAN, Jeremy
Migrants awake: the 1980

Johannesburg Municipality strike. VI, 7 (May, 1981), pp. 4 - 60.

KHANYILE, Z.A.
What is a trade union? VIII, 1 (September, 1982), pp. 85 - 88.

KHOZA, M.
see *BENJAMIN, Paul and KHOZA, M.*

KIRKWOOD, Mike
Conflict on the mines, 1974. I, 7 (November, December, 1974), pp. 35 - 42.
The Defy dispute: questions of solidarity. II, 1 (May/June, 1975), pp. 55 - 63.
The mineworkers' struggle. I, 8 (January/February, 1975), pp. 29 - 41.

KLUGMAN, Barbara
Maternity rights and benefits and protective legislation at work. IX, 3 (December, 1983), pp. 25 - 51.

KNIGHT, Margaret
The mines death benefit scheme. IX, 4 (February, 1984), pp. 42 - 53.

KOLBE, Kolya
Review of F.A. Johnstone: *Race, Class and Gold. III, 3 (October, 1976), pp. 81 - 89.*

KOOY, Alide
Notes on mine accidents. IV, 9 and 10 (March, 1979), pp. 43 - 53.
see also *CORNELL, Jud and KOOY, Alide*
see also *HIRSCH, Alan and KOOY, Alide*

KRIKLER, Jeremy
Magnificent miners. X, 6 (May, 1985), pp. 9 - 22.
Women workers strike over job evaluation. X, 4 (January/February, 1985), pp. 49 - 50.
Women workers win job evaluation battle. X, 7 (June, 1985), p. 18.

KROS, Cynthia
T.V. review: *1922.* X, 12 (October/November, 1984), pp. 119 - 122.

LABOUR MONITORING GROUP
Andries Raditsela: monitoring the protests in Natal. X, 8 (July/August, 1985), pp. 92 - 102.
The March stayaways in Port

Mineworker protest on the Witwatersrand, 1901 - 1912. III, 5 (March/April, 1977), pp. 5 - 24.

MORRIS, Kagan
IX, 2 (November, 1983), p. 102.

MORRIS, Mike
Capital's responses to African trade unions post Wiehahn. VII, 1 and 2 (September, 1981), pp. 69 - 85.
Wilson-Rowntree: history of SAAWU's organisation. VII, 4 and 5 (February, 1982), pp. 18 - 27.

MORRIS, Mike *and* KAPLAN, David
Labour policy in a state corporation: a case study of the South African Iron and Steel Corporation. II, 6 (January, 1976), pp. 21 - 33.
Labour policy in a state corporation: a case study of the South African Iron and Steel Corporation. II, 8 (April, 1976), pp. 2 - 21.

MORRIS, Mike
see also KAPLAN, David and MORRIS, Mike

MOTALA, Shereen
Repression against unions. VIII, 6 (June, 1983), pp. 5 - 8.

MOTHOBI, B.
Some reflections on management beliefs about African workers in Rhodesia. I, 9 (March, 1975), pp. 36 - 45.

MOTOR manufacturers attempt to break union. VIII, 1 (September, 1982), pp. 17 - 19.

MPETHA on bail. VIII, 7 (August, 1983), pp. 69 - 70.

MTHETHWA, Alpheus *and* MFETI, Pindile
Report on the Leyland Motor Corporation of South Africa Ltd. with special reference to its labour policies and its attitude towards the Metal and Allied Workers' Union, June, 1975. II, 5 (1975), pp. 36 - 47.

THE MTHIYA case. VIII, 8; IX, 1 (September/October, 1983), pp. 7 - 8.

MUGABE, A.G.
Some union problems amongst commercial workers. II, 7 (February, 1976), pp. 45 - 46.

MUNCK, Ronaldo

New international labour studies confront traditional unions. X, 4 (January/February, 1985), pp. 46 - 48.

MUNICIPAL and General Workers Union of S.A. on the U.D.F. IX, 2 (November, 1983), pp. 63 - 75.

MUNICIPAL and General Workers' Union rejects registration. IX, 5 (March, 1984), pp. 83 - 86.

MURRAY, Colin
The effects of migrant labour: a review of the evidence from Lesotho. VI, 4 (November, 1980), pp. 21 - 39.
From granary to labour reserve: an economic history of Lesotho. VI, 4 (November, 1980), pp. 3 - 20.
'Stabilization' and structural unemployment. VI, 4 (November, 1980), pp. 58 - 61.

MYERS, Johnny *and* STEINBERG, Malcolm
Health and safety organisation: a perspective on the Machinery and Occupational Safety Act. VIII, 8; IX, 1 (September/October, 1983), pp. 79 - 90.

NALEDI Writers Unit/Medu Art Ensemble. Working class culture and popular struggle. X, 5 (March/April, 1985), pp. 21 - 30.

NAMIBIA'S economy: Africa Bureau factsheet no. 51, May/June, 1977. IV, 1 and 2 (January/February, 1978), pp. 174 - 180.

NARSOO, Penny
Black working class women in South Africa. X, 8 (July/August, 1985), pp. 118 - 121.

NATAL LABOUR RESEARCH COMMITTEE.
Control over a work-force: the Frame case. VI, 5 (December, 1980), pp. 17 - 48.

NATAL shop workers get in touch. VII, 3 (November, 1981), pp. 14 - 15.

NATIONAL Automobile and Allied Workers' Union — Alfa in Rome. VIII, 7 (August, 1983), pp. 1 - 3.

NATIONAL Automobile and Allied

pp. 20 - 25.

OCCUPATIONAL Medicine Bill. IX, 4 (February, 1984), pp. 18 - 21.

O.K. workers push out personnel officer. VIII, 1 (September, 1982), pp. 16 -17.

O'MEARA, Dan
White trade unionism, political power and Afrikaner nationalism: a review of Louis Naude: *Dr A. Hertzog, die Nasionale Party en die mynwerkers.* I, 10 (April, 1975), pp. 31 - 51.

OMOND, Roger
Azikwelwa. I, 8 (January/February, 1975), pp. 51 - 57.

OOSTHUIZEN, Frik
Unions respond to new technology. X, 3 (December, 1984), pp. 20 - 22.

OPERATION solidarity. IX, 2 (November, 1983), pp. 14 - 17.

ORANGE Vaal General Workers' Union proposals for union unity. VIII, 5 (April, 1983), pp. 57 - 63.

ORGANISING small towns: an interview with Matthews Oliphants and Vincent Mkonza. VIII, 4 (February, 1983), pp. 70 - 73.

PARENTAL or independent parallel unions? III, 4 (January/February, 1977), pp. 7 - 13.

PARSON, Jack
The working class, the state and social change in Botswana. V, 5 (January, 1980), pp. 44 - 55.

PASSES for 'coloureds'. VIII, 4 (February, 1983), p. 15.

PENSION Bill protest was a victory for workers. VII, 4 and 5 (February, 1982), pp. 6 - 9.

PENSIONS strikes again. VIII, 1 (September, 1982), pp. 9 - 13.

PENSIONS the problem. VII, 3 (November, 1981), pp. 3 - 4.

PEOPLE'S support essential. VII, 3 (November, 1981), pp. 9 - 12.

PEROLD, Jacques
The historical and contemporary use of job evaluation in South Africa. X, 4 (January/February, 1985), pp. 72 - 82.

PHIMISTER, I.R.
African worker consciousness: origins and aspects to 1953. III, 1 (July, 1976), pp. 23 - 42.

A note on labour relations in Southern Rhodesian agriculture before 1939. III, 6 (May, 1977), pp. 94 - 104.

PICK 'N PAY workers are picking up. IX, 4 (February, 1984), pp. 54 - 57.

PICKING apples for R12 a week. VIII, 3 (December, 1982), pp. 7 - 9.

PILLAY, Nesem
see MAASDORP, G.G. and PILLAY, Nesem

PINETOWN bus strike. IX, 6 (May, 1984), pp. 8 - 13.

PLAUT, Martin
Report on the Anglo American Corporation gold mines. II, 8 (April, 1976), pp. 36 - 45.
see also PLAUT, Timothy and PLAUT, Martin

PLAUT, Timothy *and* Martin
A Review of the *Trade Union Industrial Studies Series.* III, 1 (July, 1976), pp. 63 -76.

PREAMBLE to the 1925 revised constitution (of the I.C.U.). I, 6 (September/October, 1974), p. 21.

PRESS statement on the Industrial Conciliation Act following a joint meeting between FOSATU, W.P.G.W.U., F.C.W.U., A.F.C.W.U. V, 6 and 7 (March, 1980), p. 17.

PREVENTING methane explosions. IX, 7 (June, 1984), pp. 12 - 20.

PRIOR, Andrew
Managerial ideology: a case study; an incident in a South African gold mine, 13 August, 1975. III, 8 (October, 1977), pp. 67 - 71.

PRIOR, Andrew
see PRIOR, Carroll and PRIOR, Andrew

PRIOR, Carroll *and* Andrew
Some aspects of unemployment in the Western Cape, October, 1976 -September 1977. IV, 4 (July, 1978), pp. 77 - 83.

PROFILES of Junerose Nala and Obed Zuma, II, 9 and 10 (May/June,

San Francisco dock workers fight apartheid. X, 6 (May, 1985), pp. 67 - 73.

WESTCOTT, Gill

A review of Vicente Navarro: *Class struggle, the state and medicine.* IV, 9 and 10 (March, 1979), pp. 123 - 128.

WESTERN PROVINCE GENERAL WORKERS' UNION

The Cape Town meat strike: the struggle for democratically elected workers' committees. VI, 5 (December, 1980), pp. 49 - 78.

Comments on the question of registration. V, 4 (November, 1979), pp. 114 - 134.

Letter to the *Bulletin.* VI, 1 (July, 1980), pp. 3 - 5.

The meat workers' dispute. VI, 1 (July, 1980), pp. 77 - 84.

Memoranda on meat industry dispute. VI, 5 (December, 1980), pp. 79 - 90.

Registration, recognition and organisation: the case of the Cape Town stevedores. V, 6 and 7 (March, 1980), pp. 57 - 75.

Submission to the Department of Manpower with regard to the proposed Industrial Conciliation Amendment Bill. VII, 1 and 2 (September, 1981), pp. 10 - 11.

WESTMORE, Jean

Review of Liz Clarke and Jane Ngobese: *Women without men.* II, 1 (May/June, 1975), pp. 64 -69.

WESTMORE, Jean *and* TOWNSEND, Pat

The African women workers in the textile industry in Durban. II, 4 (October, 1975), pp. 18 - 32.

WHERE are the workers? IX, 2 (November, 1983), pp. 76 - 77.

WHITE, I.D.

The changing labour process and its consequences a case study of a general engineering firm in Natal. IV, 7 (November, 1978), pp. 55 -62.

WICKENS, Peter

The organisation and composition of

the I.C.U. I, 6 (September/October, 1974), pp. 27 - 34.

WIDGERY, David

Unless we organise. I, 5 (August, 1974), pp. 33 - 40.

WIENDIECK, Gert

A review of W. Backer: *Motivating black workers.* II, 9 and 10 (May/June, 1976), pp. 110 - 116.

WILSON, Francis

Migrant labour in world perspective. I, 4 (July, 1974), pp. 18 - 26.

Notes on the migrant labour system in Lesotho. I, 4 (July, 1974), pp. 27 - 30.

Women and trade unions. VIII, 6 (June, 1983), pp. 63 - 68.

WOMEN in Southern Africa: a bibliography. IX, 3 (December, 1983), pp. 18 - 19.

WOMEN office cleaners on night shift. IX, 3 (December, 1983), pp. 74 - 81.

WORKER leader assassinated (Samson Cele). VI, 2 and 3 (September, 1980), p. 1.

WORKER organisation in Durban. IV, 8 (January/February, 1979), pp. 1 - 2.

WORKERS axed. VIII, 2 (November, 1982), pp. 1 - 3.

WORKERS held at gunpoint. VII, 3 (November, 1981), pp. 8 - 9.

WORKERS unite — don't vote (document). IX, 8 (July, 1984), p. 121.

WORKERS Voice. VIII, 3 (December, 1982), pp. 73 - 76.

WORKMENS compensation and unclaimed moneys. IV, 9 and 10 (March, 1979), pp. 7 - 8.

WORKMENS Compensation Bill. IX, 5 (March, 1984), pp. 28 - 31.

WORKMENS compensation – who pays the price? IX, 7 (June, 1984), pp. 6 -11.

WORKSHOP on women. IX, 3 (December, 1983), pp. 7 - 17.

YOUNG CHRISTIAN WORKERS.

The International week of Working Class Youth. X, 6 (May, 1985), p. 2.

Y.M.C. International Week — an evaluation. X, 7 (June, 1985), pp. 16 - 17.

Subject

pp. 75 - 86.
BANTUSTANS — Boputhatswana
Bantustan attack on trade unions. IV, 5 (March, 1984), pp. 90 - 91.
BANTUSTANS — Ciskei
Ciskei repression: joint statement. VIII, 8; IX, 1 (September/ October, 1983), pp. 96 - 97.
Ciskei U.I.F. VIII, 7 (August, 1983), pp. 62 - 63.
East London correspondent. East London and labour: 1981, a summary. VII, 4 and 5 (February, 1982), pp. 28 - 33.
East London workers U.I.F. petition. VIII, 7 (August, 1983), pp. 58 -59.
Green, Philippa and Alan Hirsch. The Ciskei: the political economy of control. VII, 4 and 5 (February, 1982), pp. 65 - 85.
Maree, Johann. SAAWU in the East London area, 1979 — 1981. VII, 4 and 5 (February, 1982), pp. 34 - 49.
Mdantsane bus boycott. VIII, 8; IX, 1 (September/October, 1983), pp. 29 - 32.
Swilling, Mark. 'The buses smell of blood': the East London boycott. IX, 5 (March, 1984), pp. 45 - 74.
U.I.F. appeal. VIII, 7 (August, 1983), pp. 60 - 61.
BANTUSTANS — KwaZulu
Claassens, Aninka. The Riekert Commission and unemployment: the KwaZulu case. V, 4 (November, 1979), pp. 49 - 64.
Clarification: Trade unions and KwaZulu politics. I, 3 (June, 1974), pp. 3 - 8.
BANTUSTANS — Labour
Bophuthatswana Industrial Conciliation Act. IX, 5 (March, 1984), pp. 36 - 44.
Clarification: Trade unions and Kwa-Zulu politics. I, 3 (June, 1974), pp. 3 - 8.
Free trade zones and homelands. VIII, 7 (August, 1983), pp. 67 - 68.
Homeland labour relations law. VIII, 8; IX, 1 (September/October, 1983), pp. 65 - 78.
Khanyile, Z.A. What is a trade union? VIII, 1 (September, 1982), pp. 85 - 88.
Maré, Gerry. The East London strikes. SALB, I, 5 (August, 1974), (Article written by R. Turnerd), pp. 26 - 32.
TUCSA and the African workers. I, 2 (May, 1974), pp. 2 - 3.

BOOK REVIEWS
Badsha, Omar. A review of Richard Hyman: *Disputes procedure in action: a study of the engineering industry disputes procedure in Coventry*. I, 5 (August, 1974), pp. 48 - 51.
Bardill, John. Review of *Development and dependence in Lesotho* by Gabriele Winai Ström. VI, 4 (November, 1980), pp. 79 - 90,
Benjamin, Paul. Review of *Labour legislation in South Africa*, by R.A. Jones and H. Griffiths. VI, 7 (May, 1981), pp. 87 - 89.
Bradford, Helen. Review of *Trade union foreign policy* by Jeffrey Harrod. V, 8 (May, 1980), pp. 68 -72.
Callinicos, Luli. Of maids and madams: a review of *Maids and Madams — a study in the politics of exploitation* by Jacklyn Cook. VI, 1 (July, 1980), pp. 85 - 88.
Callinicos, Luli. Review of Eddie Roux: *Time longer than rope*. II, 2 (July, 1975), pp. 52 - 58.
Callinicos, Luli. Reviews of M.G. Whisson and W. Weil: *Domestic servants: a microcosm of the race problem* and Sue Gordon *Domestic workers: a handbook for housewives*. II, 4 (1975), pp. 60 - 69.
Callinicos Luli. Review of Norman Herd: *1922, the revolt on the Rand*. I, 5 (August, 1974), pp. 54 - 62.
Copelyn John. A review of William Brown: *Piecework bargaining*. I, 5, (August, 1974), pp. 52 - 58.
Davies, Rob. A review of Gavin Maasdorp and A.S.B. Humphrey: *From shanty town to township, an economic study of African poverty*

(January/February, 1985), pp. 119 -120.

Lewis, Jon. Review of *Industrial relations in industrial perspective*, by K. Reese. IX, 5 (March, 1984), pp. 92 - 93.

Lewis, Jon. A review of *Labour and monopoly capital: degradation of work in the twentieth century* by Harry Braverman. IV, 3 (May, 1978), pp. 50 - 59.

Maasdorp, G.G. and Pillay, Nesem. Review of Verity S. Cubitt and Roger C. Riddell: *The urban poverty datum line in Rhodesia*. I, 9 (March, 1975), pp. 66 - 72.

Mabin, Alan. Anglo American and the rise of modern South Africa. X, 7 (June, 1986), pp. 119 - 121.

Maré, Gerhard. Up against the fences. XI, 2 (October/ November, 1985), pp. 113 - 120.

Maree, Johann. Class struggle at work. (book review). IV, 7 (November, 1978), pp. 81 - 92.

Maree, Johan. Review of Francis Wilson: *Migrant labour in South Africa*. I, 4 (July, 1974), pp. 59 - 64.

Maree, Johan. Review of I.L.O.: *Employment, incomes and equality, a strategy for increasing productive employment in Kenya*. I, 8 (January/February, 1975), pp. 72 - 77.

Maree, Johann. Seeing strikes in perspective: review of article of *The Durban Strikes, 1973*. II, 9 and 10 (May/June, 1976), pp. 91 - 109.

Mkalima, Mlungisi. Race or class?: a review of *Class, race and workers insurgency — the League of Revolutionary Black Workers*, by James A. Geschwender. VI, 2 and 3 (September, 1980), pp. 92 - 96.

Narsoo, Penny. Black working class women in South African society. X, 8 (July/August, 1985), pp. 118 -121.

O'Meara, Dan. White trade unionism, political power and Afrikaner nationalism: a review of Louis Naude: *Dr A. Hertzog,*

die Nasionale Party en die mynwerkers. I, 10 (April, 1975), pp. 31 - 51.

Plaut, Timothy and Martin. A Review of the *Trade Union Industrial Studies Series*. III, 1 (July, 1976), pp. 63 - 67.

Review of H.G. Ringrose: *The Law and practises of employment*. IV, 8 (January/February, 1979), pp. 90 - 2.

Schlemmer, Lawrence. Review of Alan S. Tiley: *Bridging the communication gap between black and white*. II, 5 (1975), pp. 67 - 69.

Simkins, Charles. Apartheid and housing in Cape Town: a review of Margaret Nash: *Home, an introduction to the housing crisis in Cape Town;* and Charles Simkins: *Socio-economic characteristics of sixteen squatter settlements in the Cape Town area in 1975*. II, 2 (September, 1976), pp. 100 - 104.

Simkins, Charles. The 2001st casualty: a review of Walker and Weinbren: *2000 casualties: a history of the trade unions and the labour movement in the Union of South Africa.* II, 6 (January, 1976), pp. 60 - 65.

Simkins, Charles. Review of R. Cohen: *Labour and politics in Nigeria, 1945 — 1971*. II, 8 (April, 1976), pp. 61 - 67.

Southall, Roger. Review article: South African labour studies. IX, 7 (June, 1984), pp. 88 - 114.

Spencer, L. A review of *A Seventh Man*, by John Berger and Jean Mohr. IV, 6 (October, 1978), pp. 70 - 76.

The Surplus Peoples Project. VIII, 8; IX, 1 (September/October, 1983), pp. 111 - 116.

Webster, Eddie. Review of H. Benyon: *Working for Ford*. I, 3 (June, 1974), pp. 53 - 55.

Webster, Eddie. Review of *Industrial relations and the limits of law: the industrial effects of the Industrial Relations Act, 1971*. V, 6 and 7

International worker solidarity? V, 8 (May, 1980), pp. 1 - 2.

Irish shop workers boycott South African goods X1, 2 (October/ December, 1985), pp. 25 - 26.

May Day 1984. IX, 7 (June, 1984), pp. 1 - 5.

May Day 1985. X, 7 (June, 1985), pp. 10 - 15.

Munck, Ronaldo. New international labour studies confront tradional international unions. X, 4 (January/February, 1985), pp. 46 - 48.

Phillippines: 350 000 workers celebrate May Day. X, 8 (July/ August, 1985), pp. 57 - 59.

We last held May Day in 1950. VII, 6 (April, 1982), pp. 28 - 30.

Webster, Eddie. The International Metalworkers' Federation in South Africa (1974 — 1980). IX, 6 (May, 1984), pp. 77 - 94.

Young Christian Workers' Communique. The international week of working class youth. X, 6 (May, 1985), p. 2.

Young Christian Workers' communique. Y.C.W. international week — an evaluation. X, 7 (June, 1985), pp. 16 - 17.

Working for Coca-Cola. X, 8 (July/ August, 1985), pp. 53 - 56.

INTERNATIONAL LABOUR OFFICE

Freedom of Association and trade unions. II, 9 and 10. (May/June, 1976), pp. 1 - 10.

IRON AND STEEL INDUSTRIES, *see MANUFACTURING — Iron, Steel, Engineering and Metallurgical Industries*

JOB EVALUATION

Cowan, Bill. Is job evaluation scientific? X, 4 (January/February, 1985), pp. 93 - 106.

Krikler, Jeremy. Women workers strike over job evaluation. X, 4 (January/February, 1985), pp. 49 - 50.

Women workers win job evaluation battle. X, 7 (June, 1985), p. 18.

Le Roux, Len. A guide to job evalua-

tion systems used in South Africa. X, 4 (January/February, 1985), pp. 83 - 92.

Mathews, Cathy. Case study: the Paterson system at a factory in Cape Town, X, 4 (January/ February, 1985), pp. 25 - 28.

Perold, Jacques. The historical and contemporary use of job evaluation in South Africa. X, 4 (January/ February, 1985), pp. 72 -82.

KADALIE, Clements

Bonner, Philip. The decline and fall of the I.C.U.: a case of selfdestruction? I, 6 (September/ October, 1974), pp. 38 - 43.

KAGAN, Morris

Morris Kagan. IX, 2 (November, 1983), p. 102.

LABOUR, *see AGRICULTURE — Labour, Bantustans — Labour, Construction — Labour, Government — Labour, Mining — Labour, Services Sector — Labour, and Under names of countries e.g. Britain — Labour, Strikes, Trade Unions*

LABOUR BUREAUX

Duncan, Sheena. The central institution of South African labour exploitation. III, 9 (November, 1977), pp. 5 - 17.

Greenberg, Stanley and Giliommee, Hermann. Labour Bureaucracies and the African reserves. VIII, 4 (February, 1983), pp. 37 - 50.

Hindson, Douglas. The new Black Labour Regulation: limited reform, intensified control. VI, 1 (July, 1980), pp. 45 - 52.

Marchand, C.G.J. A consideration of the legal basis and some practical operations of labour bureaux. III, 9 (November, 1977), pp. 18 - 40.

LABOUR FORCE PARTICIPATION

Booth Alan. The development of the Swazi labour market 1900 — 1968. VII, 6 and 7 (April, 1982), pp. 34 - 57.

Hendrie, Delia and Horner, Dudley.

of Employment Act: the position of women. VIII, 6 (June, 1983), pp. 1 - 4.

Myers, Johnny and Steinberg Malcolm. Health and safety organisation: a perspective on the Machinery and Occupational Safety Act. VIII, 8; IX, 1 (September/October, 1983), pp. 79 - 90.

Nupen, Charles. Unfair labour practices and the industrial court. VIII, 8; IX, 1 (September/October, 1983), pp. 39 - 64.

The Occupational Medicine Bill. IX, 4 (February, 1984), pp. 18 - 21.

Protection against victimisation. V, 3 (May, 1978), pp. 1 - 4.

The response of African unions to state labour policy. V, 6 and 7 (March, 1980), pp. 10 - 11.

South African Labour Bulletin Editors. Critique of the Act (Labour Relations Amendment Bill 59 of 1981). VII, 1 and 2 (September, 1981), pp. 29 - 38.

Uniply revisited. X, 1 (August/September, 1984), p. 24.

Western Province General Workers' Union. Submission to the Department of Manpower with regard to the proposed Industrial Conciliation Amendment Bill. VII, 1 and 2 (September, 1981), pp. 10 - 11.

Workmen's Compensation Bill. IX, 5 (March, 1984), pp. 28 - 31.

Workmen's compensation — who pays the price? IX, 7 (June, 1984), pp. 6 - 11.

LABOUR PROCESS

Bosquet, Michel. The 'prison factory'. III, 8 (October, 1977), pp. 50 - 66.

Cronwright, Rodney. The changing techniques of milk distribution industry over the past thirty years and the consequent labour implications, a case study, Crons Dairy, Fish Hoek. IV, 7 (November, 1978), pp. 41 - 54.

Kaplan, Dave. New technology in the garment industry. X, 7 (June,

1985), pp. 75 - 96.

Meth, Charles. Are there skill shortages in the furniture industry? IV, 7 (November, 1978), pp. 7 - 40.

Natal Labour Research Committee. Control over a work-force: the Frame case. VI, 5 (December, 1980), pp. 17 - 48.

Nonracial democracy in the workplace. IV, 7 (November, 1978), pp. 4 - 6.

Oosthuisen, Frik. Unions respond to new technology. X, 3 (December, 1984), pp. 20 - 22.

Sitas, Ari. Rebels without a pause: the M.W.U. and the defence of the colour bar. V, 3 (October, 1979), pp. 30 - 58.

Technical Advice Group. Case study: introducting work study at a factory in the Transvaal. X, 4 (January/February, 1985), pp. 41 - 45.

White, I.D. The changing labour process and its consequences: a case study of a general engineering firm in Natal. IV, 7 (November, 1978), pp. 55 - 62.

LABOUR STATISTICS, *see STATISTICS — Labour*

LEBOEA, Paul

Obituary: Paul Leboea and Theboho Noka. VIII, 6 (June, 1983), p. 81.

LESOTHO

Gay, Judy. Wage employment of rural Basotho women: a case study. VI, 4 (November, 1980), pp. 40 - 53.

Murray, Colin. The effects of migrant labour: a review of the evidence from Lesotho. VI, 4 (November, 1980), pp. 21 - 39.

Murray, Colin. From granary to labour reserve: an economic history of Lesotho. VI, 4 (November, 1980), pp. 3 - 20.

Showers, Kate. A note on women, conflict and migrant labour. VI, 4 (November, 1980), pp. 54 - 57.

LOCK-OUTS, *see STRIKES*

MC CARTHY, Eddie

Eddie Mc Carthy 1943 — 1985. X, 4

1985), pp. 43 - 49.

STRIKES — South Africa
Briefings: responses to the work stoppage called by the African Food and Canning Workers' Union following the death in detention of Neil Aggett. VII, 6 (April, 1982), pp. 5 - 28.

Cooper, Carole. Details of strikes during 1978. V, 1 (May, 1979), pp. 57 - 66.

Cornell, Jud and Kooy, Alide. Wiehahn part five and the White paper. VII, 3 (November, 1981), pp. 51 - 74.

Ensor, Linda. Labour repression. I, 7 (November/December, 1974), pp. 50 - 51.

Gottschalk, Keith and Smalberger, John. The earliest known strikes by black workers in South Africa. III, 7 (June/July, 1977), pp. 73 - 75.

Haysom, Fink. The right to strike in South African law. V, 1 (May, 1979), pp. 67 - 80.

1982: a record strike year. VIII, 5 (April, 1983), pp. 12 - 13.

The right to strike. V, 1 (May, 1979), pp. 1 - 4.

Strikes and the African worker. III, 7 (June/July, 1977), pp. 1 - 4.

STRIKES — South Africa — Chemical
Ensor, Linda. Rumblings of discontent. I, 7 (November/December, 1974), pp. 43 - 49.

Ensor, Linda. The strike at Sterling Winthrop. I, 6 (September/October, 1974), pp. 50 - 53.

Joshi, Ravindra. Forbo Krommenie strike case. IV, 8 (January/February, 1979), pp. 87 - 89.

STRIKES — South Africa — Clothing
Nicol, Martin. Strike at Cape underwear. X, 2 (October/November, 1984), pp. 87 - 108.

STRIKES. — South Africa — Construction
Golding, Marcel. BCAWU strike at Pilkingtons. XI, 1 (September, 1985), pp. 34 - 38.

Rocla workers strike for recognition. X, 8 (July/August, 1985), pp. 3 - 4.

STRIKES — South Africa — Docks
Maree, Johan. The Cape Town stevedores ban on overtime. I, 8 (January/February, 1975), pp. 58 - 63.

STRIKES — South Africa — Durban
Ensor, Linda. Recent strikes in Durban. I, 4 (July, 1974), pp. 49 - 56.

Ensor, Linda. Recent strikes in Durban. I, 5 (August, 1974), pp. 41 - 44.

Mawbey, John. Industrial disputes in Durban during 1975. II, 6 (January, 1976), pp. 40 - 55.

Mawbey, John. Strikes in Durban. January to April, 1975. I, 10 (April, 1975), pp. 52 - 60.

STRIKES — South Africa — East London
East London Correspondent. East London and labour: 1981, a summary. VII, 4 and 5 (February, 1982, pp. 28 - 33.

Labour situation: East London (document). VII, 8 (July, 1981), pp. 8 - 17.

Maré, Gerry. The East London strikes. I, 5 (August, 1974), pp. 26 - 32. (Article by R. Turner.)

Maree, Johann. SAAWU in the East London area, 1979 — 1981. VII, 4 and 5 (February, 1982), pp. 34 - 49.

STRIKES — South Africa — Electronics
Metal and Allied Workers' Union. Workers under the baton: an examination of the labour dispute at Heinemann Electric Company. III, 7 (June/July, 1977), pp. 49 - 59.

STRIKES — South Africa — Food
Bakers Biscuits strike. X, 5 (March/April, 1985), pp. 9 - 11.

The Duens Bakery dispute. II, 9 and 10 (May/June, 1976), pp. 71 - 77.

Duens Bakery workers victorious. III, 2 (September, 1976), pp. 98 - 99.

Editorial comment on strikes. VI, 6 (March, 1981), pp. 1 - 2.

Hosken, Liz. Strike at Rainbow Chickens Hammarsdale, Natal,

Maree, Johann. The 1979 Port Elizabeth strikes and an evaluation of U.A.W. VI, 2 and 3 (September, 1980), pp. 13 - 30.

Mthethwa, Alpheus and Mfeti, Pindile. Report on the Leyland Motor Corporation of South Africa Ltd. with special reference to its labour policies and its attitude towards the Metal and Allied Workers' Union, June, 1975. II, 5 (1975), pp. 36 - 47.

People's support essential. VII, 3 (November, 1981), pp. 9 - 12.

Roux, Marianne. Daily events of the wildcat strike (Ford Co). VI, 2 and 3 (September, 1980), pp. 3 - 12.

Strikes in the motor industry. VI, 8 (July, 1981), pp. 71 - 76.

STRIKES — South Africa — Municipal Workers

Comment: one coin — two sides. VI, 7 (May, 1981), pp. 1 - 3.

Keenan, Jeremy. Migrants awake: the 1980 Johannesburg Municipality strike. VI, 7 (May, 1981), pp. 4 - 60.

Labour Research Committee. State strategy and the Johannesburg Municipal strike. VI, 7 (May, 1981), pp. 61 - 86.

STRIKES — South Africa — Non-metallic Mineral Products

Glass and Allied Workers' Union. Report on the strike at Armourplate Safety Glass from 6 September, 1976 to 1 November being the first legal strike by black workers in South Africa. III, 7 (June/July, 1977), pp. 60 - 72.

Golding, Marcel. BCAWU strike at Pilkingtons. XI, 1 (September, 1985), pp. 2 - 4.

Golding, Marcel. SAAWU in the western Cape — the continental China strike. X, 7 (June, 1985), pp. 57 - 74.

STRIKES — South Africa — Orange Free State

Hudson, Peter. Strikes in the Transvaal and the O.F.S. I, 5 (August, 1974), pp. 45 - 47.

STRIKES — South Africa — Paper and Packaging

Baskin, Jeremy and Bissell, Ian. Sundumbili general strike of March 1982. VIII, 1 (September, 1982), pp. 26 - 33.

STRIKES — South Africa — Public sector

Hudson, Peter. Post office strike. I, 2 (May, 1974), pp. 35 - 38.

STRIKES — South Africa — Rubber

Monitoring the Sarmcol struggle. XI, 2 (October/December, 1985), pp. 89 - 112.

Sitas, Ari. The Dunlop strike: a trial of strength. X, 3 (December, 1984), pp. 62 - 84.

STRIKES — South Africa — Services

Budlender, Debbie. RAWU victory at Dairybelle. X, 1 (August/September, 1984), pp. 21 - 23.

Golding, Marcel. Groote Schuur hospital workers strike. X, 2 (October/November, 1984), pp. 75 - 86.

Golding, Marcel. Hospital strikes in Durban. X, 5 (March/April, 1985), pp. 57 - 76.

Potchefstroom municipality workers' strike. X, 5 (March/April, 1985), pp. 17 - 18.

STRIKES — South Africa — Sugar

Ensor, Linda. Rumblings of discontent. I, 7 (November/December, 1974), pp. 43 - 49.

STRIKES — South Africa — Textiles

Strikes in 1980: an introduction. VI, 5 (December, 1980), pp. 1 - 3.

Case study: the functions, nature and effectiveness of the statutory liaison committee — Pinetex. II, 9 and 10 (May/June, 1976), pp. 41 - 58.

Ensor, Linda. Rumblings of discontent. I, 7 (November/December, 1974), pp. 43 - 49.

Legal strike at Natal Thread. VIII, 8; IX, 1 (September/October, 1983), pp. 13 - 23.

Mawbey, John. The 1980 cotton workers strike. VI, 5 (December, 1980), pp. 4 - 16.

Natal Labour Research Committee.

racy: the case of the J.M.C.E.U. X, 5 (March/April, 1985), pp. 31 - 39.

Western Province General Workers' Union. Letter to the Bulletin. VI, 1 (July, 1980), pp. 3 - 5.

TRADE UNION FEDERATIONS — South Africa

Lever, Jeff. Functional federations and consultative councils. XI, 2 (October/December, 1985), pp. 11 - 14.

TRADE UNION RECOGNITION

The Case for African unions. I, 1 (April, 1974), pp. 3 - 55.

Chemical Workers' Industrial Union. Workers' struggle at Colgate. VI, 8 (July, 1981), pp. 18 - 33.

Comment: Management's dilemma. II, 3 (August, 1975), pp. 1 - 2.

Critique of 'Problems of African trade unions'. I, 5 (August, 1974), pp. 10 - 14.

Ensor, Linda. The problems of African trade unions. I, 2 (May, 1974), pp. 39 - 48.

Ferreira, F.H. Collective bargaining: dealing with a black union. VI, 2 and 3 (September, 1980), pp. 78 - 83.

Fisher, Foszia. Parliamentary debate on labour. II, 1 (May/June, 1975), pp. 47 - 50.

Horne, Pat. PWAWU: organising Mondi. X, 2 (October/ November, 1984), pp. 37 - 43.

The legal status of African unions. IV, 6 (October, 1978), pp. 1 - 5.

Legassick, Martin. The record of British firms in South Africa in the context of the political economy. II, 1 (May/June, 1975), pp. 7 - 36.

Roux, Andre. SAAWU consolidates. X, 2 (October/November, 1984), pp. 25 - 28.

Webster, Eddie. Towards a stable truce. III, 1 (July, 1976), pp. 43 - 51.

Western Province General Workers' Union. Registration recognition and organisation: the case of the Cape Town stevedores. V, 6 and 7 (March, 1980), pp. 57 - 75.

TRADE UNION REGISTRATION

Adler, T. Letter to the editor. VI, 8 (July, 1981), pp. 4 - 7.

Benjamin, Paul and Cheadle, H., Khoza, M. A guide to the Labour Relations Amendment Act (1981). VII, 1 and 2 (September, 1981), pp. 18 - 28.

Bonner, Phil. Independent trade unions since Wiehahn. VIII, 4 (February, 1983), pp. 16 - 36.

Cheadle, Halton. Letter to S.A.L.B. V, 6 and 7 (March, 1980), pp. 7 - 9.

Cornell, Jud and Kooy, Alide. Wiehahn part five and the White paper. VII, 3 (November, 1981), pp. 51 - 74.

Federation of South African Trade Unions. Resolution of the proposed Amendment to the Industrial Conciliation Act No 28 of 1956 passed by the Central Committee at its meeting April, 1981. VII, 1 and 2 (September, 1981), pp. 16 - 17.

FOSATU Central Committee statement on the Amended Industrial Conciliation Act that forms the basis for the joint stand with other unions. V, 6 and 7 (March, 1980), pp. 14 - 16.

Fine, Bob. Trade unions and the state once more: a reply to our critics. VIII, 1 (September, 1982), pp. 47 - 58.

Fine, B., de Clercq, F. and Duncan Innes. Trade unions and the state: the question of legality. VII, 1 and 2 (September, 1981), pp. 39 - 68.

Food and Canning Workers' Union and African Food and Canning Workers' Union. Memorandum of objections to the Director General, Manpower Utilisation regarding the draft Bill (Industrial Conciliation Act no 28 of 1956). VII, 1 and 2 (September, 1981), pp. 5 - 9.

General Workers' Union. G.W.U. Yes to registration X, 8 (July/August, 1985), pp. 5 - 6.

Parson, Jack. The working class, the state and social change in Botswana. V, 5 (January, 1980), pp. 44 - 55.

Simkins, Charles. Labour in Botswana. II, 5 (1975), pp. 28 -35.

The views of the chairman of the Botswana Federation of Trade Unions. V, 5 (January, 1980), pp. 56 - 61.

Cooper, Dave. Unions in Botswana: comparisons with Lesotho. X, 8 (July/August, 1985), pp. 103 - 114.

TRADE UNIONS — Brazil

Fig, David. Brazil labour movement and the crisis. IX, 6 (May, 1984), pp. 28 - 57.

TRADE UNIONS — Britain

British miner in South Africa. X, 3 (December, 1984), pp. 13 - 19.

Firth, Jim. British trade unions in the seventies: from moderation to militancy. II, 3 (August, 1973), pp. 40 - 49.

TRADE UNIONS — Canada

Mabin, Alan. Issues in the Canadian union movement. VIII, 5 (April, 1983), pp. 34 - 47.

Operation solidarity. IX, 2 (November, 1983), pp. 14 - 17.

TRADE UNIONS — Craft

De Clercq, Francine. The organised labour movement and state registration: unity or fragmentation? V, 6 and 7 (March, 1980), pp. 18 - 43.

Greenberg, Stanley. Open and closed unionism in South Africa. I, 8 (January/February, 1975), pp. 6 - 23.

Greenberg, Stanley. Open and closed unionism in South Africa. I, 10 (April, 1975), pp. 18 - 30.

TRADE UNIONS — Europe

Douwes-Dekker, Loet. Are works committees in other countries effective? I, 3 (June, 1974), pp. 22 - 35.

Fisher, Foszia. The industrial relations system in Germany. I, 8 (January/February, 1975), pp. 42 - 50.

TRADE UNIONS — Industrial

De Clercq, Francine. The organised labour movement and state registration: unity or fragmentation? V, 6 and 7 (March, 1980), pp. 18 - 43.

Greenberg, Stanley. Open and closed unionism in South Africa. I, 8 (January/February, 1975), pp. 6 - 23.

Greenberg, Stanley. Open and closed unionism in South Africa. I, 10 (April, 1975), pp. 18 - 30.

TRADE UNIONS — International Confederation of Free Trade Unions

Douwes-Dekker, L.C.G. Notes on international labour bodies and their relevance to South Africa. V, 8 (May, 1980), pp. 34 - 53.

Migrant workers' charter of the International Confederation of Free Trade Unions. I, 4 (July, 1974), pp. 42 - 48.

Waterman, Peter. The foreign impact on Lagos dockworker unionism. V, 8 (May, 1980), pp. 16 - 33.

TRADE UNIONS — Lesotho

Southall, Roger. Trade unions and the internal working class in Lesotho. X, 3 (December, 1984), pp. 85 - 113.

TRADE UNIONS — Mozambique

Socialist trade unions: battle against poverty. IX, 4 (February, 1984), pp. 85 - 98.

TRADE UNIONS — Namibia

Unions in Namibia. IX, 6 (May, 1984), pp. 14 - 16.

TRADE UNIONS — Nigeria

Waterman, Peter. The foreign impact on Lagos dockworker unionism. V, 8 (May, 1980), pp. 16 - 33.

Waterman, Peter. H.P. Adebola: The man, the myth, the movement. IX, 6 (May, 1984), pp. 103 - 112.

TRADE UNIONS — South Africa

Altman, J.R. Leadership problems of registered trade unions in South Africa. III, 2 (September, 1976), pp. 35 - 41.

Bonner, Phil. Independent trade unions since Wiehahn. VIII, 4

(February, 1983), pp. 16 - 36.
Comment: Name game. II, 6
(January, 1976), pp. 1 - 5.
Copelyn, John. Problems in collec-
tive bargaining. VIII, 1
(September, 1982), pp. 69 - 80.
De Clercq, Francine. The organised
labour movement and state regis-
tration: unity or fragmentation? V,
6 and 7 (March, 1980), pp. 18 - 43.
Ensor, Linda. The problems of estab-
lished trade unions. I, 3 (June,
1974), pp. 17 - 21.
Fisher, Foszia and Nxasana, Harold.
The labour situation in South
Africa. II, 2 (July, 1975), pp. 43
- 51.
French, Kevin. Workers' Charters in
South Africa. IX, 4 (February,
1984), pp. 58 - 71.
Greenberg, Stanley. Open and closed
unionism in South Africa. I, 8
(January/February, 1975), pp. 6
- 23.
Greenberg, Stanley. Open and closed
unionism in South Africa. I, 10
(April, 1975), pp. 18 - 30.
Kaplan, David and Morris, Mike.
Manufacturing capital and the
question of African trade union
recognition 1960 — 1964. VII, 1
and 2 (September, 1981), pp. 86
- 107.
Khanyile, Z.A. What is a trade
union? VIII, 1 (September, 1982),
pp. 85 - 88.
Labour Monitoring Group. Andries
Raditsela: monitoring the protests
in Natal. X, 8 (July/August,
1985), pp. 92 - 102.
Lewis, Dave. Registered trade unions
and Western Cape workers. III, 2
(September, 1976), pp. 42 - 61.
Lewis, Dave. Trade union organisation and economic recession.
VIII, 5 (April, 1983), pp. 20 - 26.
Lewis, Jon and Randall, Estelle. The
state of the unions. XI, 2
(October/December, 1985), pp. 60
- 88.
Moodie, Dunbar. The Afrikaner
struggle for an effective voice in
the South African economy prior

to 1948. I, 7 (November/
December, 1974), pp. 31 - 34.
Morris, Mike. Capital's responses to
African trade unions post
Wiehahn. VII, 1 and 2
(September, 1981), pp. 69 - 85.
Motala, Shereen. Repression against
unions. VIII, 6 (June, 1983), pp. 5
- 8.
Njikelana, Sisa. The unions and the
front: a response to David Lewis.
IX, 7 (June, 1984), pp. 76 - 83.
Security action and trade unions.
VIII, 3 (December, 1982), pp. 11
- 13.
Southall, Roger. Review article:
South African labour studies. IX,
7 (June, 1984), pp. 88 - 114.
Stein, Mark. Max Gordon and
African trade unionism on the
Witwatersrand, 1935 — 1940. III,
9 (November, 1977), pp. 41 - 57.
Summary of recommendations by the
South African Labour Bulletin
Board to the Wiehahn Comm-
ission. IV, 5 (September, 1978),
pp. 75 - 80.
The trade union struggle continues.
III, 4 (January/February, 1977),
pp. 1 - 4.
Union repression escalates. VIII, 8;
IX, 1 (September/October, 1983),
pp. 9 - 12.
The U.D.F. on the unions: interview
with Mosiuoa Lekota. IX, 2
(November, 1983), pp. 78 - 84.
Webster, Eddie. Management's
counter offensive. II, 3 (August,
1975), pp. 29 - 39.
Webster, Eddie. A profile of unregis-
tered union members in Durban.
IV, 8 (January/February, 1979),
pp. 43 - 74.
Webster, Eddie. Towards a stable
truce. III, 1 (July, 1976), pp. 43 - 51.
Welcher, Larry. The relationship
between the state and African
trade unions in South Africa 1948
— 1953. IV, 5 (September, 1978),
pp. 15 - 48.
Where are the workers? IX, 2
(November, 1983), pp. 76 - 77.
TRADE UNIONS — South Africa —

Federation of South African Trade Unions

Adler, T. Letter to the Editor. VI, 8 (July, 1981), pp. 4 - 7.

Baskin Jeremy. Growth of a new worker organ: the Germiston Shop Stewards' Council. VII, 8 (July, 1982), pp. 42 - 53.

Bonner, Phil. Focus on FOSATU. V, 1 (May, 1979), pp. 5 - 24.

Federation of South African Trade Unions. Report November, 1980 — November 1981. VII, 4 and 5 (February, 1982), pp. 104 - 116.

FOSATU and the 'New Deal'. XI, 2 (October/December, 1985), pp. 76 - 81.

FOSATU on unity. VIII, 5 (April, 1983), pp. 68 - 69.

Forster, Joe. The workers' struggle: where does FOSATU stand? VII, 8 (July, 1982), pp. 67 - 86.

TRADE UNIONS — South Africa — Food and Canning Workers' Union

Baskin, Jeremy. Factory workers in the countryside: the Food and Canning Workers' Union in Ceres and Grabouw. VIII, 4 (February, 1983), pp. 51 - 58.

Democracy in trade union work. VIII, 5 (April, 1983), pp. 63 - 68.

Documents: speeches prepared for the funeral of Neil Aggett on 13 February, 1982. VII, 6 (April, 1982), pp. 167 - 75.

F.C.W.U.: annual conference. XI, 2 (October/December, 1985), p. 2.

Food and Canning Workers' Union. Search for a workable relationship. VII, 8 (July, 1982), pp. 54 - 58.

Food and Canning Workers' Union Communique: unity is strength. X, 7 (June, 1985), p. 9.

Obituary; Neil Aggett 1953 — 1982. VII, 4 and 5 (February, 1982), pp. 117 - 119.

Strike and lock-out at L.K.B. East London. VIII, 4 (February, 1983), pp. 59 - 63.

McGregor, Liz. The Fatti's and Moni's dispute. V, 6 and 7 (March, 1980), pp. 122 - 131.

TRADE UNIONS — South Africa — Furniture and Timber Workers' Union

Ensor, Linda. A look at the open trade unions. I, 3 (June, 1974), pp. 46 - 52.

TRADE UNIONS — South Africa — Natal Garment Workers' Industrial Unions

Garment union capitulates. I, 8 (January/February, 1975), pp. 2 - 4.

TRADE UNIONS — South Africa — Garment Workers' Union of South Africa

Bolton, Harriet. Tribute to a fighter: Johanna Cornelius. I, 3 (June, 1974), p. 62.

Brink, Elsabe. Plays, poetry and production: the literature of the garment workers. IX, 8 (July, 1984), pp. 32 - 53.

Lewis, Jon. The new unionism: industrialisation and industrial unions in South Africa, 1925 — 1930. III, 5 (March/April, 1977), pp. 25 - 49.

Lewis, Jon. Solly Sachs and the Garment Workers' Union. III, 3 (October, 1976), pp. 67 - 80.

Mawbey, John. Afrikaner women of the Garment Union during the thirties and forties. II, 4 (1975), pp. 33 - 50.

TRADE UNIONS — South Africa — Garment Workers' Union of the Western Province

Maree, Johann. Problems with trade union democracy: case study of the Garment Workers' Union of the Western Province. III, 2 (September, 1976), pp. 62 - 73.

TRADE UNIONS — South Africa — General Factory Workers' Benefit Fund

Ensor, Linda. A look at the open trade unions. I, III, (June, 1974), pp. 46 - 52.

Ensor, Linda. Reynold's: scene of struggle. I, 3 (June, 1974), pp. 36 -39.

TRADE UNIONS — South Africa — General Workers' Union

Baskin, Jeremy. G.W.U. and the Durban dockworkers. VIII, 3